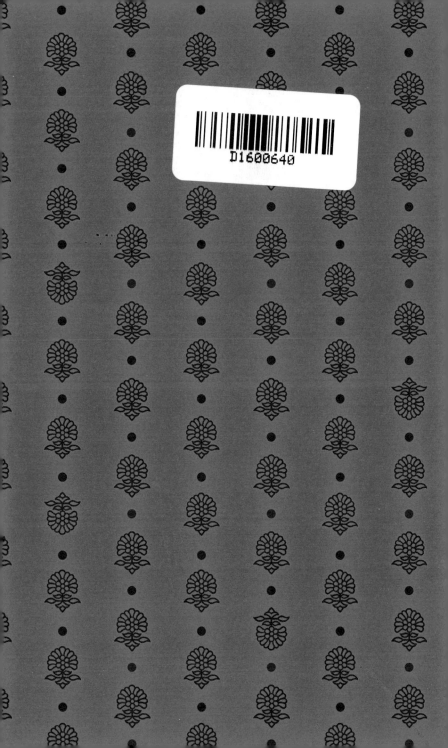

GATHERING THE ASHES

GATHERING
THE ASHES

Amritlal Nagar

TRANSLATED BY
MRINAL PANDE

LONDON NEW YORK CALCUTTA

SERIES EDITOR
Arunava Sinha

Seagull Books, 2016

First published in India in 2014 by Harper Perennial
An imprint of HarperCollins *Publishers*

Original © Amritlal Nagar, 2014
English translation © Mrinal Pande, 2014

Printed in arrangement with HarperCollins *Publishers*.
This edition is not for sale in the Indian subcontinent (India, Pakistan,
Sri Lanka, Bangladesh, Nepal, Bhutan, Myanmar and the Maldives),
Singapore, Malaysia and the UAE.

ISBN 978 0 8574 2 392 4

British Library Cataloguing-in-Publication Data
A catalogue record for this book is available from the British Library.

Typeset in 11/14.2 Goudy Old Style by Saanvi Graphics, Noida
Printed and bound by Hyam Enterprises, Calcutta, India

To all those who have fought successfully or otherwise, for their rights and India's freedom

CONTENTS

AUTHOR'S NOTE

As I began collecting information for a novel I wished to write about the ghadar, the great public uprising of 1857 in Awadh, I began to feel increasingly dissatisfied with the material that came my way. It was evident that my task would remain incomplete until I visited the actual area where the ghadar had taken place a hundred years ago, and gathered the memories and local legends from authentic local sources that were fast fading into the mists of time. Since so little about the ghadar has been written down by our own people, the only way to understand the historic event as the local public experienced it, was to follow the orally transmitted memories and legends that had survived among ordinary families and clans in the countryside.

Therefore in 1957, as the nation was getting ready to celebrate the ghadar's first centenary, I began to think of travelling through rural Awadh to gather memories of the uprising that had been transmitted over the years. I felt the same sense of duty and veneration that families carry as they set out to gather the ashes of a dear departed one.

There was one problem though. The extensive travelling required for this task needed resources that were beyond me.

Here I was helped greatly by Bhagwati Sharan Singh, director of information for the government of Uttar Pradesh and his departmental colleagues. Together, they facilitated my travels and meetings with people. Bhagwati bhai is a close friend and I am sure, expects no effusive and formal expressions of gratitude from me.

I began writing this book on 21 July 1957, and completed it within three months, on 16 September. Gyanbhadra Dixit wrote out the entire manuscript for me, by hand. My younger brother, Madan has managed to reproduce an enlarged portrait of the late Begum Hazrat Mahal, using a very small and faded photograph I acquired through her great grandson and my dear friend, Sahibzada Kaukab Qadr. I am truly indebted to all of them.

Amritlal Nagar
The Chowk
Lucknow

(*The writer's preface to the first imprint of* Ghadar Ke Phool *published by the Publications Division of the Department of Information , Government of Uttar Pradesh in 1957-58*)

1

BARABANKI

The route adopted by Amritlal Nagar for his travels does not follow the order of events in 1857. The ghadar had first erupted in the army camp in Meerut and then spread simultaneously towards Delhi and Lucknow, the capital city of Awadh. When Lucknow was reclaimed by the British after a long and bloody siege, the rebels fled to the countryside of Awadh where the battle continued for almost a year before the revolt was finally quelled. For various reasons, Nagar began his travels in the reverse, starting with the rural areas of district Barabanki. It is only in the last chapters that he talks at length about the events surrounding the ghadar years, the decline and fall of the nawabi regime of Awadh with its old hybridized culture and the rise of a new anglophile elite led by the now all powerful British in his beloved city of Lucknow. It was a city with which he had a very long association, and where his many friends from various communities and different strata of society had been helping him gather rare material for years.

During the ghadar years, Barabanki was one of the four districts in the Faizabad division. It is a fertile area fed by the rivers Gomti, Ghaghra and Kalyani. According to the 1871 census, the district then had thirteen large towns and four tehsils or subdivisions. It had fifty-three major talukedars who headed the rural socio-economic infrastructures and commanded a lot of respect from farmers in their areas. As a class of rural elite, the talukedars of Awadh were created by Saadat Khan, the founder of the nawabi dynasty of Awadh and a representative of the Mughal king in Delhi. Khan opted for a hereditary band of revenue collectors from among the major local landlords and later also entrusted them with the task of maintaining law and order in their allocated area. Given the immense powers they now came to exercise, the talukedars were frequently also referred to as raja.

Around the time the Nawab of Awadh was dethroned by the East India Company, these rajas owned half the land and over sixty per cent of the villages in the area, and were contributing ninety per cent of the assessed revenues to the royal exchequer at Lucknow. The clans the talukedars belonged to, had come into Awadh in waves all through the seventeenth and eighteenth centuries. Once they had settled in, they invited their clansmen to join them, providing them with ample farming land and strengthening the kinship ties further by marrying into their families. The loyal band of brothers thus created over generations formed a security ring around the talukedars and members of this charmed circle were ever ready to go to war on behalf of their raja.

In addition to powerful talukedars, there were also 5397 wealthy zamindars and small cultivators in this region. They employed some 1354 landless labourers, mostly from the dalit communities to work in their farms. All cultivators paid a rent to the talukedar and had the right to mortgage their land in times of need, and then the person to whom that land had been mortgaged, began paying rent to the talukedar. Since the higher castes considered it shameful to hold the plough, they mostly found landless men from lower castes to till the farms and sow and reap their crops. For this, often a big loan was paid to the man's family who then became a bonded labourer for the loan giver. It was an exploitative system since all cultivators were dependent on the raja and their tenant farmers for vital livelihood.

But it protected the small farmers and landless families against even more cruel moneylenders and the corrupt and exploitative officers of the Crown.

After the rebel forces lost Lucknow, the rebel leader-in-chief, Begum Hazrat Mahal issued a fervent appeal for help to talukedars in the rural areas in the name of her infant son Birjis Qadr who had been declared the regent by rebel leaders in Lucknow. By now the peasantry had also begun to exercise a great moral pressure on the rajas for throwing caution to the winds, begging them to come out in defence of Awadh and its infant nawab.

Dariyabad, the then district headquarters, was the scene of one of the major battles in rural Awadh. After the natives were defeated, the victorious British forces mercilessly pillaged and destroyed Dariyabad. Several minor battles were also fought in the nearby villages of Bhitauli and Ram Sanehi Ghat (also known as Rudauli), and the British armies, led by Sir Hope Grant finally got the rebels to surrender in Nawabgunj. Major rebel leaders like Nana Saheb and Begum Hazrat Mahal, however, managed to escape into the adjacent state of Nepal along with a few loyal armed men. After the ghadar, the district headquarters were shifted from the ruined town of Dariyabad to Nawabgunj, and ultimately to Barabanki.

Present-day Barabanki district has 1.68 per cent of the total population of the state of Uttar Pradesh, two parliamentary constituencies and seven state assembly seats. The rebel genes obviously got passed down across generations because six decades later, people from this region joined Mahatma Gandhi's 1921 Civil Disobedience movement. Many protesters were jailed when they actively protested against the Prince of Wales's visit to India. Among them was Rafi Ahmed Kidwai, from the well-known Kidwai clan of Bhayara village, who later rose to be a major public leader in Independent India.

Mrinal Pande

My friend Athar Abbas Rizvi, an undersecretary in the Department of Education had once shown me a couple of letters exchanged between two of the local heroes of the ghadar, Raja Veni Madhav Baksh Singh of Shankarpur and Maulvi Ahmedullah Shah of Lucknow. The two leaders: one Hindu and the other a Muslim, had discussed at length a military strategy for an impending battle between the native people of Awadh, and the British East India Company. The correspondence dispelled the commonly accepted theory propounded by the likes of the Bengali historian Dr Ramesh Chandra Majumdar, that the 1857 ghadar was by and large a limited, sudden and sporadic revolt limited largely to the native sepoys of the British army against the British. It was, in Awadh at least, a people's uprising indeed.

As a student I had also read Sir Hope Grant's memoirs and excerpts from Sir William Russell's diary describing the decisive battle of Nawabgunj in some detail and how the British forces finally managed to defeat the rebel native armies after a pitched battle. It was also at Barabanki that a young Rajput ruler of Chahlari, Balbhadra Singh Raikwar had challenged the British army near Dariyabad and was killed in battle. Like him, several other talukedars like Raja Veni Madhav Baksh Singh of Shankarpur and Raja Devi Baksh Singh from the neighbouring districts of Rae Bareilly and Gonda had taken up arms against the British. In 1957, the state government of Uttar Pradesh (UP) decided to work towards preparing an authentic record of the ghadar of 1857 as experienced by the people of Awadh and asked for my help.

Why did I begin at Barabanki?

I must confess to having some misgivings about the project as I set out. Suppose, I wondered, I do not find any supportive evidence about the fabled rural battles? Or worse, if the material I finally unearth in the district of Barabanki contradicts what I have been led to believe about the local bravehearts I had grown up worshipping? Would it still be justifiable to continue my travels and visit other parts of Awadh? Do I have the right to spend public money on what may well turn out to be just a personal whim? But then I reassured myself. Surely there must still be some witnesses or their descendants who can provide some hitherto unrecorded local details about the mutiny years. And even if the district of Barabanki does not yield much by way of local lore, why should one assume that there is nothing available in any of the other districts of Awadh?

When the easy-going ordinary farming folk in the rural areas of Awadh picked up arms against their rulers' armies, their anger must have had a long history of bureaucratic oppression and social alienation. To be sure, the ordinary people of Awadh harboured a deep resentment against the increasing interference in their community life and religion by the British, who had constantly humiliated their much-loved local rulers. There was also a deep suspicion against the increasing interference by Jesuit priests in the community life and religion of both Hindus and Muslims. Not only the capital city of Lucknow, but the entire Awadh region was a veritable tinderbox ready to explode with the tiniest movement. In Barabanki, the necessary push came at the battle of Dariyabad where a young and brave lad was reported to have died protecting the honour of the helpless begums of Talukedar Farzand Ali Khan, who while fleeing the palaces, were said to have been terrorized by a posse of armed British soldiers. As the news spread about the wily British gunning down the eighteen-year-old Raja of Chahlari who rushed to protect the women like a true Rajput, the anger simmering below the surface suddenly erupted throughout the region, leading to much death and destruction. Most people may not know that in 1857, Chahlari was a part of the neighbouring district of Seetapur. It was only when the ghadar was quashed and the districts were reorganized in 1858 that Chahlari was included within the district of Barabanki.

The district of Barabanki in 1857 was called Nawabgunj. Both Banki and Bara villages, which lent the new district its present day name, are actually located quite far away from the district headquarters. The young District Information Officer Lakshmi Sahay Gupta who imparted this piece of information, appeared to be an enthusiastic fellow and shared with me a whole lot of interesting local lore about the mutiny. He told us that the idea of putting together a public history of the 1857 uprising was first broached at a meeting of district officials here. At that point, doubts were voiced about the martyrdom of the teenage hero, Thakur Balbhadra Singh of Chahlari because after killing him, the British built a grave over the raja's mortal remains. To some it meant that they must have considered the dead man a friend of theirs, who had been killed by mistake.

According to British sources, the death of the raja was due to a certain misunderstanding. Balbhadra Singh was actually passing through the area with a wedding procession when he was suddenly challenged by the British forces who thought that the raja was leading a posse of rebels. At the time, marriage processions of local rulers from various Kshatriya clans were usually accompanied by a large armed contingent of fellow Rajputs, and preceded by armed riders, liveried sepoys and brass bands playing marching songs. The rear was brought up by drummers and soldiers firing guns in the air. Watching such a procession during the ghadar, the British commanders may have assumed that it was another motley group of armed natives coming to attack them. This is perhaps why instead of humiliating the dead by defacing the bodies, their guilt drove them not only to cremate the young ruler but also build a grave over his remains. This lenient view however, was hotly challenged by a certain Acchan Sahib. He said he had heard many tales in and around Barabanki about the brave ruler of Chahlari. His uncle (mother's brother) had even sent him a popular Alha ballad about the bravery of Balbhadra Singh in the battle of Barabanki. I decided that at some point I must accept the offer to work on a monograph on Awadh during the 1857 ghadar. At least then I would meet this uncle and get hold of the fabled Alha about a local martyr and god knows what else.

The district information officer and I arranged to begin with a visit to Dariyabad, where the mutiny was said to have first erupted in Barabanki. By now several local people, including a few journalists who were said to be knowledgeable about the area, and Jagannath Prasad Nigam, a local Member of the Legislative Assembly (MLA), had also joined us. Nigam claimed to have many unknown facts about the uprising in his possession. He said he had dredged them painstakingly from old gazettes and local lore. As proof of his gathered fund of knowledge, he often fished out a little pocket diary and quoted various dates and details as our procession moved towards Dariyabad.

Located at a distance of eighteen miles from Lucknow along the road to Faizabad, Dariyabad was settled initially by one Dariya Khan, a subedar from the armies of the Sharki ruler Muhammad Ibrahim. With time, it became an imposing township with thirty-four gates. The elaborate names of its old residential localities are indicative of a lost glory: Muhalla Muharriran or the locality of clerics, Muhalla Makhdoomzadan or the locality of the revered holy clans, Muhalla Chaudhariyan or the locality of eminent landlords, Muhalla Mughlan, etc. Nobles from the Sooryavanshi (solar) clan of Hadaha and the Kayastha families of Dariyabad Khas were some of the well-known factions of this area during the ghadar years in Awadh.

Ram Sanehi Ghat

We aimed to begin at Ram Sanehi Ghat, a man-made ghat located on the banks of the Kalyani river, some twenty-six miles from the district headquarters. I was told that Baba Ram Sanehi, after whom the place is named, was a highly evolved saint who had fought fiercely against the British armies with his band of devotees and fellow sadhus. After his death in battle, he was not cremated but buried in a samadhi as befits a sanyasi. I was told that after the mutiny, the British wanted to build a road through the area where this tomb stood. But the local labourers who were asked to remove the tomb, refused to participate in its demolition. They told their gora supervisor that the holy monument contained the remains of a revered local saint killed during the ghadar. They would not start the work they said, unless the gora sahib himself wielded a pickaxe first and hammered the first blow. It is said that the gora supervisor who foolishly tried to dig the earth at the spot came to a sorry end. Eventually, the government passed an order stating that the monument was to be left untouched even if this resulted in the road becoming a little misaligned at the spot.

We explored Ram Sanehi Ghat to find out more about the miraculous baba and his participation in the mutiny. The ghat itself is a beautiful spot with the river running between lines of magnificent forest trees. Baba's tomb sits atop a high mound near a Dak bungalow with a garden of sorts around it. One felt tempted to halt and spend a few days at this serene spot. However, the first sight of the samadhi made me doubt the local lore about the circumstances of baba's death. It was a small, domed monument and the top looked like a feeding trough for cattle placed upside down. In India, this kind of architecture is usually seen at a site where a sadhu has taken voluntary samadhi. To do this, folklore states that the sadhu wishing to give up his life will first sit in a lotus posture (Padmasana) and then use his yogic powers to release his last breath by opening up an unseen hole (Brahmrandhra) centred in the middle of his forehead. Once the soul has departed thus, instead of being cremated like an ordinary Hindu, the yogi is laid to rest sitting, and a samadhi is built around his body to mark the spot. This sort of monument would not have been built, had Baba Ram Sanehi been martyred in a battle. How did the baba actually die? I decided to pose this query to an aged gardener tending to plants in a garden nearby.

'Ah, the baba!' the gardener said. 'He was a great soul. How could anyone have killed him in battle? He died like a yogi and left his body when he wished to do so, by going into a voluntary samadhi at the ghat. There he released his soul through the Brahmrandhra and was interred by his disciples. Baba's relatives live nearby, across the road,' the old man added. 'Why don't you go ask them?'

We crossed the road to Baba Ram Sanehi's thatched house, an ancient baked brick structure. Children were playing outside and a dishevelled old woman sat working with cow dung on the side. We stood at the bottom of the mound and Shri Nigam raised his voice to summon the inhabitants. We were told they were all away. We then decided to climb up and quiz the old lady who was shaping cow dung into pats.

'Who really was the baba and how did he die?'

'He was a saint, don't you know?' she shot back angrily. 'How could ordinary mortals have killed him in battle? He took samadhi as everyone knows.'

She then went on to repeat the story about the hapless gora supervisor and his foolish attempt to dig up baba's tomb. This was somewhat disappointing, particularly for my journalist companions, some of whom had already been led to publish stories about baba's bravery and martyrdom during the ghadar. We decided to move on.

Our team was now headed towards a doctor's clinic located in the main bazaar. The good doctor, we were told, was an old man and an avid collector of local lore about the past. They felt he was sure to provide us with exact details about the circumstances of Baba Ram Sanehi's death and his martyrdom. The journalists accompanying us still held to their original theory about the baba being martyred in battle. Many sadhus and fakirs, they said, had fought in the ghadar against the British, so it was not unusual for Baba Ram Sanehi to have taken up arms as well. But alas, even the good doctor said that the story about baba being a hands-on participant in the ghadar was not verifiable on factual grounds. He said that baba's martyrdom was one such incident where in time the names of local celebrities begin to be associated with any major happenings in the region, and thereafter myths and fables end up overshadowing historical facts. So that was that.

Dariyabad

We arrived at Dariyabad, a town full of old ruins dating back to 1857. Nigam-ji took us to see the local fort where a relatively new school building also stood. A white banner outside the building proclaimed that the Bharat Sevak Samaj was holding a camp there. A large field stretched between the school and the fort with a few rooms at the other end. The field extended well within the ruins of the fort which was all gone but for one wall to the south-west. Three parts of a small and old cannon still lay there. It could have shot ammunition not larger than the size of cricket balls. After climbing up the mound from the western side lined with mahua trees, we peeped down below and saw the remnants of an old moat that must have once protected the fort. A large maidan stretched beyond.

A hundred years ago, from here to the Katra Roshan Lal in the city, human settlements covered the entire stretch, we were told. In 1857, the British who wanted their cannons to target the rebels in this fort, demolished the houses that obstructed their view. Nigam-ji took out his little diary and read out aloud that the original fort dated back to the twelfth century when Mohammad of Gor's forces had attacked northern India. Later, during the reign of the Mughal emperor Akbar, a certain Mirza Abdul Rehman was the local chieftain of Dariyabad for the king. The fort then had a moat around it and no less than six domes mounted with guns. In 1857, Har Prasad Chakledar, an in-charge of the fort was killed when the British cannons demolished the fort. The main gate was then located on the east side and the ruins adjacent to it are still known locally as the cannon room (topkhana). About fifteen families live in thatched mud houses around the area.

At this point, a man in his mid-sixties, emerged from one of the houses and volunteered to act as our guide. He introduced himself as Mohan Lal and began describing in the local dialect how this was once a grand fort. Even now, he said, a close inspection of the ruins would reveal the intricate work that had marked the old buildings. To prove his point, he led us to the remains of an ancient sitting platform that still had patches of a lime plaster. Mohan Lal ran his fingers along the side and announced that the remains of carved flowers and leaves could still be traced with one's fingertips. Who can get such fine work executed any more, he asked no one in particular.

When Nigam-ji wanted to know if any old cannon balls or shells were still to be found around the area, Mohan Lal got up with an effort. He walked up to a house and indicated a spot near the wall where they were found from time to time. A spade was then yelled out for, and a hasty digging began. However, it revealed nothing that resembled cannon balls. 'These young boys!' Mohan Lal remarked in exasperation. 'They will leave nothing intact anywhere.'

By now I was getting worried that the mud wall would collapse if the hole near it was dug any deeper. I told Mohan Lal that risking the demolition of someone's house only to get a glimpse of some old shells was not worth it. Visibly agitated, he grabbed the spade from the digger and lifted it, only to be restrained by us. We told him that there was no need to dig, and we believed his story about the cannon balls being buried here. 'It is not just one or two, sir. There are sacks full of them, down under,' Mohan Lal said emphatically. Nevertheless, he stopped digging and we moved on towards the school with Mohan Lal in tow. Just next to its gates, there was a forlorn looking old grave. As we passed it, Mohan Lal informed us in solemn tones that his father thought this was a fake grave. It didn't really contain any human remains, but a whole cache of the rebels' weapons.

As we entered the premises, Tulsi Ram, a school teacher also joined our group. He began recounting to us the history of the locality of clerics, Mohalla Muharriran where Gulab Singh, the brother of the ruler of Kapurthala in Punjab was killed. The Chhatta Manzil here, we learnt from Tulsi Ram, housed the head offices of the district. When the British arrived here, Sheikh Najaf Ali Muharrir was the chief cleric in charge of official records. The British asked him to submit everything, to which he politely requested to be given two days so he could put all the papers in order. His request was granted. As soon as the British officials left, Najaf Ali rushed to meet Raja Sher Bahadur Singh of Kamiyar for hasty consultations. The raja told him that the British must not get their hands on valuable estate papers. It wasn't long before the raja sent several palanquins to Chhatta Manzil to fetch Najaf Ali's wife and children alongwith all the important documents. The remaining papers were packed into bundles, sealed, coated with wax and buried underground. Once this was done, the loyal Sheikh fled to an undisclosed destination. This spelt doom for Chhatta Manzil though. When the British arrived and found the offices emptied out, they were livid and avenged themselves by demolishing the grand old office building with their cannons. Today a barren field stretches where the Chhatta Manzil once stood. And all that remains of the once bustling locality of Mohalla Muharriran, is a bunch of ruins.

Land-grabbing in Roshan Lal Ka Katra and songs about a ghadar hero and villains

We then proceeded towards the heart of Dariyabad, to an area now known as Roshan Lal Ka Katra. We entered the katra through a grand gate, perhaps built by Dariya Khan who first built this settlement. The locals, however, insist that the katra was built later by Lala Roshan Lal, the Hindu dewan to the local landlord, Almas Ali. As proof, they pointed out that Katra Roshan Lal still has a mosque and inn named after Roshan Lal.

Further queries however revealed that Lala Roshan Lal, a kayastha by caste, was a wily operator. Over the years he had hoodwinked his gullible and somewhat laidback lord Almas Ali, and discreetly managed to grab some land and build a rather lucrative inn on it. When some of his known adversaries rushed to Almas Ali to report the Lala's unauthorized land grab, Ali decided to pay a surprise visit to Dariyabad. Roshan Lal, who had been tipped already by his moles about the impending inspection, quickly started building a mosque next to the disputed inn. When asked what was all this hullaballoo about unauthorized constructions on his lands, the wily Roshan Lal replied humbly that he was actually just getting a mosque built for his lordship so that whenever he was passing by, he could offer his namaz comfortably.

Almas Ali was pleased by the Lala's thoughtfulness and the matter of the inn was buried quietly. There is still a carved stone upon the wall of the mosque proclaiming that the mosque was built in the Hijri year of 1203, sixty-nine years prior to the mutiny at Almasgunj. This confirmed that the original name of the Katra Roshan Lal was indeed Almasgunj. By now the MLA,

Nigam-ji, Tulsi Ram and our self-appointed local guide Mohan Lal were in full form, each capping one story with another. About 125 years ago, Nigam said, this area had a population of 25,000 and in the evenings Katra Roshan Lal was like the bustling chowk area in old Lucknow where one could barely walk about among the large and milling crowds.

Did anyone remember some local folk songs or long sagas that may have been composed in the local dialect about the mutiny? I asked. Mohan Lal immediately exclaimed that had he been informed earlier, he could have easily summoned a dozen men who could still recite a popularly sung local Alha poem that detailed the martyrdom of the Raja of Chahlari. But he assured us, he did remember a few couplets that he would recite to us. He then cleared his throat, clapped his right hand on his right ear, extended his left and burst into a stirring couplet:

> The women were from Sahgunj,
> the launda that ran away from Bhitauli
> The one that dug in and unsheathed his sword
> Was our Raja of Chahlari.

Who was this *launda* who had abandoned the poor women and ran off? I was curious to know. Why the pejorative? It was the cowardly Raja Man Singh, the Raja of Shahgunj, Mohan Lal explained. He was called a *launda* (an imbecilic young lad) because he had let down his rebel friends despite having been entrusted by his rebel friends with protecting their begums and had chosen to flee from battle to save his life unlike a true Rajput. It was then that the Raja of Chahlari, who was passing by, stepped in and gave his life like a true Kshatriya warrior trying to save the honour of women.

Mohan Lal informed us that Thakur Rampal, a man in a nearby village had a whole stock of such ballads. But when we asked to be taken to him, we were told that he was unavailable.

At Mohan Lal's request, Tulsi Das recited another short poem:

> *The Raja of Chahlari talked to his men,*
> *We shall attack their cannons that are aimed at us, he said,*
> *We shall put their gunners to sword and grab the cannons,*
> *And then kill and feed the firangees to the vultures.*
> *These firangees from London that are leading the Company's forces*
> *We shall make the ground soft with their blood,*
> *I am the son of Shripal of the Raikwar clan*
> *I must build a dam to block their moves.*

I was keen to hear more, but that's all Tulsi Das could recall. Many lines were within his heart, he said, but none would rise to the surface.

Could someone then refer us to some of their elderly relatives who may have witnessed the battle in Dariyabad or had been given first-hand information by those that had participated in it? Could we at least learn names of the local folk who had participated in the battle?

We were given a long list of ordinary villagers: Beni Pathak and Thakur Awtar Singh of Tarapur village, Ramsevak Pande of Hansor and Jhau Lal Pathak had fought in the battle of Barabanki, and then among the rebels from the upper classes there was Rai Abhiram Bali of Dariyabad, Ajab Singh, the landlord of Sikraura village and his bosom friend Allahbaksh. The last named, we were told, was killed fighting the British at the Barren Bagh road near Kayampur. His friend Ajab Singh impressed the British so much with his bravery, we were told, that after they had beheaded him, the goras carried his head to Lucknow where it was displayed at the museum for many days.

We had by now returned to the school in Dariyabad where tea awaited us. Word had also gone around about our visit, and several locals awaited us with a treasure of tales about the martyrs from the mutiny. We now picked some interesting and innocent local lore about various small rulers like the local raja of Hadaha state. He was rather immature, we were told, but his wife Rani Ratan Kunwar was a sharp one and what she actually wanted was to oust Muslim rulers from the area and establish Hindu rule. But since the British won the battle, that particular plan failed to fructify. This version was hotly contested by some, who said that the plan to restore Hindu hegemony was an earlier one and it was not the Rani of Hadaha but the ruler of Amethi who had launched it. The aim then, was to tackle Maulana Amir Ali, not because he was a Muslim, but because earlier in 1853 he had declared a jihad against Hindus in Ayodhya and posed a threat to the lives of people there.

Everybody however agreed that in 1857, the Hadaha Rani had joined the group of local feudal rulers led by Rana Veni Madhav Baksh Singh that also included the Thakur of Barkataha, the talukedar of Ranimau and Sher Bahadur Singh of Kamiyar. All of them later fought in unison against the British forces.

The grandson of the Chief Gunner of Dariyabad and Rudauli, also survivors from the Bali family, saved by the family goddess and English tuitions

We took to the lanes once again and met one of the oldest citizens of Dariyabad, Shri Paltani, a man in his nineties. He was the grandson of Bechan Chaudhary, the gunner in charge of the topkhanas of both Dariyabad and Rudauli in 1857.

'The gora soldiers had camped in the public gardens,' he said, 'but they were massacred by the rebels and the treasuries were looted. The next day when the British forces arrived to retaliate, people began to run and hide. Many from Dariyabad hid in Kamiyar and I had heard from the family elders that the heads of rebels were cut and hung upon six gates in the city, as a warning.'

'What gates were these?' we asked.

'All that I don't know. Whatever I had heard from our elders, I have told you,' said Paltani-ji and lapsed into silence.

Our next stop was at the house of the Bali family. They belong to a powerful kayastha clan and one of their members, Rai Rajeshwar Bali had been a minister in the local cabinet during the Raj days. Their ancestors had arrived in Dariyabad as legal advisors to the British. Surendra Nath Bali, a member of this clan has held a senior post in All India Radio in Delhi and is a friend of mine. I have known him as a connoisseur of music who has organized many memorable musical gatherings at his house in Lucknow for friends. The Bali family is a devotee of Shakti and Lord Krishna and has named many of the local villages after areas in western UP that were Krishna's pet haunts. So this region has its own Gokula, Nandgaon, Barsana and Vrindavan.

At the Bali residence I once again raised my query about the six gates where the rebels' heads were hung by the British. We were told that six principalities—Paska, Kamiyar, Shahpur, Dhanava, Ata and Paraspur—were known as the six gates to the area. The erstwhile ruling families in these villages were all friends with the Bali family and Thakur Sher Bahadur Singh of Kamiyar enjoyed the rank of a commander-in-chief among them. During the mutiny, members of the Bali family had sought refuge in Kamiyar. An old member of the Bali family *(unfortunately, his name, hastily scribbled with a pencil, has become illegible)* talked about Pratap Bali Singh of his clan who was the manager of the estate and was in possession of the keys to the treasury.

'It is believed that a posse of British officials flourishing naked swords, had surrounded him and asked him to hand over the keys, to which Pratap Bali's reply was that he was a mere manager and did not handle any keys. When the British made threatening gestures towards him, Pratap chanted the name of the family's guardian goddess Ishta Devi for help. When Pratap's mother heard about the firangees threatening her son, she went into the prayer room to seek the goddess' blessings but found the statue of the goddess missing. Her son's life was under threat and she feared that the goddess had deserted them! The poor mother began to weep and wail. But suddenly she saw that the statue was back where it had always stood. She was astounded by the miracle. After a short while her son arrived. The mother hugged him and told him what had happened. Pratap Bali told her that when he had called out to the goddess for help, she must have left her abode and saved his life, this was why she must have gone missing.'

The story is a good example of how a tribe whose self-respect has been trampled upon again and again, may fight extreme adversity by an unshakeable faith in divine intervention. Against the background of an uprising that was triggered off by a perceived threat to the natives' dharma, the rise of several such stories is neither strange nor rare. The goddess is said to have manifested her powers yet again in the post-mutiny years after the British had once again found their bearings. They had chosen the palace of the Bali clan as their office, and tried converting the holy room of the deity deliberately into a stable, to desecrate it. The day they did this, it is said that all their horses died overnight. Those with knowledge of this incident used it to tell the gora sahibs about how powerful the goddess was and warned them against incurring her wrath. After that, the practice of tying their horses in that particular room came to an abrupt end.

The palace soon became home to many British families. A certain Mr Shamier, who later became a divisional commissioner, was born there. Once when he visited the palace he expressed a desire to see his birthplace and when he saw the room, he remarked, 'Oh, so this is where I was born!'

There was a jail located outside the palace. Ranjit Singh, one of the guards who protected its gates was educated and had learnt the English language. He went and colluded with the British, and in exchange for his swapping his loyalties, the British rewarded him with a gift of five villages that had belonged to the Bali family.

I also enquired about Abhiram Bali, who I had heard had participated in the ghadar against the British. I was told that he was the nephew of Rai Pratap Bali but he had not participated in the uprising. Apparently, no one from the Bali family had. Then why were five villages snatched away from them? Nobody had any answers. Perhaps, it was because in the post-mutiny phase, the British rulers redistributed the land and titles, but the principality of Bondi—the meeting point of one of the biggest gathering of native rebel leaders under Begum Hazrat Mahal, the rebel queen of Awadh—was amalgamated totally with the Crown's properties.

Mahadeva Village

Some parallel theories regarding the possible route taken by Begum Hazrat Mahal to the Nepal border, and the alleged sighting of the mysterious rebel leader and last Maratha Peshwa, Nana Saheb, by locals performing a Shraddha

On our way back from the palace of the Bali family, Ram Swarup Vajpai recounted some more details about the uprising. He said that Begum Hazrat Mahal of Lucknow had actually passed via Barabanki and not Sitapur, as is generally believed. She arrived at Barabanki on 23 March 1858 and reached Bhayara village via Deva, where she crossed the Kalyani river. Thereafter on 16 April 1858 she reached Hazratpur, which is named after her and lies near the village of Badosarai. At an assembly there she conferred with the local rulers and they all concluded that they would not be able to take on the mighty British forces. The Begum then left for village Mahadeva and thence to Bhitauli, where she sought shelter with Raja Devi Baksh Singh of Bhitauli in Gonda district. After Bhitauli was razed on 5 December 1858 by the British army chasing the Begum, she escaped to a place called Nanpara and then crossed into Nepal.

I was not entirely convinced by this travel trajectory. According to facts referred to in a collection of letters written by various begums of Awadh, *Begumate Awadh Ke Khatut* (Chapter 10) while fleeing from Lucknow, Begum Hazrat Mahal had proceeded via the village of Biswan to Badi in Sitapur district. Another book, *Kaisar Ut Tavareekh*, also corroborates this route from Lucknow towards Sitapur. But when I pointed this out to him, Vajpai-ji stood by his story, saying that if folks in Mahadeva believed that the Begum came to Barabanki, she must have.

Deen Dayal Dixit, whose ancestors had participated in the war of independence in 1857, and who was himself now employed in the department of political pensions at the state secretariat, confirmed the story about Hazrat Mahal travelling to Nepal via Barabanki. When I contacted him and requested him to describe and confirm the participation of his ancestors in the ghadar, he wrote me a letter that said:

There is a place called Hazratpur in the district of Barabanki located to the north of Bado Sarai, some two miles south of the river Ghaghra. Originally a fort during the ghadar, Hazratpur had thick brick walls and four domes, of which only ruins remain now. After the fall of Lucknow, this was where the rebel leaders: Begum Hazrat Mahal, Prince Birjis Qadr, Nana Dhondu Pant Peshwa, Rana Veni Madhav Singh, Raja Hardutt Singh of Bondi and Raja Devi Baksh Singh and the Raja of Gonda held a secret conclave. Their loyal followers kept vigil at crucial points such as Nawabgunj and Behrat Ghat to protect their leaders from enemy forces. A posse of trusted men willing to lay down their lives for their beloved native leaders stood guard at the gates of the fort. Pandit Bhawani Shankar Dixit and his elder son Prayag Dutt of village Arya Mau, Shiv Ram Upadhyay of village Tasipur and some elders from the village Khor participated in the vigil.

The leaders and their men crossed the Ghaghra river by boat from Sardaha Ghat at 2 a.m. arriving at the palace of the Raja of Bondi at dawn. Begum Hazrat Mahal rewarded all those who had stood guard through the night, with her own priceless jewels. The loyalists had successfully held back the British forces beyond Behram Ghat and Nawabgunj area. The leaders then entered the district of Bahraich on their way to Nepal, with the British forces in hot pursuit. After they razed the fort of Bondi to the ground, Raja Devi Baksh Singh of Gonda decided to dig in his heels and defend his kingdom while the others proceeded to Tulsipur and Devi Patan from where they finally managed to escape into Nepal. The Queen of Tulsipur was killed while giving cover to the rebel group that included Nana Saheb, the Raja of Bondi, Begum Hazrat Mahal, Prince Birjis Qadr and a few of their trusted men including Bhawani Shankar Dixit and his son Prayag Dutt.

After they entered the dense forests of Nepal, many members of the team fell sick and died. Begum Hazrat Mahal and Nana Saheb developed differences and the Begum, her son and others left for Kathmandu while the Nana and Bhawani Shankar Dixit moved north-west. Bhawani Shankar Dixit died during the journey and was cremated by his son Prayag Dutt within the forest. At this point Nana Saheb advised Prayag to leave them and settle down in some village in Nepal and perform the necessary rituals for his father. He also ordered Dixit's sons to ensure that at least one of them go to Gaya (in Bihar) at some point and perform a shraddha for his father there to finally set his wandering soul at rest. As for himself, Nana himself decided to renounce the world, become a sanyasi and go on a pilgrimage to various holy cities until death claimed his body. It is said that he had given a secret mantra to Prayag Dutt, which, when chanted at a pilgrimage spot, would get them a darshan of Nana. The secret mantra used the imagery of wild rice on which Nana had subsisted since they left Tulsipur. It is said that if one chews upon the root of this plant, it can control hunger for many days.

The principalities of Gonda and Bondi were both amalgamated into the British empire after the mutiny was over. The village of Arya Mau that had belonged to Bhawani Shankar's family, was handed over to the Raja of Hadaha. Shankar's sons migrated and settled in the principalities of Baroda in Gujarat and Udaipur in Rajasthan. It was only after twenty-five years that the Dixit family regrouped in

Arya Mau. Prayag Dutt had already returned to his native village from Nepal. As per custom it was necessary that a shraddha be performed in Gaya by the sons of Bhawani Shankar Dixit before they could stake a claim to any family property, and that could be done only after the one who performed the shraddha had visited all the necessary pilgrimage spots. Prayag therefore gave the magical mantra to his younger brother Lalta Prasad who was willing to do what was ordained. It is said that he used the secret mantra upon reaching the holy city of Allahabad and was indeed rewarded with a darshan of Nana as promised.

Nana Saheb was pleased at his reverence for his father and presented him with a copy of the holy Ramayana. Lalta Prasad then set out on a pilgrimage with Nana to the holy town of Badrinath in the Himalayas, but unfortunately he died on the way.

Upon receiving news of his death, another brother, Mahavir Prasad Dixit completed the remaining part of the pilgrimage and then performed the shraddha at Gaya. It is said that he too used the magic mantra in the forests of Naimisharanya and when Nana came as promised, he was informed that the Gaya shraddha for his companion Bhawani Dutt had been performed properly as per his orders. Nana lived for several more years and some newspaper reports claim that he died in 1936 in Naimisharanya itself. The year could not be independently confirmed but what is undisputed is that his remaining years after the mutiny were spent as a sanyasi visiting pilgrimage spots.

This writer is the great-grandson of Bhawani Shankar Dixit and this story was recounted to him by his father Pandit Mahavir Prasad Dixit. Some of the weapons that had been salvaged after the 1857 mutiny are still buried under a wall in his ancestral house. Another cache lies in a well that Bhawani Prasad Dixit had dug in one of the orchards he owned. This writer had himself immersed the copy of the holy Ramayana in the Ganges, the same copy that Nana had presented his grand-uncle. The immersion was necessary since the volume by

*now had disintegrated completely and the pages turned to dust upon
touch. Perhaps if some old sanyasi in the Naimisharanya area were
to be quizzed, more trivia about the band of rebels led by Nana could
be unearthed.*

While reading this letter, I'd made up my mind to arrive at
Naimisharanya and probe Nana's sudden disappearance.
However I remain sceptical about the Begum of Awadh arriving
in Bhitauli via the Barabanki route. The book *Savanhat-e-
Salateen-e-Awadh* records clearly that the Begum-e-Aliya's
procession left Alam Bagh in Lucknow, arrived in Bharawan,
then left for Khairabad via Badi. She stayed at the palace of Raja
Sahib of Mahmudabad as a guest. She then left for the Bondi
meet with other native princes via Bhithauli. In a letter written
by Sarfaraz Begum Lakhnavi, (one of the Nawabs of Awadh,
Wajid Ali Shah's begums) to a co-wife, Begum Akhtar Mahal
who was incarcerated at the Matia Burz in Calcutta with her
exiled husband, I found this:

'... Hazrat Mahal (the begum who had stayed behind to claim
the throne of Awadh for her young son Birjis Qadr) left in a
palanquin from Alam Bagh. When she departed from Lucknow,
she was accompanied by Mammoo Khan on horseback. The
zamindar Raja Mardan Singh gave her the cold shoulder but
Maulvi Amaduddin Devi alias Maulvi Muhammad Nazim came
to meet her all the way from Biswan-e-Badi some six miles away.
It was then decided to head towards Bareilly.'

I feel it was the great affection the people of Awadh
harboured for their Nawab and his family, that has led to
conflicting and unsubstantiated claims about the Begum

or Nana Saheb Peshwa having visited 'their area'. And the stories about the slow disintegration of the Nawab's family who was humiliated and sent to Calcutta in exile, contributed tremendously to the popular ire against the British that erupted all over Awadh a few months later.

As we proceeded further, it was becoming clear that the alien rule was not the only factor that drove the people of Awadh into revolt. Their caste-based feudal social structure failed to challenge an increasingly weak state where bureaucratic corruption was rampant. But for a handful of nobles, life had remained hell for the poor for as long as they could remember. Had it not been so, immediately after the ghadar, sociopolitical equations could not have changed so radically in such a short span of time. Within a decade of the ghadar, in 1865, some 5,000 young students in Awadh had voluntarily left their traditional learning systems and were attending 1,400 government-run schools where they were taught to read and write in English, the language of the firangee rulers that eventually replaced Persian as the formal language of power. Had such a deep desire for a new society and new learning signified by English not been lying in the heart of the society in Awadh, would such changes have been possible?

2

BHAYARA

The raja-cum-talukedar in Awadh had been the customary recipient of various kinds of dues from his subjects, both in cash and kind. The Kidwais of Bhayara and the young martyr, Raja of Chahlari both belonged to this category. Like others of their class, they hired the services of men from lower castes–koeris, kachhis, barbers and others– who tilled the soil for them as loyal bonded labour. These men were paid mostly in kind and occasionally in cash and granted full protection against the petty government functionaries. On certain occasions, able-bodied men from among them were recruited into a loosely structured armed militia for the raja. They were given perfunctory training in use of arms, but they spent most of their time working on the fields as farmers.

Mrinal Pande

We left early in the morning for Bhayara village in Barabanki district. During the nineteenth century, in addition to being a hub for growing sugarcane, Barabanki was a major producer and supplier of opium to the decadent nawab's court at Lucknow, the capital of Awadh. Just as hills attract us with their dark, mysterious profiles, their serpentine roads and snow-capped peaks, flat plains bearing the unending and vast generosity of Mother Nature enchant the mind in a unique way. The soil in the area appeared sandy but was obviously fertile. Vast fields surrounded by tall trees and rows of hills along the horizon gave this land the look of a vast platter with raised rims. We travelled down a road that ran along a canal and was flanked by lush sugarcane fields on either side.

At Bhayara, we finally halted at the panchayat house, right next to a canal. It was a surprisingly modern building replete with a children's playground that sported swings, a merry-go-round and a see-saw. The homes of the villagers meanwhile, were humble mud huts with thatched straw roofs. Perhaps in another decade or so, I thought, when the panchayat building would begin to look old and weathered, these homes would be reconstructed with stone and cement and have running water and electricity, and the playground may not appear so out of place here.

We had come to this village looking for an Alha poem about one of the heroes of the ghadar. Many such long poems about ancient wars and legendary warriors, I was told, are still sung in the villages of Awadh. These are set to a specific metre and narrated dramatically in public, accompanied by drums and cymbals. I was keen in particular to listen to Alhas that described the feats of the Raja of Chahlari, a near-forgotten young hero of the ghadar who was killed battling the British and buried close by in Barabanki. My friend Acchan Sahib had mentioned to me in Lucknow that his maternal uncle Sheikh Abdul Ali Kidwai, an erstwhile landlord of the Bhayara village, possessed a bunch of rare local Alhas dating back to 1857 when the ghadar erupted in Awadh. He had informed Sheikh sahib of my impending visit and awaited our visit.

His house, a simple dwelling with a thatched roof, stood close to the panchayat house and Sheikh sahib sat outside on a simple bamboo charpoy. He welcomed us politely and after the customary exchange of formal salutations, I asked him about the Alhas and the legends about the ghadar he may have heard from his elders. Sheikh sahib told me that with age, his memory was failing; so sometime ago he had written down whatever he could remember of the ghadar and sent the papers to his nephew and my friend Achhan who was to have them published. However, since we had chosen to come all the way to meet him, he said he would try to recount whatever remained in his memory. He began without much fuss:

'After the banished Nawab Wajid Ali Shah's wife Begum Hazrat Mahal lost the throne of Lucknow to the Company's men, she sent out an appeal for help to various princes in Barabanki, including the Raja of Chahlari. They all decided to gather at Mahadeva village to prepare a strategy that would help the Begum defeat the armies of the East India Company and restore the rule of nawabs. By now, the signs of an impending public revolt in the entire countryside of Awadh were clearly visible. A local Maulvi, Ahmedullah Shah from Faizabad district had been going around urging local Muslims to unite with their Hindu brethren, cutting across barriers of religion to overthrow the British. His fiery speeches left a deep impact on the locals and they signalled that they too were ready to merge as one with the native forces led by the Begum of Awadh.

'Begum Hazrat Mahal's coalition by now also included local Hindu rulers of Bondi and Charda states along with my paternal grandfather Sheikh Yaseen Ali Kidwai, a major landlord from the well-known clan of Kidwais. He and his trusted men joined the rebels at Mahadeva village, an old and popular pilgrimage spot in Barabanki named after an idol of Lord Mahadeva (Shiva). The temple was ancient and the statue was said to have been installed by the legendary Pandava warrior Yudhishthira over a thousand years ago. This village became the epicentre where a united front of Hindus and Muslims was forged formally. To seal their pledge, the Hindus went into the temple and placed their hands upon the idol of their lord, while the Muslims held copies of the holy Quran, and together, all vowed to fight the firangees unitedly till their last breath.

'When I was a child, we had an old family retainer by the name of Bhaggu Naai, a Muslim barber by profession and a poet by passion. He had long served the Kidwai clan in the house of Shujat Ali, who was the great-grandfather of the well-known Congress leader Rafi Ahmed Kidwai who participated in the freedom struggle with Jawaharlal Nehru-ji. Bhaggu witnessed the ghadar himself, and being poetically inclined, he composed a stirring Alha about the battle of Barabanki in 1857. After the ghadar, Bhaggu resigned from his job at our house and chose to become an *attar* (a seller of perfumes). He did drop by whenever he was in the neighbourhood and when he came, we, the children would ask him to narrate some of his stirring stories and Alhas to us and he was only too happy to oblige.

'I have already put all this on paper along with the entire Alha about the Raja of Chahlari for your friend and my nephew Acchan. But since you have been kind enough to come all the way, I will try and recite to you whatever I can recall of that ballad now. When you go back to Lucknow, you may ask Acchan to show you the bunch of papers. I should also add that Alha singing is a special gift and a good Alha singer can recreate an entire battle to an extent that you feel you are witnessing it with your own eyes. Bhaggu Nai, as he sang the Alha, slipped into a trance. His posture and voice changed, and he became charged with a strange emotion as he reached the part about the young Raja of Chahlari's last hours, so much so that tears rolled down his cheeks and his voice choked faltered with genuine grief. This is how the Alha goes:

> As the sahibs pitched their tents in Obree,
> Princes of the land joined hands in the name of Rama.
> The guns of the sahibs boomed and shrapnel flew
> It was as though the apocalypse was nigh, O Rama.
> In an instant those that were hit died
> Bits of their bodies littered the countryside.
> Rajas and others ran away screaming to save their lives,
> Among them the cowardly Hardutt Singh, Raja of Bondi,
> And Raja of Charda Jot Singh by name.
> The one that stayed back to face the enemy and met his doom
> Was our Raja of Chahlari, Balbhadra Singh, a young bridegroom
> His wedding headgear and lucky amulet still in place as he was killed.

> As the enemy's men ran towards the royal elephant
> And the worried mahout asked his lord's permission to turn back,
> The proud raja waved a 'No!' and spoke angrily to his man,
> That fleeing from battle was unbecoming of the Kshatriya clan.
> 'Send me my horse!' he ordered, and when it was brought in,
> The raja handing his loyal mahout his gold bracelets said 'Go!'
> Then leapt upon horseback and was soon deep in battle as though
> A fearless hound was tearing into a pack of frightened sheep.

> All by himself the young Raja of Chahlari dodged the enemy for hours,
> When he fell, he had slain eleven British officers and many men.
> Only when they all piled on him, could the brave raja be
> brought down.

By then he had killed no less than fifty men.
The martyred raja's fame spread far, upto London and all around
Vilayat where the firangees conceded that no one had fought them
As had the brave young Raja of Chahlari on the battleground.

By the time Sheikh sahib stopped reciting these lines, tears were rolling down his own cheeks. 'I feel as though I am talking about my own grandfather,' he said, wiping his eyes. 'We are an old family. My grandfather Sheikh Yaseen Ali Kidwai belonged to a long line of Kidwais of Bhayara, whose origins remain vague. All I know is that around 1857, the Kidwai family had been residing in the principality of Awadh for some 750 years. My grandfather was born and lived all his life in Bhayara village and was well-known as a major landlord of the area. When thousands of Hindu-Muslim rebels who had taken to arms against the British crossed the Kalyani river at Bhayara, my grandfather also decided to throw in his lot with the native forces and joined them with a bunch of his trusted men. According to an old couplet we, the Kidwais were the owners of fifty-two villages in the district:

Fifty-two villages make up Kidwara,
The largest of them being village Bhayara.

'Since major events of the ghadar are already known, let me give you my version of why the natives of Bhayara and their partners finally lost to the British. The men from Bhayara and their comrades were undoubtedly brave, but despite their noble intentions, they were too emotionally charged and untrained for organized battle. Our side was no match for the the much smaller but disciplined and well-trained British soldiers. Our local leaders mostly panicked under pressure and abandoned their soldiers at the mercy of the enemy to save themselves. The rajas of Bondi and Charda were quick to flee, and as Bhaggu's ballad says, only young Balbhadra Singh of Chahlari fought back and gave all he could.

'My grandfather too fought hard, but his unskilled men were soon mowed down by the firangee soldiers and he was shot and badly wounded. Despite being unconscious, he survived only because his horse managed to carry him to the safety of a sugarcane field. Later, after dark, when some of his cultivators located him lying unconscious in the field, he was carried to safety. Such a close brush with death can do strange things to a man. For one, he begins to dread any kind of painful death, especially death by hanging. When the British had crushed the ghadar comprehensively and bloody reprisals against the native rebels were unleashed, my grandfather was frantic to escape the noose. Later, in the jubilee year of Queen Victoria, when the British announced amnesty for all those who had not killed any firangee man, woman or child outside of the battlefield, my grandfather promptly presented himself in the court and gave an affidavit swearing his innocence. He finally managed to save his life but it cost him most of his family lands.'

When I asked whether any other member of the clan had participated in the ghadar, Sheikh sahib's answer was as interesting as it was blunt:

'The Kidwais had had an uneasy relationship with the nawabs of Lucknow since the famous battle of Buxar (1761). As a result they refused to pay the annual revenues that the representatives of subsequent nawabs sought. It got so bad that occasionally, a group of armed officials from Lucknow was sent to collect taxes from the Kidwais. The reason for their anger against the nawabi government was that during the battle of Buxar, 1,700 men of the Kidwai clan had supported Nawab Shuja-ud-Daula of Lucknow as volunteers when he joined Shah Alam to try and wrest power from the firangees. As the cowardly nawab lost the battle and decided to flee, the Kidwais admonished him saying, "If you, the leader, desert your men thus, you may regain your shame later as you are the badshah. But how will we, ordinary recruits in your army go back and show our face in public? We simply cannot run away!" The nawab chose to ignore their plea and fled. All 1700 of our best young men chose to stay on and fight the enemy to save their honour, only to be slaughtered in battle. We have heard from elder women in our family how an enormous wailing broke out of the Kidwai haveli, as the young widows of all those martyrs smashed their glass bangles in the courtyard. The uncaring nawab did not lift a finger to compensate the bereaved families or provide protection and care for the orphaned children of those who had fought so bravely for him.

'After that, the animosity between the Kidwais and the Lucknow nawab only grew until our fortunes and the number of men dwindled. Some members of the clan soon began to drift apart and seized opportunity when they saw one. We are practicing Sunnis but several Kidwais, including our cousins in Jehangirabad, chose to get themselves registered at the durbar as Shias (the sect to which the nawabs of Lucknow belonged). Despite this transition, as far as I know, barring my grandfather, none of the other Kidwais from the area or Jehangirabad took to arms in support of the Begum of Awadh during the ghadar. The

Kidwais of Jehangirabad were among the richest landlords but they never sided with the nawabs after one bitter experience.'

It was a pleasure to meet a man so refreshingly honest and frank. Sheikh sahib had spoken to us with an intimacy and warmth one reserves for one's own kin. As we reluctantly took our leave he said, 'I am glad you are writing all this down for posterity before it gets lost. In many ways, I have felt closer to the martyr Raja of Chahlari than my own clan. The story of his bravery connects me with my grandfather as nothing else does. Another member of my clan I am proud of, is Rafi Ahmed Kidwai. He has continued our glorious tradition.'

Jehangirabad

How Sir Hope Grant nearly lost his life, and the intriguing tale of the inimitable rise of a scoundrel, Raja Naushad Ali

After Bhayara we headed for Jehangirabad, one of the biggest talukas in the district. In his book *The Sepoy War*, Sir Hope Grant has spoken rather derisively of the double-faced Raja Razzak Baksh, the ruler of Jehangirabad. He writes how he had heard of the impregnable clay fort of Jehangirabad among dense impenetrable forests, and also how the wily ruler of Jehangirabad had been playing both sides. Earlier the ruler had apparently visited Sir Grant and shown him great courtesy, bowing to him again and again and swearing everlasting loyalty to the British. He claimed he was visiting to offer them three cannons to help them crush the rebellion. But when Sir Grant and two of his battalions reached the gate of the so called fort, they found it surrounded with a thicket of bamboos and thorny shrubs.

After they crossed it successfully, they were informed that the promised cannons had already been sent to the divisional commissioner. In the meantime, Grant's men had ferreted out two cannons hidden in the thickets, and another aiming at the road they were to take on their way out. This one had a slow burning fuse lit inside. It was only then that they learnt that some of their officials had chanced upon papers within the fort, that listed seditious plans against the British.

Sir Hope rushed back to Nawabgunj and sent an army under the leadership of his trusted brigadier that burnt the forest and decimated the entire fort. I had also gathered from other sources how the victorious British had first hung the raja and eighty of his men from trees, and later disposed off their dead bodies by throwing them into the burning forest. Afterwards the gurkhas and the Company's forces had gone on a rampage, looting the raja's treasures and raping the women from his palace.

This incident prompts an obvious question. Was Raja Razzak Baksh of Jehangirabad a patriot or a British loyalist? And what about his son-in-law Raja Farzand Ali alias Naushad Ali?

It is entirely possible that Raja Razzak Baksh, from whose palaces seditious material was seized and who was later found to have made meticulous plans to kill Sir Hope and his men, was sympathetic to the native cause because of his intense dislike for the British. The way he and his men were punished also makes it amply clear that the British did not consider him an ally either. But then what can explain the British appointing Naushad Ali as the next ruler of Jehangirabad, after killing Raja Razzak Baksh and his men so brutally?

The rise of Naushad Ali is an utterly intriguing story. In Bhayara, Sheikh sahib had told me that Raja Naushad Ali began life as a commoner named Farzand Ali. The story of how he managed to marry Zaibunnisa, the only daughter of Raja Razzak Baksh is shrouded in mystery. The match though, is corroborated by *The Golden Book of India* by Sir Roper Leithbridge, wherein the writer refers to Zaibunnisa (born on 28 October 1855) as the queen of Jehangirabad who should actually have inherited the throne of Jehangirabad upon her father's death on 7 April 1881, when she was twenty-six years old. The roots of her marriage and the subsequent elevation of Naushad Ali as successor to Raja Razzak Baksh upon the throne, however remain shrouded in mystery. What is clear though, is that before he got married, Naushad Ali was a pampered man at the court of Nawab Wajid Ali Shah and had managed to acquire the title of a raja from the nawab even before he had acquired a principality to rule. What is even more unusual is that his title was also confirmed later by the British as his family title, on dubious grounds that he had married a royal.

Farzand Ali alias Naushad Ali's known story pans out like this. Before he married Zaibunnisa, this handsome young man was the lowly caretaker of the Sikander Bagh gardens in Lucknow. His boyish good looks attracted the attention of Wajid Ali Shah when the latter was once walking in the gardens. The enchanted Nawab thereafter sent Farzand Ali some rich gifts and offered him a place in the court. The obvious interest shown in him by the Nawab Badshah of Lucknow opened the gates to good fortune for the handsome and ambitious young man. Khwajasara Bashir-ud-Daula , an influential eunuch at the nawab's court is also said to have been charmed by Farzand Ali and it was through his efforts that he was felicitated with the title of 'raja' by Wajid Ali Shah.

It is quite possible that to elevate him and help him enter the privileged ranks of nobility of Awadh, the Nawab Wajid Ali

Shah and his powerful Khwajasara may have pressurized Raja Razzak Baksh, to marry his only daughter to the commoner Farzand Ali. His status as the Raja of Jehangirabad's son-in-law would then lend credibility to the title of 'raja' conferred upon him by the Nawab.

When the Nawab of Lucknow was dethroned in 1857 and sent to Calcutta, Farzand Ali was part of the select group of nobles that the British permitted to follow the exiled Nawab. He stayed in Calcutta during the ghadar. As soon as the revolt had been quashed, Naushad Ali changed tack publicly and became a loyalist to the victorious British. This move not only helped him get his title as the Raja of Jehangirabad confirmed, the British also entrusted him with the additional powers of an assistant collector. I had gathered from Sheikh sahib that the direct descendants of Raja Razzak Baksh still lived in the village and that it was widely suspected that when Naushad Ali accompanied the deposed Nawab Wajid Ali Shah to Calcutta, he was feigning loyalty to the Nawab. All along, his real loyalties lay with the British who had embedded him in the unsuspecting Nawab's entourage as their spy. And once his father-in-law Raja Razzak Baksh had been disposed of, Naushad Ali received the throne of Jehangirabad as a handsome reward from the British for his loyalty.

If the above stories are true, what was Naushad Ali's relationship with his father-in-law really like? If indeed Raja Razzak Baksh was forced by the Nawab to give his only daughter Zebunnisa in marriage to this handsome bisexual, the nobleman may well have harboured a big grudge against this wily commoner. But in that case, Razzak Baksh could have easily offered Sir Hope Grant an easy access to the fort and helped him discover the cannons and other seditious material hidden within, and confessed that this was done by his son-in-law who was a known groupie of the deposed Nawab and wished to upstage those that had forced him into exile.

Strangely, when Sir Hope Grant and his men arrived at Jehangirabad, Razzak Baksh lured the British army and its officials into the forest with a view to segregating and killing their leaders. When the plan backfired, he and his trusted men were brutally butchered by the British.

Could this be taken as proof that Raja Razzak Baksh was a man of principles who risked everything he loved to support his native brethren against the British? The son-in-law Farzand Ali was certainly not loyal either to his mentor or to his native brethren. He was just a ruthless and ambitious young man who used his charm and was further aided by good luck to rise from a lowly caretaker of the royal gardens to a raja and deputy collector to Her Majesty's government. Ultimately he emerges in native lore as a weak man with strong ambition.

History, ancient and modern, now began to unfold before our eyes as the grand Jehangirabad palace became visible among tall clusters of palm trees.

Several ancient groves of bamboos were visible near the river that ran along the ruins of the old fort at Jehangirabad. They framed several old mosques and patches of brown earth. Flames of the forest were in bloom here and there and they added a touch of crimson to the scene.

'This is the old area of Gadhi that Hope Grant had decimated,' Indu Prakash pointed out. 'Once this was a favourite haunt of the British governors who came here to relax and hunt. People milled around the fort all day, as they do in Kaiserbagh in Lucknow. They would cross the bridge over the canal and walk right upto the palace. The bamboo groves that I saw earlier when I came here before Independence, are mostly gone now.'

We crossed the bridge and moved onward towards Naushad Ali's palace that stood flanked by an unfinished mosque to its right. This palace is still an imposing building. I thought of Sir Hope Grant and his ire against Raja Razzak Baksh. He would perhaps have been rather pleased to note how well the hated raja's son-in-law and his heirs had done for themselves. Come to think of it, most princes in the Awadh area seem to have not done too badly after the ghadar, considering the pace at which several such palatial buildings sprouted up soon after the mutiny. They were offset by ruins of palatial homes of rebels torn down by Sir Hope Grant and his men when retaliations began.

The palace of Naushad Ali was deserted. We learnt that the members of the erstwhile royal family and their managers had all departed for the hills. We came across an official who was in charge of the *maal khana* (the godowns). He accompanied us to the old Gadhi Maidan but said he knew nothing about the ghadar other than local hearsay about the properties that originally belonged to the royal house of Jehangirabad. He told us that the old palace of Raja Razzak Baksh that was demolished by the firangees was built of mud and clay. There was a reason for this. The rajas in Awadh under the rule of the nawabs had become increasingly assertive of their own authority. They seldom paid the necessary taxes to the Nawab badshah of Lucknow and when the badshah's men turned up with armed guards to collect taxes by force, the rulers would run deep into forests and hide in mud palaces constructed as temporary hiding holes. Even around the new palace of Naushad Ali that had replaced the old one, one could make out the remnants of them. The bamboo groves though were drying up fast, and most had been cut to create cultivable fields. They must have thrived while the area was forested, but were now nowhere to be seen as the forests that sheltered them had disappeared.

When asked if he had heard of Raja Razzak Baksh and his clash with the British general, the royal godown keeper flipped open a pouch and carefully extracted some chewing tobacco. 'I know nothing about history,' he said finally, swirling the rich juices in his mouth, 'but I have heard that Raja Razzak Baksh was a religious man. He lived a simple, austere life, like a fakir and had many friends amongst Hindu priests. Holy men like the Mahants of Rampur and he visited each other regularly. May his soul rest in peace.'

Kursi, The Village of Fools

Ghadar tales from the Chaudhary, the Maulvi, the Haji and Khurshid, the tailor about the fleeing rebels and those that helped themselves to their gold and jewels and lived happily ever after

I was still mulling over the tragic stories of high intrigue and betrayals that had originated in the palaces of Jehangirabad as we headed for Kursi, a village where residents have a reputation for being comical dimwits. A recent joke about Kursi has it that one of its residents was seen having a sharp exchange of words with his neighbour and soon thereafter, an unidentified body was recovered from the village well. One of the Kursi residents told the police constable that the dead one had to be the man who was recently seen in a nasty argument with his neighbour. The police immediately arrested the alleged perp even though the poor fellow kept insisting that the man next door was very much alive. The police, the alleged killer and the usual crowd of onlookers from the village landed at the police station only to discover that the allegedly murdered man was very much alive and sitting at the thana. After the police refused to listen to the entreaties of the arrested man, his alleged victim had been brought to the police station by the family of the arrested man as living proof of his undead state. The magistrate, before whom the convict was presented, instead of reprimanding the local police for not verifying the death properly, had a good laugh and said with a few expletives, 'Brothers! This is what Kursi waters will do to your brains!'

To be sure, the butt of various jokes, Kursi, is actually an ancient village that was earlier known as Luv Kushi after its founders, the twin sons of the legendary Lord Rama. It is said to have once been a stronghold of learned Brahmins but by 1030 AD, when the Muslim invader Syed Salar Masud attacked the area, it had lost its reputation for learning and was being ruled by a king of the Bhar dynasty. The Bhars or Bhar Shivas were a caste of celebrated warriors during the medieval ages, whose history is yet to be traced properly. But the stigma of Kursi being a village of buffoons is confirmed because a Mughal document, the *Jehangirnama* also refers to the Ahmakana-e-Kursi (idiots of the Kursi area).

Located barely sixteen miles from Lucknow and not being too intellectually inclined, Kursi was drawn into the whirlpool of the ghadar somewhat reluctantly. According to the district gazette, on 12 March 1858, after the fall of Lucknow, the rebel native armies crossed the stone bridge towards Barabanki and headed north, towards the Ghaghra river. When word came that some 4,000 rebels had gathered at Kursi and were waiting to mount an attack on the British, the then Brigadier Hope Grant, ordered his men to rush to Kursi and scatter the natives. In the early hours of 23 March, he succeeded in driving the ranks of the rebel army into total disarray. True to its reputation, Kursi, I soon discovered, has chosen to more or less forget the nasty war fought at its doorstep.

We first arrived at the house of Chaudhary Mehmood Hassan, a major landowner and the village head of Kursi. After being told of the purpose of our visit, Chaudhary sahib said he had no idea about the involvement of his village in the ghadar. Queries to his family retainers yielded a few names of the village octogenarians but none of them, it seemed, were fit enough to come and meet us.

Was I sure this fact was reported in the district gazette? Chaudhary sahib wanted to know. I told him that indeed it was, and that I wished to meet those in the age group of seventy to eighty in particular, who may have some rare legends about the ghadar that were passed down to them by their family elders. Our man said that this was the first time he had heard about Kursi's martyrs, but anyway since we had trudged all the way to his house, he would accompany us to the village cleric Maulvi sahib, who possessed many old books. The rest of the villagers are useless idiots, he added as an afterthought.

The village lanes we passed through, were full of old ruins bearing witness to the historical importance of the area. We settled down at the raised brick platform outside the government seed store. Soon two elders turned up. One of them was Haji Abdussamad. He had a clean-shaven head, a white beard and was dressed only in a lungi. He walked with a stoop, and his aged body and bandaged foot depended on a cane for support as he hobbled up. In a tired and barely audible whisper, he told us that the ghadar tales he had heard were all based on hearsay and he had forgotten most of them. We requested him to tell us whatever he could recall.

'Well, my mother used to say that the goras had entered the village from the point behind the mosque where the topkhana stood. The locals ran off towards Mitaila as the gora army marched in. Mitaila was a little lake at Kazi Bagh, about one and a half miles from Kursi. Finally the goras surrounded the locals near the lake and butchered them mercilessly. My mother said that ever since that massacre, the villagers were constantly scurrying here and there to save their lives.'

As Haji continued his story, I noticed that about half a dozen others had collected at the spot. An old man who must be a little younger than Haji sahib, said that the British had been ruling the area even before the ghadar. During the revolt, for three months, the villages were vacated and it was only later that the villagers were allowed back. Haji Sahib added that one of their family retainers who had saved himself by diving into the Ghaghra river and swimming across to the other side, reported that the rebels, having chased the British, had turned into violent thugs and spread panic among villagers. Their lawless ways made it easier for the British to return to power.

At this point, Khursheed miyan, the village tailor made an appearance. He was said to be around ninety years old but seemed in better health than Haji sahib. Khursheed miyan told us that the simpletons from Kursi village had indeed clashed with the goras in Khursheed Bagh. They were massacred by the British soldiers in a locality known as Madarpur. The rebel native troops were chased thereafter to the Mitaila lake and finally defeated in battle. At this point the tailor broke off and looked to Haji miyan for approval, but after he saw that miyan kept rubbing his bald pate absentmindedly, he continued. 'In those days the village had a topkhana and a permanent army contingent whose offices were located where the Chaudhary sahib now resides. The army stayed at the topkhana and during the ghadar, some soldiers from the Nawab's army had also taken up residence at Kazi Bagh.'

Haji sahib quipped that in those days, the Nawab's men used to tour the area at regular intervals to inspect the crops and assess the annual taxes payable to the royal treasuries. The land in the area was all najul category (administered directly by the Nawab's representatives) and there were no zamindars here. He said that his grandfather, a short-tempered man, was once taken into custody by the Nawab's officials and asked to do wageless labour. This made him so angry that he jumped into a dry well and said, 'If you want me to work for free, try to pull me out at the risk of drowning! I'd rather die than work without being paid.' A leader of the nawab's contingent (Risaldar) lived in this village. His mistress's grave can be found in the topkhana area, Haji sahib said.

I steered the conversation back from the Risaldar's mistress to the ghadar and asked how long the battle at Mitaila had lasted.

'Ah, it was over in just a day,' the elders said and lapsed into silence. It was obvious—this was all they could tell us.

Chaudhary sahib now accompanied us to the house of the learned Maulvi sahib with the library. He belonged to the family of the elder guru of the famous saint Waris Ali Shah and lived in his ancestral house near a mosque whose origins dated back to the days of Mughal emperor Babar. When we reached Maulvi sahib's house, it was being sprayed with DDT to fight malarial mosquitoes and he was busy supervising the somewhat intricate campaign against the nasty bloodsuckers. He excused himself as we approached and welcomed us warmly. As we got talking, he told us that he knew little other than the fact that after the fall of Lucknow, when the palaces were being looted and set on fire, many begums from the deposed Nawab Wajid Ali Shah's harem, had run to Kursi to save their lives. As the poor, disoriented women ran into unknown forest areas, many became easy prey for dacoits and soldiers that lay in wait there and were subjected to many unspeakable humiliations.

When they heard that the British were chasing them, the royals abandoned the cartloads of gold coins and precious jewellery that they had carried out of their palaces. Apparently, a man by the name of Dullu, the father of Lallu, managed to scuttle away one such cart full of gold coins from the Nawab's palace, and subsequently became rich.

The Maulvi sahib had a precious collection of old handwritten religious texts in Persian and Arabic. Several of these were by well-known professional calligraphers who had flourished in Lucknow under the nawabs. Chaudhary sahib tried to nudge him into requesting all of us to find good buyers for these precious volumes. The ample money that their sale would bring could erase all his debt and make him very rich, he said. But the Maulvi sahib had the easy nonchalance of an intellectual. 'Ah, sir,' he said to the Chaudhary, 'Time takes care of such matters. Why should you and I get into all that? When He wills, and the time is right, they will sell on their own.'

It was a pleasure to meet the learned man. I noticed that his house was paved with the kind of large lakhauri bricks one does not see any more. I asked him if he had had them baked especially for his courtyard. He said that the house we sat in was an ancient one. It was built on a spot where an old fort of the Bhars stood earlier. During the digging, a lot of beautifully baked small and large bricks were unearthed, and utilized in building the house.

As we were about to leave, word came in that Haji sahib and Khursheed miyan wished to meet us again as they had suddenly remembered a few important facts about the ghadar subsequent to our meeting. Ageing brains often work in cycles and perhaps talking to us about the past had triggered some dormant memories. So we retraced our steps, thanked them as we sat down once again, me with my pen hovering over paper, waiting for the two old men to speak.

Haji sahib said that after we left, he had suddenly recalled his mother telling him how the Begum of Awadh, when she arrived here with her young son Birjis Qadr, had kept dropping little bundles containing gold coins and her fabled jewels into various wells as she moved on. He'd also heard that before they decided to send him into exile, the wily British had asked Nawab Wajid Ali Shah to choose between twelve kosas (about thirty-five square miles) of land, or Rs 1.25 lakhs in cash as compensation for being divested of his throne. At this, his wife, Begum Hazrat Mahal's reaction was, 'What sort of measly compensation is this for a vast empire?' Finally it was Wajid Ali Shah's own father-in-law and vizier Naqui miyan (Nawab Ali Naqui Khan), who as the intermediary, was responsible for making the badshah hand his kingdom over to the British and accept that petty amount. When Prince Birjis Qadr later questioned this act, the badshah had said to him, 'What could I do? It was your grandfather who made me give away my kingdom.'

The tailor Khursheed miyan recounted another story. 'Ganga Baksh and his son, residents of the Behta village nearby went and kidnapped a white man and his memsahib. They tortured the two horribly and it is said they even drove nails into their private parts. Later, the father and son were captured by the British and they were beheaded publicly near a nullah in Lucknow, now known as Sar Katta Nullah.

I then asked if anyone had heard about natives looting or torturing other natives during the ghadar.

Khursheed miyan said that the begums of Awadh were robbed repeatedly when they were on the run to to save their lives. A man named Dullu apparently hijacked a bullock-cart loaded with precious gold and gems belonging to the begums.

'Was it the same Dullu, father to one Lallu?' I asked.

'Yes, yes, he was Lallu's father.'

I thanked the two gentlemen profusely and left.

After that I met Asghar Ali, an octogenarian living in Topkhana mohalla. He pointed out to us the near extinct graves of the then commander's favourite nautch girls and a few crumbling watchtowers. As we were about to leave, he mentioned that his father had told him how Begum Hazrat Mahal had sought shelter in Bondi village when the British came.

'Was there looting here during the ghadar?' I asked.

'No. We were told that when the soldiers arrived here, the villagers had already escaped into forests with all their belongings,' he said.

Thus the Ahmakan-e-Kursi!

Obri Village

Meeting with an actual eyewitness, Sahibdeen the centenarian

Ram Swarup Vajpai, who had been waiting for us at the district headquarters at Barabanki, asked us to meet a 114-year-old resident of a nearby Obri village, a fellow by the name of Sahibdeen. We were told that he had seen the battle of Nawabgunj with his own eyes and when the officials wanted to commemorate Raja Balbhadra Singh of Chahlari, it was he who had pointed out to them the actual spot where he was killed. Prayers and flowers were thereafter offered on 10 May, the date that marked the beginning of the ghadar a hundred years ago. We welcomed the offer and left almost immediately to meet him. It was around five in the evening when we arrived at our destination, Obri, a small village with clean and well-kept mud houses. It was here, in a large maidan, where a battle against the foreign army was fought. A battle overlooked by British and Indian scholars and forgotten by all but the common folk of the area. We crossed a lane and entered the courtyard of the house where Sahibdeen lived with his family. We saw a skeletal man lying upon a plank bed under the thatched roof of the veranda. The skin hung around his emaciated body like a loosely draped sheet and he was panting. Asthma, we were told.

It is strangely exciting and somewhat awesome to meet and listen to someone who has lived for over a century. One feels like a child in that person's presence, a person who has withstood the passage of a hundred years and lived to tell the tale. Sahibdeen wore a string of tulsi beads around his thin and wrinkled neck. His face had become hairless. His body, now almost a skeleton, had seen better days. Signs of ageing marked his skull-like face with unmoving and opaque eyeballs, and his puckered mouth showed a few dark stumps which once may have been his teeth. Seeing us near him, he began to speak in a surprisingly strong voice. I asked him how old he was. 'I am fourteen, or maybe just turned fifteen,' he said. He was not rambling. Once someone has completed a hundred years, it is customary in our villages to count each year afresh thereafter, starting with one. Sahibdeen, therefore, by his own admission, was 115 years old. He also informed us that his wife, who was his third, was also around eighty. They had four sons and countless grand and great-grandchildren.

Sahibdeen, we were told, still managed to do all his own work unassisted, including cooking his sole meal of the day with his own hands. His major complaints were that, one, he could only manage to have a single meal daily, and two, that ever since he had crossed a century, the most he could do was doze sporadically, and he could no longer get a good night's sleep any more. Other age-related problems like failing eyesight and getting hard of hearing were comparatively minor problems. A good, uninterrupted sleep was what he craved.

As soon as he was told that we had come to him to listen to him recount the story of the Raja of Chahlari, Sahibdeen's breathing quickened and his body seemed to find a new wave of energy.

'Where shall I begin?' he asked us, panting with excitement. 'I still remember it all.' I kept my pen and paper ready to jot down the facts as they came out. Sahibdeen began:

'The British cannons were installed at Kadir Ghat and the Nawab's cannons at the Company gardens. There were three cannons. All right? The British lost the first round and they were really put off by their defeat. To make up for the loss, they sent for two more regiments and it was only then that they were able to defeat Hindustan and all those eminent nawabs and kings. All right? There were no papers in those days, so the list of the participants was written down on *bhoj patra* (papyrus like bark of the bhoja trees). Raja Balbhadra Singh of Chahlari was one of them. He was only eighteen years old and was just about beginning to show a moustache on his upper lip. He had got married just a day earlier. All right?'

Here Sahibdeen stopped, somewhat out of breath. After a short while, he resumed: 'When his elephant was surrounded by enemy forces in battle, his mahout asked him if he had permission to turn the elephant around and escape. At this the proud young raja said, 'I am a Kshatriya. If I run away from battle, how will I ever face my people? Make the elephant sit!' After the elephant knelt, the raja instead of holding a shield in one hand and a sword in another, leapt off it holding just a sword in each hand. After that, he began to mow down the British like a reaper in a field of millet. Ah, what a warrior god had created in him!'

There was silence as an emotionally overcome Sahibdeen began panting again. He resumed his story after a while. 'So the raja was fighting with both hands as the sun circled overhead. All right? The British officer decided not to kill him. However a soldier broke ranks and delivered a fatal blow to his back. The raja did not collapse immediately. Everyone who was watching the battle from a distance saw the headless body striding ahead! The British, now scared, quickly had the almanac read and upon advice, sent for a woman. It was only when she touched the body that it fell.

'After the battle, the new administrative arrangements implemented by the angrez collapsed. They tried implementing it again. Even that did not work. The third time it began to work. All right? After that, they laid the railway lines. The sahib who was in charge used to live in a bungalow near the railway station.

'The princes insisted that there should be a tehsil headquarters for each cluster of thousand villages, others disagreed, saying there should be a tehsil for each group of five hundred villages. So finally the angrez created the necessary divisions without grabbing even a biswan (a basic unit for measuring land) from anyone.'

As Sahibdeen paused for breath, I asked him, 'Did you live here at that time?'

'No, during the ghadar I lived in the village of Jagnehata. I was born there.'

'Where exactly is that located?' I enquired further.

'At the border between Barabanki and Bareilly.'

'So you stayed there through the ghadar?'

'No. Since those days were a period of great uncertainty, my father escaped with his family to Bhitauli village for a month.'

The name Bhitauli rang a bell. I asked the old man if he had seen the Begum of Awadh while she camped there.

'Who? The Begum?' Sahibdeen thought for a moment and suddenly his face lit up with a smile. 'Yes, I did see her while we were at Bhitauli. She was a fair and slender woman of medium height and did not use the veil. She was a truly grand presence. Almost like a goddess.'

Vajpai-ji decided to return to the topic of Raja Balbhadra Singh and asked Sahibdeen where exactly his body had fallen.

'I told the sahib the other day. He fell close to a cluster of five mango trees in Obri, then known as Obagadh.'

We took Sahibdeen's leave and went to see the spot at Obri.

The place lies to the west of Barabanki railway station and further towards the north-eastern direction, one can see the railway bridge. Kadir Ghat and the royal bridge referred to by Sahibdeen are about half a mile away. As correctly described by Sahibdeen, a cluster of five mango trees marked the spot. Between these and two teakwood trees that stood at a little distance, lay the site where Sahibdeen said the headless body of the young raja had finally collapsed. A few wilted flowers and clay lamps, offered at the site on 10 May, still lay scattered in the dust there.

For a short while my mind was lost in images brought on by Sahibdeen's stories. I could imagine hundreds of soldiers on horseback and on ground, mounting attacks on their enemies as the drums and bugles sounded and cannons thundered in the background. And then a tall, young man thundering ahead and being beheaded with one swoop of a nameless arm.

Mahadeva

How Pandit Lodheram dug out Lord Shail Mallikarjuna and built the temple where Hindus and Muslims swore unity in 1857

On 6 June, we were about to leave for the village Mahadeva. My guide, Gupta-ji had entered his house to sort out something and I opened my little pouch to roll myself a fresh paan. I saw a notebook next to the roll of paan leaves. Let's see what I manage to jot down in the pages of my copy today, I said to myself. For no particular reason I also remembered how in school, our English teacher used to lay great stress on our referring to school notebooks as copy books. But boys will be boys. To them, all stitched exercise books, whatever the size, quality or number of pages, were copies. The word copy is now part of the average Hindi speaker's lexicon. So much so, that even an illiterate man, who does not know what words like copy book or notebook mean, understands that the word copy denotes a certain number of paper sheets stitched together and used for writing in.

Like the word copy, the Urdu word ghadar too has mutated in our regional languages. It no longer denotes only an uprising, but any kind of unexpected and sudden chaos. Dr R.C. Majumdar, a learned scholar, objected to the use of the word ghadar for what he saw as a disorganized and limited revolt by the disgruntled native sepoys of the British army. But during my travels in the villages of Awadh, story after story talked about ordinary local people, farmers and princes and landlords, who fought against the British forces. Begum Hazrat Mahal had toured extensively through the area, winning popular support for her cause. Folks in Barabanki held fervently to the belief that the feisty lady and her young son Birjis Qadr had visited their district during the days of the princes' conclave at Bhitauli village. It is possible that while camping at Bhitauli, the begum may have toured the nearby areas soliciting popular support, and these roadshows may have resulted in the sightings that residents of Hazratpur and Mahadeva still talk about.

The ghadar of 1857 therefore, must not be seen as only an impulsive sepoy uprising. The ease with which leaders like Maulvi Ahmedullah Shah and Tatya Tope managed to collect and mobilize local forces against the British, shows that it was a far more comprehensive uprising.

Ramnagar

How Hazrat Mahal's father stayed back with his gold.
The grand conclave of the nobility at Mahadeva village, a missing
raja, tale of the Faujdar Fakir who never sheathed his sword again
right till the day he died, a reclusive mahant and a talkative
chief priest

Our next stop was Ramnagar. We were a little disappointed to find that our local contacts were not available and the erstwhile Raja of Ramnagar was out travelling. We finally landed at the house of a local block development officer where several curious locals had gathered. They were keen to know what we sought and what mysterious ghadar tales we had unearthed in our travels so far. Memories of the ghadar are never forgotten, we were told solemnly. To illustrate the point, we were told about Faujdar Shah Fakir, a local soldier who had refused to put back his sword in the scabbard when the rebels were on the run and had arrived in Bhitauli with his naked sword. This he had carried unsheathed till his dying day and was buried with it as willed.

We then left for the holy pilgrimage spot Mahadeva, and once in the village, headed for the house of the mahant. Huge gates led us into a large house where the mahant sat against a bolster with ochre covers. He appeared to be a simple and distracted man hailing from some place around Haridwar. He insisted we have lunch and when we said we had already eaten, he sent for some sweets and urged us to eat them. He said he had been living in the village only for the past two decades and knew nothing about its past during the 1857 ghadar. What he knew, though, was that the statues in the temple were

very old and could date back to the age of the Mahabharata.
After the expected visit to the temple, the chief priest Mahavir
Prasad Awasthy took us to his quarters and I brought out my
notebook and pen to write what he could tell us. The mahant
had requested him to share with us all local lore about the
ghadar that he knew. It didn't take long to realize that Awasthy-ji
enjoyed telling a good tale:

'After the Chinhat battle was over,' he began, 'those people—
the Begum, Raja Hardutt, Raja Devi Baksh and Raja Guru
Baksh of Ramnagar—arrived here at Mahadeva. They sat upon
the Ram Chautara where Ram Leela is staged during Navratri,
and began to strategize how to continue the war against the
enemy. Raja Devi Baksh was a great devotee of Bhole Baba
(Lord Shiva). All these fine carvings in stone that you see within
the temple, were commissioned by him. He had also awarded
500 beeghas of land to our priest Gauri Shankar's ancestor, the
then priest, Shiv Gulam Panda. The silver-plated doors you see
at the main temple were donated by Udit Narayan-ji, the Raja
of Ramnagar, ancestor of Raja Guru Baksh Singh. The begum
stayed at his Sattaisee Ka Kila at Bhithauli. An area of twenty-
seven (*sattais*) is known as Sattaisee here. Bhithauli belonged to
one such group of twenty-seven villages, so the fort here is also
known by that name. When the British passed through the area,
they blew the fort to smithereens with powerful cannons. The
village also saw plenty of fire then. The Raja of Ramnagar, Guru
Baksh Singh had two other forts across the Ghaghra river. Since
his elder son Sarvjeet Singh wanted to save those from the wrath
of the British, he is believed to have distanced himself from
his father who had resided in Sattaisee before he fled. Sarvjeet
himself had remained loyal to the British and those two forts
that belonged to him should be spared, he reasoned with the

British. After this incident, Sarvjeet came to be recognized as the local raja and his father Guru Baksh, despite coming out of hiding, could never reclaim his throne.

'Raja Sarvjeet had a mistress called Kadir Jehan. He was so smitten by her that he gifted her his entire kingdom. His son Udit Narayan however challenged his father in court and won back the kingdom. He gave five villages to Kadir Jehan and told her that as his father's wife she was a mother to him and the income from these villages should see her comfortably through her remaining years. As thanksgiving for his victory at the courts, he mounted the doors and door frame of Baba's temple with silver. This temple is very old and its original name was Shail Mallikarjuna, counted among the famous twelve jyotirlingas of Lord Shiva. They say a time came when the temple disappeared from the spot. After many years a well-known saint arrived here and began to live where the temple once stood. One day he had a dream in which Lord Shiva arrived and told him, 'I am buried in the fields of Pandit Lodhe Ram Awasthy, please take me out.' Pandit Lodhe Ram Awasthy was one of my ancestors and reputed to be a learned, virtuous and noble Brahmin. The saint approached him and told him about his strange dream. The spot was dug and the statue was indeed recovered. Ever since, this spot is also known as Lodheshwara. The offerings to the temple are divided equally among the mahant and the clansmen of Lodhe Ram Awasthy.'

We took leave of the priest and left Mahadeva. I wished we could have also visited Bhithauli but it lay beyond the river, across another rivulet and we would have to traverse four arid miles of scrub land on foot. I also had to leave out a visit to Hydergarh where the Rana Jang Bahadur of Nepal and his soldiers had fought a pitched battle against the rebel forces of

Barabanki. Considering that I had a deadline to meet and also had to get back to my own writing that fed me and my family, with a heavy heart I cancelled our visit to both these places, even though they promised much by way of ghadar lore.

At the Soldier Board guest house where we camped, someone showed us a large brass medallion. Such medallions, we were told, were awarded to each of the families of the soldiers who had died fighting for the British forces. The engraving on it said that the awardee had died defending 'his honour and self-respect'!

At the request of Shiv Prasad Pandey, the young and enthusiastic deputy commissioner of Barabanki district, we spent an additional night at Barabanki. They were celebrating Martyrs' Day to mark the centenary of the ghadar and there was a big parade and several functions to be held, the largest one in the maidan in front of the fort. Shri Kayamuddin, an old Congress leader from Fatehpur tehsil was presiding. Even he admitted that Begum Hazrat Mahal had passed through Fatehpur and her father, Ustad Maulvi Abdul Qasim had chosen to stay back with a bullock cart loaded with gold coins. Later when the reprisals began, eighty-three men from the village were hung from a neem tree because the British were enraged by the shelter extended to Begum's old father by the local folk.

Once the centenary celebrations were over, it was time for us to leave for Faizabad.

3

FAIZABAD

When Governor Saadat Ali Khan created the Subah of Awadh in 1722, this area granted to him by the Mughal emperor had seventeen districts. One of the districts he founded was Faizabad which became the capital city of Awadh till the third Nawab Shuja-ud-Daula shifted the royal durbar to Lucknow. Saadat Khan's adroit handling of the area resulted in a sizeable increase in revenues for the Crown, winning him the title of Burhan-ul-Mulk from the emperor. Soon after, Saadat Khan built himself a fort at Faizabad along the Ghaghra river and also established an army cantonment and barracks there.

Even after the capital shifted to Lucknow, Saadat Ali Khan's widow (Bahu Begum) who was wary of her grandson's lifestyle, continued to stay in Faizabad. She owned a considerable number of properties there. The relations between the Begum and Lucknow being what they were, she made a will bequeathing most of her properties to the British Resident at Lucknow in exchange for considerable and regular financial protection from him. After her death in 1815, the British handed over her estates to her estranged grandson, but asked for a loan of half a million pound sterling in exchange, so that the Resident could continue to fund the late begum's charitable works at Faizabad. As a result of this deal, the British Resident in Lucknow came to enjoy the prestige of a powerful monarch in Faizabad and the sole dispenser of royal donations and pensions worth a million sterling.

The native recruits from Awadh in the British army (about 50-60,000) then enjoyed a special privilege. They could submit petitions about their domestic matters (often concerning petty village officials and disputes about land tenure) for quick decisions to the Resident who referred them directly to the nawab. Some British residents, who were privileged members of the Lucknow's high society, used these petitions to actively interfere in various cases for monetary considerations and even held Saturday durbars in Faizabad. This duality of authority naturally created friction between the Nawab and the Resident and it kept growing year after year. Eventually, the privilege of petitioning through the Resident was abolished under Col Sleeman.

This move cleansed the sytem somewhat, but the sepoys of Awadh, used to jumping the legal queues via Faizabad, were displeased as they lost considerable prestige in their native villages. Sleeman's stern and cold regime seemed racist and censorious of all natives and further fomented a deep dislike and suspicion for the British.

Purifying crusades generally have a tendency to breed their own vices and it will always be open to question whether the old abuse of power in Faizabad by friendly and corrupt previous Residents was worse than the racial arrogance and the sense of moral superiority that the relatively cleaner duo of Sleeman and Outram displayed. The constant friction between the Resident and the Nawab and his talukedars contributed substantially to the avoidable rise of communalism in the religious town of Ayodhya. The issue of a mosque built over the spot the Hindus believed to have been a temple marking Lord Rama's birth, suddenly became a point of agitation between Hindu sadhus of Ayodhya and Muslim maulvis of Faizabad and Amethi. In 1853, ugly sectarian riots broke out in Faizabad provoked by rumours and fomented by vested interests. Further animosity was created when the

British forces, summoned by a petrified nawab in Lucknow, killed a
Muslim jihadi leader Maulvi Amir Ali of Amethi, leading a group of
jihadis against the band of Bairagi Hindu sadhus of Hanumangarhi
fortress in Ayodhya.

Amir Ali's death led to another mysterious arrival upon the scene—
Maulvi Ahmedullah 'Danka' Shah, who claimed to have been sent
by the higher powers to avenge the death of the jihadi from Amethi.
Described in the records as a tall, lean, muscular man with deep-set
large eyes, Ahmedullah Shah went on to play a crucial role during
the public uprising four years later in 1857. He became a powerful
and feared figure in Lucknow who even challenged the authority of
the Begum and the coronation of her infant son. He claimed he had
divine will behind him, and was heard giving contradictory orders to
the native army during the famous siege around the Residency. The
mysterious Maulvi however fled to the Rohil Khand region after the
fall of Lucknow and continued to fight the British until he was killed
in June 1858 by a paid assassin in Shahjehanpur.

Mrinal Pande

Intezam Ullah Shahbi's *Begumat-e-Awadh Ke Khutoot* is an
interesting compilation of letters exchanged between Nawab
Wajid Ali Shah exiled at Matia Burz in Calcutta, and his
numerous wives and mistresses left behind in Awadh. In one
of the compiled letters, Begum Shaida describes the somewhat
mysterious Fakir Maulvi Ahmedullah Shah. It is interesting that
in Awadh, Faizabad's name was linked with the events of the
ghadar via this self-proclaimed cleric, despite him not hailing
from Faizabad. Of this mysterious Maulvi Ahmedullah Shah,
also known as Faqir 'Danka' (drum) Shah, Shaida Begum writes:

'Ever since the Maulvis have gathered at the Ghas Mandi
area, one has been hearing many tales about a certain visiting

Sufi fakir by the name of Ahmedullah Shah. According to hearsay, he is the son of Nawab Cheena Teen and hails from Agra. The man is said to have acquired thousands of followers and has taken to making public appearances seated in a palanquin. Several drummers run ahead of the procession, announcing his arrival while others bring the rear.'

In another book, *Savanhat-e-Salateen-e-Awadh*, he is described thus:

'Ahmedullah Shah Fakir who originally belonged to Deccan, had been residing for many years in the Ghas Mandi area of Lucknow. It is said that he once visited Faizabad with the intention of joining the British army, but was put under arrest when he picked an argument with a British gunner. He was later released because he was considered a fakir. The British officials had briefly considered inducting him in the army, because they felt that his local knowledge and influence would be useful for them for settlements to be made after the ghadar. But they decided against it when they were informed that the fiery man was a well-known Hindu baiter and had been overheard saying that he wished to settle scores some day with those Bairagi sadhus of Hanuman Gadhi. The British did not wish to risk a bitter clash between Hindus and Muslims after the bitter experience of the ghadar. Accordingly, the proposal to appoint Ahmedullah Shah as an official in their army was quietly shelved.

In Faizabad, several stories about Ahmedullah 'Danka' Shah had been doing the rounds for years among the locals. Some of these described him as a relative of King Tipu Sultan, while others traced his roots variously to Arcot or Chingalpet in the Deccan. In Lucknow, the elderly still refer to him as Danka Shah because his dramatic public processions were invariably accompanied by a host of drummers. He had acquired a large following among the superstitious common folk in Awadh and his disciples would attract large crowds at his rallies by performing miracles in public such as chewing up live cinders and spouting fire. These disciples informed the public that they had gathered around the Maulvi to launch a jihad against the resident Bairagi sadhus of Hanuman Gadhi in Ayodhya.'

The atmosphere in Faizabad district underwent a sea of change between 1853 and 1857. In 1853, sectarian riots led by Amir Ali had rocked the entire area. But by 1857, the need for communal harmony was acute as the ire against the British mounted in Awadh. The Muslim leader Maulvi Ahmedullah Shah spoke against the suspected designs of the firangees for converting all natives to their own Christian faith and since the enemy's enemy is one's friend, he went out of his way to win the support of Awadh's restless Hindu nobility. The Maulvi had already forged an alliance with Begum Hazrat Mahal, whose minor son Birjis Qadr had been anointed as his father's successor to the throne of Awadh. This brought the Hindu princes closer to the Muslim nobility and the people followed.

As he started touring Awadh, Ahmedullah Shah began with a long correspondence with an influential Hindu rebel leader, Raja Veni Madhav Baksh Singh of Sitapur. He addressed several stormy public rallies in Faizabad, Unnao, Rae Bareilly, Sitapur and Lucknow. He was reputed to be a popular and fiery orator and the fun-loving people of Awadh flocked to hear him in droves. Their biggest attraction however, was the miraculous feats performed by the Maulvi and his disciples.

During my visit to Ayodhya, I was keen on gathering information both about this mysterious fakir and the bitter 1853 communal rioting between armies of Hindu rajas and

Muslim jihadis led by Amir Ali. I also wanted to understand how the same Hindu princes of Awadh that had picked up arms against their Muslim brethren in 1853 in defence of their faith, suddenly had a change of heart during the ghadar and joined forces with them to fight under the green flag symbolizing the combined leadership of two Muslim rulers: Begum Hazrat Mahal of Awadh and Bahadur Shah Zafar, the last Mughal emperor in Delhi. How did this miracle happen?

Ayodhya

Ayodhya was first formed by the ancient King Manu on the banks of the river Sarayu. King Dashrath, father to Lord Rama, spruced it up even more and is believed to have made it a cultural capital of sorts. The poet dramatist Kalidas and the Chinese traveller Fa Hien have similarly waxed eloquent about the beauty and importance of this holy city. The Buddhist scriptures refer to Ayodhya as Saket, meaning a city that was self-created (*Swayamagatam, swayamagatam Saket Saketamiti sangya samvrita*).

The deterioration of Ayodhya as a spot of holy pilgrimage for both Hindus and Buddhists probably began after the Mughal king Babur's general (Mir Baki) demolished the ancient temple of Lord Rama to build a mosque over the spot. Whether entirely true or not, stories of this alleged vandalism and the desecretion had led to much bad blood between the communities since. Such disputes never quite die out. The sagacious Mughal emperor Akbar, grandson to Babur, sensing the Hindus' sense of hurt, ordered that a platform be built near the ruins of the old temple, next to the mosque and the statues of Ram and his family be reinstalled thereupon. This noble gesture that could have appeased the public sentiment to a large degree over time, was sadly undone by Akbar's conservative great-grandson, Aurangzeb. By the time Nawab Wajid Ali Shah ascended the throne of Awadh, instability and lawlessness marked the entire area. As often happens during a period of unease and suspicion, various untreated old wounds had once again begun to fester and this was what resulted in ugly sectarian clashes in 1853.

Ayodhya looks nothing like how one would imagine the capital of the legendary King Rama. The very name Ayodhya means a city against which no one can wage a war. But in the summer of 1957, a hundred years after the ghadar, this city looked incredibly gloomy. Even the temples that had come up in recent years looked forlorn. The neighbourhoods were colourless and full of old ruins. Where was prosperous and well-protected Kosala that the poet Valmiki's epic Ramayana celebrates?

According to an article published in the *Pioneer* on 20 June 1902 (by a British author and excerpted in the *Awadh Gazetteer*), the 1853 communal clashes in Ayodhya originated from unsubstantiated rumours spread first by a certain Bairagi sadhu of Hanuman Gadhi. This sadhu had been expelled by the head of the sect (mahant) from its headquarters in Hanuman Gadhi for some misdeeds and he therefore harboured a deep resentment against not just the mahant, but the entire Bairagi sect. To avenge his humiliation, he first converted to Islam and then travelled from Faizabad to Lucknow, the capital of Awadh. After his arrival in Lucknow, he started a chain of ugly rumours about how the Bairagi sadhus of Hanuman Gadhi had long been finalizing a plan for mounting a sudden armed attack against the capital to avenge the earlier demolition of the temple at Ayodhya by Muslim invaders. Upon hearing this, Maulvi Amir Ali of Amethi, a Muslim cleric residing in Lucknow, was said to have become so incensed that he in turn declared that he'd personally lead a jihad against the Bairagi sadhus of Hanuman Gadhi.

The article in the *Pioneer* also hints subtly that Nawab Wajid Ali Shah may have been playing a double game, since he had ordered an enquiry into the matter at Faizabad but also continued to patronize Amir Ali. A fuming Amir Ali soon left for his home town in Amethi, and having collected a large militant band of supporters, began leading a march against the Bairagi sadhus in Ayodhya. Somewhat taken aback by these sudden developments, the nawab sent his trusted man Basheeruddin to try and pacify Amir Ali and bring him back to Lucknow. But by then, Amir Ali and his jihadis were beyond reasoning and so the mission failed and the maulavi and his mujahideen continued their march towards Ayodhya shouting jihadi slogans. The Nawab then sent another body of clerics to try and reason with the fiery Maulvi and his men, and help cool their tempers especially because incensed Bairagis in Ayodhya were gearing up for a violent fight. Sensing imminent danger, the Nawab requested General James Outram (resident chief commissioner of Awadh) to help quell a situation fast running out of control.

Although the clerics managed to calm most of the belligerent jihadis and talked them out of their violent plans, their leader Amir Ali refused to back down. A posse of soldiers was then sent under the command of Colonel Barlowe and in the violent clash that followed, Amir Ali and some two thousand of his men were killed. The year was 1853, four years prior to the ghadar of 1857.

As I left for Hanuman Gadhi, I hoped that I would learn from the present day Mahant of the Bairagi sect in that town about what exactly had transpired between 1853 and 1857 that had suddenly led to renewed goodwill between Hindus and Muslims. What, if any, were the reasons for Amir Ali and Ahmedullah 'Danka' Shah, two Muslim leaders from the same area of Faizabad, for taking two dramatically different approaches to communal provocation emanating from rumours? How come Amir Ali had been so incensed by rumours that he chose to lead a jihadi march against the Hindu sadhus, while four years later, in the same area, rumours about Indian soldiers being given cartridges laced with lard and cow fat had led Ahmedullah Shah to forge closer ties with Hindu leaders? What united them during the ghadar, so much so that Hindus and Muslims fought the firangees together under the green flag (of Bahadur Shah and Begum Hazrat Mahal)?

Ayodhya has remained a somewhat edgy town for centuries. Several years ago, a Vaishnavite Tamil Brahmin friend, who was a great devotee of Lord Rama, had visited Ayodhya and told me that it did not resemble the reposeful Ayodhya of the scriptures at all. Whatever it may once have been, today it is a city of ruins and graves, he said. He also felt that it was ironic that the statues of Rama and his family should be standing forlornly under a thatched roof upon an open platform, while the statue of his humble servant, Hanuman, should be housed within an armed fortress.

Hanuman Gadhi, from a distance at least, appears more like a fortress than an old monastery for sadhus. One can still see a few ancient cannons on rooftops of shops dotting the base of the fort, ostensibly placed there to fire at the enemy in case of an attack. Among the centres of pilgrimage in India, Ayodhya, the birthplace of Rama, can perhaps be counted as one of the most forlorn and run-down spots today.

Truth be told, it is not Hanuman but circumstances that had the Hanuman Gadhi erected, segregating the devotee from his lord. Hanuman Gadhi was built in an age when buildings took shape under various real or imaginary threats posed to non-Muslims by Islamic rule. Over centuries, Muslim rulers had displayed varying attitudes towards touchy sectarian issues. As a reaction to harsh measures that discriminated against non-Islamic subjects and threatened their religious spots, several *akhadas* (organized sects) of sadhus who were fence-sitters in matters of Hinduism, and may have worshipped specific Hindu gods or non-sectarian reformist gurus, began believing, unlike mainstream Hindus, that they had a right to defend their faith, if need be, with arms.

The Sikhs were one such sect, and just like them, many armed sects of sadhus who remained outside the pale of the Brahminical (Sanatani) Hindu caste structures also considered themselves the guardians of all weaker sections of the land. The mainstream Sanatani Hindus who may not have shared close ties of bread and daughters (roti-beti) with them, had come to see these militant men in saffron as rather noble, though somewhat deviant brothers. As misrule in Awadh became more and more pronounced and these militant sects were deprived of the essential sobering discipline of larger associations of caste and clan, some sects became dangerously aggressive. Sworn to celibacy, many young members of such sects lacked family ties that could have tamed their youthful aggression and linked them to the larger society. One can find many instances where saffron-clad sadhus had been hired as mercenaries by rulers seeking revenge against each other.

The statue of Lord Hanuman stands on the first floor within the Gadhi. As I climbed upstairs, I remembered my Tamil friend's ironic quip again about the incongruity of the lord residing under a thatched roof whereas his humble servant standing tall within a palatial fort. It was hard work dodging the milling beggars and greedy Brahmins asking for money and offering help for performing various cleansing rituals. Finally I managed my way to the upper floor. Here I saw a platform, in the middle of an open yard that led to the temple, with a mattress placed over it. The elderly head-priest (mahant) sat not upon this mattress but on the bare floor. I repeated my usual queries to him but he remained somewhat non-committal and said, 'We sadhus living here only sing devotional songs to the lord, we do not care for history or hearsay.'

I tried to soften him by talking about the religious past of the city and the militant version of dharma as interpreted by the then sadhus of his akhada, but he remained unmoved. 'The sole dharma for us sadhus consists of praying to Lord Rama and taking a dip in the holy river each day,' he said.

'How many sadhus live here, Maharaj?'

'About 500.'

'And how long have you been residing here yourself?'

'We sadhus do not keep track of time.'

'I understand. But even so? A rough estimate?'

'Must be at least forty or forty-five years.'

I thought it was safe now to come out with the real reason for my visit. I asked him if any old records or papers could still be available at the Gadhi that could tell us something about the past. The mahant made a face and said, 'Arrey baba, I told you, didn't I? We sadhus do not keep or preserve any records. All that is known about Hanuman Gadhi is that this land was given to the sect for free, sometime during the reign of the Yavanas.'

I was convinced by now of the futility of extracting any interesting information from the gritty sands of Vairagya. I stood up, folded my hands in a farewell gesture and left. Perhaps it was destined that I would not to be able to extract any information about the ghadar and Ayodhya at least at this Gadhi.

Of the two other likely sources lined up for us at Ayodhya, it turned out that one man had gone to Faizabad and the other had left town to attend a wedding. No, it was certainly not my day for gathering stories. In the end I decided that it would be somewhat more prudent to head for the district headquarters at Faizabad. So having put off a detailed visit to Ayodhya for the next day, I got back into the car.

On the way, as he drove us to Faizabad, the old driver expressed his deep sympathy at my obvious frustration. 'You have come so far,' he said, 'and I feel personally humiliated that the place did not yield the information you sought. Perhaps we could look up Priya Dutt Ram Sahib at Ayodhya and also call upon Dadua Sahib, the Raja of Ayodhya. They are both eminent and learned men, and may be able to help you. After having come this far in search of material about the ghadar, you deserve to get it,' he added. After mahant-ji's curt attitude, this old man's simple warmth touched me. 'I will go wherever you take me,' I told him.

We arrived at the large house of the Raja of Ayodhya. A high-ranking official from his secretariat, dressed like a pandit himself, met us and informed us that no papers were available with them nor did Dadua Sahib possess any special information regarding the matter.

Having drawn a blank at the palace, we left, somewhat disappointed. For some unexplained reason, I found us escorted to a local lawyer's residence. He was about to leave for work in his car and asked us to follow him to the district courts. There is a lawyer there, he informed us helpfully, who could introduce us to someone who hailed from the family of Raja Man Singh of Ayodhya (the ruler at the time of the ghadar) and as a member of an old local family, he might be able to provide us with some answers to our queries. We chose not to follow him.

By now I was convinced that Lord Rama's Ayodhya would not yield any secrets about the ghadar to me easily. This realization made me more determined to continue my search. I decided to take a chance with any octogenarian I came across in town, given that most of them are lonely men who like to ramble on about times gone by. As soon as our car arrived near the Chowk area, I saw an old man with a walrus moustache walking straight ahead with his head bent, without looking sideways. My sudden arrival by his side made him halt on his tracks like a screeching old car. 'Ghadar? Yes sir, as a child I heard many tales about it but I am now past eighty. I remember some details, but most of it I may have forgotten. Anyway, I will tell you whatever I can recall,' he said and began crossing the road, motioning towards us to follow him.

The Survivors

Pandit Ganjoo's tales about the clever Kashmiri boy, a precious necklace and the two young missing daughters of the British officer

We arrived at a shop that apparently belonged to a dentist. There were no patients to be seen anywhere and the dentist himself sat playing a lonely game of patience on his table. It turned out that the subject of my pursuit was called Pandit Sooraj Kishan Ganjoo. With the familiarity of an old acquaintance, he pulled out a chair and sat down with his back towards the good doctor, nodding at me to do likewise.

'So,' he said as I settled in another chair, 'prepare to write down what I shall dictate to you about an incident during the ghadar. You see, there was this old woman from a domiciled Kashmiri Muslim family, who had a son serving in the army. This son found out late one night that his fellow soldiers were planning to rise in revolt against the British the next day. He saddled his horse and left for home right away. After he got there, he confided to his mother that there was going to be mayhem the very next day, so she should bundle up all her precious belongings and leave town with his younger brother as quietly as she could, that very night. Then he rode back to his barracks. But you know how talkative women are, especially old women. The old mother could not keep the secret. Instead, within a short while, she informed all her friends and neighbours that something terrible was going to happen, and also that she and her younger son were leaving town with their precious belongings. Several of her female friends who could not leave town, came over and handed her their own jewellery and money in little bags for safekeeping. She tied up various bags in a large bundle. Knowing that well-dressed folk invited the attention of dacoits, she ground some coal and smeared it on her face and hands, and did the same to her son. That night, they put on tattered old clothes and left town with their large bundle, looking like a pair of beggars. They walked all night and when it was almost dawn, they stopped somewhere deep within the forest, where she made her son dig a deep hole and buried all her precious bundles in it.

'While the son was filling the pit back again, he asked his mother casually if she had remembered to pack in a priceless necklace of pearls presented to his father by the badshah. The old lady collapsed with grief for she had left it behind. When she recovered her wits, she wept and said that perhaps this was part of god's design and they should now just forget about it. At least they had saved their lives, hadn't they? But the son, like many sons, said that was nonsense. The pearl necklace was their only truly precious possession, how could he leave it behind for the marauding bands? He declared that he would find a way to go back and retrieve it, whatever the odds. The poor old lady kept crying and begging her son not to risk his life but the headstrong young lad was adamant and soon left for the city.

'As he entered Faizabad, the boy saw that the looting and vandalism had already begun and people were running helter-skelter to save their lives and possessions. The city had turned into a ghost town overnight and most homes stood empty. Soldiers, both Indian and British, had turned into wild bandits and were entering homes to loot whatever they could lay their hands on. The boy took off all his clothes except a dirty loin cloth and headed for his house behaving like a deranged man, gesticulating and talking gibberish. Some soldiers and looters tried to halt him but soon let him go, convinced that the poor man was not quite right in the head. The boy had a good time mimicking the gestures of the soldiers, talking nonsense, and occasionally sticking out his tongue at them and rolling his eyes. If some soldiers took offence and attempted to hit him, their fellow soldiers urged them to focus on pillaging instead of wasting their time in grappling with some aimlessly wandering lunatic.

'So sahib, in this way, the clever Kashmiri boy managed to not only sneak into his house unharmed, but also retrieve the precious necklace which he hid in his loin cloth, and as he came out, began to rant and rave all over again. His impersonation of a mad man fooled the armed soldiers yet again and soon he managed to sneak back into the forest with the priceless necklace nestled between his legs.

'And now you must really excuse me. I am getting late going home myself. I had just finished a meal and have yet to rinse my mouth.'

But even as he stood up to leave, he suddenly exclaimed, 'Ah, the mother!' and sat down yet again to round off his tale. 'In the forest,' he began, 'ever since her boy had left to fetch the family necklace, the poor helpless mother had been crying constantly. When she saw her son emerge from the trees and greet her, she clung to his neck saying over and over again how she had thought she'd never see him again. "Son," she said to him repeatedly, "Don't you forget! To your mother, your life is infinitely more precious than some strings of pearls."

'And now janab, I must leave. As I told you, I have not even rinsed my mouth after a meal.' Janab Sooraj Kishan Ganjoo got up and descended the steps quickly while I gathered my papers. But obviously he was not yet done. After going halfway across the road, I saw him scurrying back to the shop. He said he had remembered another vital detail about the story that I must note down as well. I lost no time in pulling out my papers from the bag and readied my pen.

'So after the ghadar subsided, or as you may safely say now, was "quelled mercilessly", the old woman and her son returned to their house within the city. As the news of their arrival spread, all the women of the area who had handed their jewellery to the old woman for safekeeping, ran to her house and began to clamour for their stuff. A bit irritated, the old woman told them that she was not going to run off. She needed to catch her breath first and they should allow her to rest a bit. The young women dispersed respectfully. After she had rested, the old woman sent for them to come and get their things. She sat with the various bundles lined up in front of her and asked each woman what colour her bundle was. Could she name and describe at least two pieces of jewellery in her bundle, detailing their shape and whether the said piece was studded with green stones or red or yellow ones. Having satisfied her, each woman was given her precious bundle intact.

'Those were the days, sir, when people were scrupulously honest and did not cheat each other. But now I really must go. I am yet to rinse my mouth!' Having said that, when Ganjoo sahib sat down once again and remarked that he might as well get just one more story recorded, I remained happily unsurprised. He began:

'There was this angrez who was a big official in his district those days. As the ghadar fires spread and panic set in, he discovered that two of his daughters were missing. As soon as the ghadar was quelled, he ordered his men to go locate the girls. So janab, they found that one girl had been given shelter in the home of a brahmin. The sahib immediately left for the place. But, as you know, most brahmins live in utter poverty. This poor fellow was no exception. The sahib found that he had no furniture in his hut; just a few prayer mats and dhurries. Seeing the sahib at his doorstep, he produced a bamboo cot and declared humbly that that was all he could offer his honoured guest. The sahib said it was good enough for him and sat down. Then he began asking the brahmin if his daughter, lost during the riots, was indeed staying in this house as per information received. The Brahmin replied in Awadhi saying that during the chaos he had given shelter to a young girl, but he did not know whose child she was. She had since then been living with his family and he would fetch her. Saying so, he entered the house and emerged with a girl who indeed turned out to be one of the lost daughters of the sahib.

'As soon as the girl saw the sahib, she ran to him and clung to him with tears running down her cheeks. You can imagine how happy the father must have felt to see his child unhurt, but being an angrez, the sahib wasted no time in becoming emotional and weeping softly. He seated himself on the bamboo cot and asked his daughter to sit next to him. Then he asked her how she had been looked after in that house.

"Papa," said the girl, "Pundit-ji was like a real father to me and has cared for me just as a father cares for his own daughter."

"Do you know what a father's caring means?" the sahib asked her. The girl said, of course she did. She said that he was exceptionally caring about her exotic food habits and had even told her in Awadhi that he knew that the British ate differently. Being strict vegetarian brahmins, they could not allow meat or eggs for her in their house, but if she missed that kind of food, he would personally take her to some eatery that served meat and eggs, and after her craving was satisfied, he would escort her back.

'So janab, even the angrez was deeply moved when he realized how in that poor household his child had been well cared for. Before they left, the girl took leave of each member of the family with tears in her eyes. It was almost as though a daughter of the house was leaving. The old pundit stood in a corner wiping his eyes and his numerous children all wailed, 'Hai Jijji, Hai Jijji!' (Ah big sister!) Even his wife quietly sobbed behind her veil. Had he not seen this and listened to what his own daughter had to say about the love and care she had received, the angrez, like others of his kind, may have kicked aside the howling crowd of natives, calling them dirty names. But the sight of his own daughter hugging the family members and weeping as she left, convinced him of the deep sincerity and true moral values of the natives of Awadh.

'Anyway, not all are alike. Word reached the sahib that some rich zamindar had taken his other daughter in. He arrived at the zamindar's house immediately. He asked the same question of his daughter as she came and sat next to him: "How were you treated here?" The poor girl looked down and whispered, "Like a wife, papa." The father jumped up, as if stung. He glared at his daughter with bloodshot eyes and asked, 'Do you realize what that implies?'

"Yes papa," said the poor girl, sobbing.

The angrez only said, "I see," and left immediately for his residence with his daughter. As soon as he reached home he issued immediate orders that the entire property of the zamindar be confiscated and handed to the poor brahmin who had looked after his other daughter like a father.

'This is another ghadar story I had heard as a child.'

Undoubtedly, meeting Pandit Sooraj Kishan Ganjoo was a real treat. He was a wonderful teller of tales and although it is possible that some of his facts may have gotten altered in the telling, he was able to conjure up right in front of my eyes, a whole era and the life and times of those violent and turbulent years.

At a shoe shop in the Chowk area, I met another elderly Muslim gentleman, dressed in khadi and talking animatedly to a customer. He was identified for me as Ghulam Hussein. I entered the shop and waited till he was done with his conversation, and then asked him my usual questions. Did he know of any local stories, especially those that could shed light on life in rural Awadh during the ghadar years?

Hussein said he had heard from his grandfather, that during ghadar days, Maulvi Ahmedullah Shah had arrived in town with his men and stayed in an area known as Pukhta Sarai Chowk. His men, when surrounded by the British army, fought back valiantly, but were killed in battle. The Maulvi was treated harshly thereafter. He was taken prisoner and paraded through the town in shackles. 'That,' he said, 'is all I know.'

Faizabad and the matter of Ayodhya according to Akhtar sahib, editor of Akhtar

In the same shop I met Akhtar sahib, an open and friendly local man, the publisher and editor of a family-owned local newspaper, *Akhtar*. He said that he had several papers and other material that he had collected about the ghadar years. 'Leave me

your address,' he said, 'and I will send you all those by mail.'
When I told him that I would be grateful for whatever he could
make available to me right away, as I had to meet a deadline for
the publication of my book and may not be able to wait that
long, Akhtar sahib asked how much could one gather anyway
in just one hurried visit?

'Go home and you will find that the material has arrived
before you did,' he said.

He also told us that many decades ago, thousands had stayed
in what was now his house. It was actually a palace that had
once belonged to Burhanul Mulk, one of the nobles of Awadh.
He said that I must visit it.

'We had a maid called Banijaan,' he added, as we walked.
'She used to say that during the ghadar when the British soldiers
forced an entry into the house and came into her kitchen, she
had thrust a burning piece of coal in the mouth of the first
gora soldier.'

Seeing that I was interested, he said, 'Nagar sahib, I have
hundreds of such stories of skirmishes between the locals and
the Company's armies during the ghadar. I have done a lot of
research on Awadh and have been amazed to find how cultured
the people of Awadh were, thousands of years ago. Such levels
of prosperity and refinement are impossible to achieve, don't
you think? Unless people have achieved a high level of culture.
I made a trip to Ajudhiya Ji (Ayodhya) for this very reason.
There I saw the ancient grave of Hazrat-e-Sheesh, said to be
the firstborn son of Adam. So you can see immediately how
old our civilization is. And how Awadh may have seen the first
manifestation of human civilization anywhere in the world.'

When he was talking of Hazrat-e-Sheesh, I told him that the
monument could well be that of Lord Shesha, a manifestation

of the divine serpent, whom the Hindus worship. Laxman, the younger brother of Lord Rama is said to have been an incarnation of Lord Shesha, the serpent.

'Could it be,' I asked him, 'that once upon a time, a temple of Lord Shesha may have stood in Ayodhya which may later have been co-opted by Muslim brethren as the site for Hazrat-e-Sheesh's grave, due to a similarity in the names?'

Akhtar sahib looked a bit uncomfortable at this question. 'If that was indeed the case, how come the structure looks Islamic?'

'Perhaps,' I said, 'when the Muslims came to Ayodhya in the fourteenth century, they may have been attracted by the similarity of names between their great spiritual leader and the Hindus' and decided to adopt the spot as a holy spot for mussalmaans as well. They might have erected a grave to protect the holiness of the spot and later replaced the temple with a tomb?'

Just when Akhtar sahib's cheerful face had begun to look somewhat sombre and tense, an old acquaintance of his, by the name of Dr Shafi Hyder dropped by. Akhtar sahib told him about the purpose of my visit.

The ghadar years according to Dr Shafi Hyder of Jaunpur

Dr Shafi Hyder said he had some knowledge of the happenings in his native area around 1857, but that, unfortunately, was not part of the principality of nineteenth-century Awadh. I told him that if I had the time and resources, I would have cased the entire area from east to west, from Barrackpore in Bengal to Ajnala in Punjab. But unfortunately that was not the case, so I would have to be satisfied with whatever I could lay my hands on in Awadh.

'The incident I am going to recount,' Dr Hyder said, 'has a link with Awadh. I come from the eastern district of Jaunpur where Shamsher Jehan, the crown prince and son of Idarat Jehan, the ruler of the state of Mahul had turned rebel and robbed the royal treasuries of Faizabad during the ghadar. After the mutiny was suppressed, the angry British hanged Idarat Jehan from a tree. It is believed that the royal elephant that he rode to the spot also collapsed and died there itself.

'After this, the British had the royal palaces razed to the ground. However, the loyal courtiers managed to sneak out the sister of the prince, who was my father's mother, along with the crown prince. They were given shelter in the house of a Hindu landowner Thakur Amreth Singh of the village Bada Gaon. Soon the British arrived there and asked that the royals of Mahul be handed over. Prince Shamsher Jehan was prepared to die as a martyr but he feared that the British may do terrible things to his sister before killing her, so he decided to kill her before courting arrest. When the thakur heard this, he rushed in and caught hold of Shamsher Jehan's wrist. He assured him that he had managed to send away the British officials.

"How did you manage this?" the prince asked in amazement. The thakur laughed and said he had pretended to be appalled at the suggestion by the British commander that he, a high-caste Hindu would even consider giving shelter to a Muslim under his roof. The British officials left, convinced they had been misinformed, because they believed that the fissures between the Hindus and Muslims were unbridgeable and deep. But the fact remains, during the entire ghadar, both Hindus and Muslims had maintained a deep sense of respect and love for each other.'

Shri Priya Ram Dutt, a respected citizen of Faizabad, told us that when he was a child they had a peon in the house who narrated many tales about the ghadar and also sang out special Alhas and Birahas composed by the village poets.

'I have forgotten most of them now. You see, after the merciless quelling of the uprising, ordinary people were scared of their children learning about the martyrs and turning rebellious once again. So we were prohibited from listening to stories about the ghadar from adults. Those were different times you see, and children from good families were raised to be proud and aloof. But I am happy to see that you are going about collecting stories from far-off villages. You should try to meet people in their eighties and nineties in the area. There is a man by the name of Shreepal Singh in Mubarak Ganj, then there are Rameshar Naki Miyan and Randheer Singh of Ramnagar. And yes, also Thakur Bajrang Singh who lives in the palace of Hindu Singh. These elders would all be good sources to tap. In the villages of Chirra, Jagatpur and Raurahi you can meet another storehouse of information, Nawab Gajnafar Hussein of Moti Masjid. And yes, make sure you also meet Pannagesh-ji.'

I dutifully jotted down everything but I knew that I would be lucky to meet even two of these men. I was running out of time, and a lack of proper facilities for covering the entire district had handicapped me further. Priya Ram Dutt-ji sent me to a few homes but the people I expected to meet were unfortunately not available. Nevertheless, I jotted down their names and addresses in the hope that some day they may come in handy for researchers with more time and resources than me.

Hero or turncoat? The unsolved mystery of Raja Man Singh

I came back to the guest house feeling a little unhappy about not being able to meet the descendant of Raja Man Singh, a man whose role in the history of the ghadar in Awadh remains somewhat strange. According to the historian R.C. Majumdar, he was involved with the seditionists in planning the uprising. But we also find him mentioned as one of the supporters of Begum Hazrat Mahal of Lucknow. In the battle of Char Bagh, he is said to have fought bravely against the British.

In a letter to Begum Akhtar Mahal, exiled in the Matia Burz in Calcutta with Nawab Wajid Ali Shah, Sarfaraz Begum Lukhnavi writes of him, 'With only 9,000 soldiers in his command, Raja Man Singh fought hard and managed to chase away the British by evening. Janab-e-Aaliya (Begum Hazrat Mahal) rewarded him by presenting him a title lauding his bravery in battle, in addition to a shawl, a handkerchief and a special scarf. She spoke most warmly about his valour in battle.'

The *Awadh Gazeteer* says that when the civil officer in charge of the district of Faizabad realized that difficult times were coming, he requested Raja Man Singh to assume responsibility for ensuring the safety of the British women and children in the area. The request was readily accepted. The sepoys' attitude towards the British had become alarmingly threatening and the British officers had no reliable men who could help them discipline the rebel sepoys. Initially, Lucknow ordered the Commissioner and Superintendent Colonel Gold to arrest Raja Man Singh, who was suspected of being a sympathizer of the rebels, but even though he was arrested as per orders, the assistant commissioner immediately wrote to Lucknow protesting the arrest of a valuable ally. He was permitted to release Raja Man Singh just in time for him to be chosen as the mentor protector for the women and children who were then sent to his fort in Shahgunj for safety.'

It seems Raja Man Singh may have been playing a double game here, like several other native princes who pretended to be loyal subjects to the British but were really supporting the cause of the rebels. It is quite possible that after his arrest, Raja Man Singh may have decided to become a British loyalist.

Several British men, women and children who were captured in the fort of Kaiser Bagh by the Raja of Mitauli, were murdered by the rebels when the ghadar was at its peak. At that point, it is believed that Raja Man Singh managed to escort several of the prisoners to safety at the Residency. In Lucknow, I also heard how Raja Man Singh had tricked the native rebels by substituting straw for gunpowder in their magazines. A folk song in praise of the bravery shown by Rana Veni Madhav Baksh also sneeringly refers to one nakki, Raja Man Singh and the one-eyed Sudershan as turncoats who chose to become British lackeys when no one was looking. The song confirms the public opinion about Raja Man Singh being a traitor.

In the evening, I once again set out to roam in the lanes of the city. I have always been a wanderer and I quite enjoy the experience of moving about in an unfamiliar city and absorbing the atmospherics whenever and wherever I please. This once, I was on a mission of finding out about the secret life of Maulvi Ahmedullah Shah. The suspense and the excitement added to my joy.

Among the various Indian heroes of the ghadar, Maulvi Ahmedullah Shah and Tatya Tope are two of the most charismatic figures. There is no denying that both of them were natural-born leaders. Other commanders like Bakht Khan may have been brave soldiers but men like these two, and Babu Kunwar Singh and Rana Veni Madhav Baksh Singh could just walk into an area and become the natural rallying point for fighters of all castes and communities.

There is no denying that many of the ghadar heroes displayed not just the popular anger against the British but also the weaknesses Indians from Kashmir to Kanyakumari share. But I was somewhat dismayed when I read the conclusions Dr R.C. Majumdar had arrived at, because his account of the ghadar reads almost as if the rest of the country was sitting with the good doctor in a theatre, watching the drama of the ghadar unfold like a small, somewhat embarrassing and inconsequential play choreographed by the sattu eaters of the northern plains. I find it hard to believe that his scholarly mind did not see how the revolt of men and women like Tatya, the Maulvi, Rana, Kunwar Singh, the Rani of Jhansi and the Begum of Awadh, made them the precursors of men like Yatindra Nath Das and Sukhdeo, Bhagat Singh, Rajguru and Azad who led the war of independence successfully a century later.

Chowk Bazaar, Faizabad

A futile search for Nanhey Miyan, the attar seller, Pannagesh-ji, the poet and Ram Gopal Pande; 'Sharad', ex-manager and writer of A Book on the Bloody History of the City of Ayodhya

I arrived at the Chowk Bazaar of Faizabad. In its layout, this civic area was certainly better conceived than the Chowk Bazaar of Lucknow where rulers like Nawab Asaf-ud-Daula were more obsessed with building and beautifying grand palaces and Imam Badas. Many of Lucknow's now well-known localities came up haphazardly under his rule as there was no proper master plan for the city. The Chowk in Faizabad however, is well-planned. It forms a neat semi-circle marked by three gates, the central one being the largest. Each gate bears the Islamic star and half-moon pattern, the famous coat of arms of the nawabs of Awadh (a bow and arrow and the fish). One gate though, has an inverted coat of arms.

I saw an elder man with a stick crossing the road slowly. He had a hennaed beard and was dressed in a lungi and a long kurta with a Lucknow-style cap on his head and a handkerchief draping his shoulders. I went up to him and after a respectful exchange of salutations, asked him my usual question about the locally preserved memories of the ghadar. He peered at me closely for a few moments and then asked me where I was coming from.

'From Lucknow, sir.'

'Just for doing this?'

'Yes, sir.'

'Are you a government servant?'

'No, sir. I am doing it on my own initiative but the government is helping me a great deal. The government is also very interested in putting together a native version of the incidents that took place in Awadh during the ghadar,' I replied.

The old man was quiet for some time. Then he looked up and told me he approved of my working on the subject. The nation was slowly forgetting about the great contribution of our previous generations to the creation of a free nation. But he also added that it was already a little too late to try and dredge up old history, and this delay was the reason why the country was going downhill. The elders who had seen the ghadar with their own eyes were mostly no more and he himself was there for the past few months to visit his son from Sultanpur.

In Sultanpur, the British had razed the entire town as revenge for the rebels killing their men. But in the villages, many tales about the bravery of the natives and what the British did, may still have survived the passage of time. Those needed to be collected.

Another man who dropped by as I sat in the house of Priya Ram Dutt, also said that the work I had undertaken was indeed noble but it was not an easy one. I needed a whole band of men who were willing to carry and survive on a small bundle of *sattu* (a dry gruel of roasted grams the poorest travellers ate mixed with chillies and salt) while wandering in the rural hinterland.

They were not wrong. But I had a large family to support and as much as I wished to, I could not afford to abandon my family duties and wander for too long.

It was sometime that day that I came across a person called Haji Sahib in the bazaar. He urged me to meet Nanhe Miyan, the perfume seller who was all of ninety years and lived behind Lal Bahadur's watch repair shop. Nanhe Miyan, he said, was often recounting stories about the days of the British rule to his friends. I asked my way to the watch repair shop which was not hard to find, being a landmark of sorts and located just off the main road. I was told that if I turned right at the corner, I would see a house standing where three roads met.

I reached the house only to find Nanhe Miyan missing. One of his family members helpfully provided me with the name and address of another elder, Haji Hasnoo, who lived behind Dr Jenny's. Haji Hasnoo was home but said he had no stories about the ghadar. At the most, he could tell me about the local clock tower, when and how it was made and by which chairman of the town's municipality. As for the ghadar, he was born once it had passed, and had heard nothing about it from the family elders either.

When I was asking around desperately for more names, the name of Pannagesh-ji, the ex-manager of the Kanak Bhawan in Ayodhya (also mentioned by Priya Dutt Ramji), cropped up again. I remembered that I'd also come across the name as author of some articles published in old Hindi magazines such as *Chand* and *Sudha*. I was told that his son works in the district court and Pannagesh-ji lives with his son in Rakab Gunj Niyavan. My stroke of bad luck continued, because when I reached the house, I was told he had moved elsewhere. By now it was nine in the evening, and I decided to go back to the guest house. Perhaps Maulvi Danka Shah did not want his secrets revealed to me just yet.

On 9 June, a Sunday, a young driver arrived saying that he wanted to take me for a holy dip. I told him I did not wish to bathe in the Sarayu river, but instead wanted to proceed to the city right away. So we arrived at the Guptar Ghat where an ageing Lord Rama is said to have disappeared within the waters of the Sarayu. Rama's life is a long and tragic string of various

sacrifices, trials and tribulations. He abandoned his personal pleasures for the sake of his people, even cast aside his wife Sita whom he knew to be blameless. Sita's suicide at the occasion of his Rajsuya Yagna and the death of his beloved brother Lakshman had broken his heart. It does not matter whether he actually decided to drown himself at the Guptar Ghat, but what does matter is that he saw no point in continuing as a ruler without his loved ones. The river is considered holy because of its association with a rare man like Lord Rama.

In Ayodhya, I was told about a book, *Janm Sthan Ka Rakt Ranjit Itihas* (The Bloody History of the Birthplace) by Ram Gopal Pande 'Sharad' that discussed the history of the place including the ghadar. I wanted to meet him, but upon enquiry I learnt that he too had gone out of town like many others.

A man by the name of Ram Kishore Khatri told me that his ancestors had arrived in Ayodhya after the ghadar but his neighbour Ram Das Khatri's grandfather was a treasurer to the then king of Ayodhya. In 1857, when the area began to seethe with stories of revolt, he had sent his family with all their precious possessions to the royal palace for their safety. His family thus survived the ghadar. According to Ram Das Khatri's grandmother, when the firangee soldiers entered their house, they found nothing of any value. Frustrated, they broke open her spice containers and when the family returned, she found the floors covered in turmeric powder.

We then visited the birthplace of the poet Tulsidas, the spot where Rama is said to have been born. We also saw Sita Ki Rasoi, where his wife Sita's kitchens were supposedly located. My companion, a young cyclist Gudun-ji was sorry that even after spending two days in Ayodhya I was not able to access much material on the ghadar. He assured me that after the local historian Sharad-ji returned, he would request him to mail me whatever material he had collected about Ayodhya during the ghadar. He did keep his word and I soon received a rather large letter from Sharad-ji. In the next chapter, I shall try to reproduce honestly the sum and substance of the facts shared by him.

4

THE GHADAR IN FAIZABAD

When the ghadar erupted in Faizabad four years after the sectarian clashes, the communal amity forged between the previously warring factions was particularly notable. Their joint fight against the British was marked by a singularly insane desire for revenge on both sides. The natives wanted, among other things, to avenge the brutal killings of Amir Ali, and the hanging of Mangal Pande and his friends and relatives. The British side was all for a similar settling of scores after receiving news about native sepoys killing their army officials and ambushing Col Hunt's unit on its way to Lucknow. Not only were men killed in Faizabad, their bodies were also subjected to barbaric and public humiliation. Like the soldiers, the local talukedars' grievances were both emotional and personal. They were as angry about both the Nawab being exiled and the loss they had come to suffer when many of them lost almost fifty per cent of their lands in the Summary Land Settlement brought in by the British a year earlier.

The native revolt in Faizabad began with attacks on the lines of British officers and then their residential bungalows were set on fire. Faizabad sepoy lines had also become the gathering point for rebels from as far as Benaras and Azamgarh. The mutiny was especially well-planned there and began with the sounding of a bugle at 10 p.m.

Rumour, fear and suppressed anger against the British swiftly brought the sepoys, talukedars and citizens together. After the destruction of British bungalows, the rebels, many of whom were ill-treated sepoys or urban poor frequently disgraced by the British in public, proceeded to attack the treasury and the jail–both icons of the Raj. Then human greed took over many and they went on a rampage, pillaging and looting shops and homes of the rich and pocketing precious gold and cash.

As always, there were a few survivors who were lucky to have lived through the carnage to tell some poignant tales about not just death and destruction, but also human love and compassion.

Mrinal Pande

True to his word, Ram Gopal Pande 'Sharad' soon sent me his paper on the bloody history of Ayodhya, titled *Ayodhya Ka Raktranjit Itihas*. He makes several notable points in his work. One, across all communities, the people of Awadh felt proud of the fact that the first martyr Mangal Pande belonged to their area. Two, Faizabad was the hub of several important and secret meetings held by the rebel forces and their leaders. (However, I am surprised that Maulvi Ahmedullah 'Danka' Shah's name does not figure in these reports.) Three, the ghadar was driven at the top, not by the feudal lords and princes, but by trained native subedars of the British army. Here I am in agreement with Dr Majumdar.

The last point, which to me is most important: by 1857, the Muslims were willing to soften their stand over the ownership of Babri mosque despite the violent riots of 1853 over the issue. When they saw the nation being threatened by the colonial British rule, the Hindus too had chosen to let bygones be bygones and joined the Muslim leaders in a joint fight against the forces of the East India Company. Contrary to the opinion of the British author of that previously mentioned article in the *Pioneer*, the last Nawab of Lucknow, Wajid Ali Shah was not responsible for igniting the communal riots in 1853.

According to Sharad, when the resentful native sepoys of the Bengal army first challenged the British rule in May 1857, the princes and their native subjects from the district of Faizabad were one of the first major group of natives who made common cause with the rebels wanting to overthrow the British rule. The draft plan for a popular uprising was first created in Faizabad and later fine-tuned by the Maratha chieftain, Peshwa Nana Saheb of Bithur. The actual execution however was spearheaded by the seasoned sepoy leaders from the army camps of Barrackpore in Bengal.

Most of these sepoys hailed from the Baiswada region that covered the south-eastern districts of Awadh and were a stronghold of the martial Bais Rajput clans, to whom caste and kinship ties were sacrosanct. The Bengal Regiment sepoys from Baiswada, mostly Rajputs and Brahmins, were entrusted with the task of deciding the final military strategy for simultaneous anti-British uprisings all over the northern plains. Certain unforeseen circumstances however, drove their original plan awry and the ghadar erupted prematurely in Meerut when the Brahmin sepoy, Mangal Pande, was so angered by certain rumours that he attacked his superior officer suddenly and shot him dead. Mangal Pande was subsequently arrested and hanged and with this, the fires of the sepoy mutiny became totally uncontrollable and unpredictable.

Had it not been for these sudden and unforeseen developments, the neighbouring district of Faizabad would have had the distinction of being the first city to rise in revolt.

Mangal Pande, the first martyr of the ghadar, was born to Divakar Pande and Abhay Rani Devi of the village of Surhurpur in Akbarpur tehsil in Faizabad district, on 19 July 1827, which according to the lunar Hindu calendar, was the second day of the bright fortnight (Shukla Paksha) in the monsoon month of Ashadh. Divakar Pande originally belonged to the nearby Duguan Rahimpur village but he settled in Surhurpur since he had inherited some land from his maternal grandfather. It was sheer luck that led the twenty-two-year-old Mangal Pande to join East India Company's Bengal army unit. It is said that while visiting Akbarpur, the young man heard that the Company's forces were marching through the area and like other villagers, he too went and stood by the roadside as a curious bystander and watched the glamourous British garrison come marching. His well-built body and height (six feet and two inches) caught the attention of an army commander who was leading the unit. He walked across and offered to recruit him on the spot. The young man happily agreed and thus began the career of one of the most celebrated soldiers from Awadh.

After hanging Mangal Pande, the British, appalled by the temerity of a man they considered a mere native sepoy, sought further revenge against other native sepoys for the death of their senior official. They arrested anyone who was rumoured to be a sympathizer or relative of Pande and all those thus held were then tied to the mouth of a cannon without a trial, and blown up publicly.

Several of Pande's relatives and sympathizers managed to escape and once they reached home, began actively fanning the fires of revolt all over the region. One such activist was the son of Mangal Pande's brother, Bujhawan. He gathered relatives and friends, and together, all of them joined the rebel native forces so they could avenge the killing of their kin. On 25 August, this motley group attacked the sepoy camp at Faizabad after sunset. They were actively helped by many other native soldiers, and this lynch mob managed to kill or capture all the British personnel and their families residing at Faizabad.

Some events from Sharad's account are also substantiated by an urgent report filed by Col Martin to his superior Col Hunt at Faizabad after the hanging of Mangal Pande. In it, he warned that the hanging of a high-caste Brahmin, considered holy and above the death penalty by all Hindus, may trigger off a violent uprising. It also pointed out, that after Pande's hanging, a series of fiery public meetings were held by the rebels all over Faizabad whereby all participants demanded swift killings of all the gora officers in the area, as a means to avenge Pande's death. Even the sepoys at Meerut were highly incensed by the brutal hanging of a fellow native sepoy and immediately went on a rampage against the British. The fires of rebellion didn't take long to reach Surhurpur village—the birthplace of Mangal Pande—and in no time, it became a veritable centre for a revolt against the British Raj.

Since the properties of Awadh begums lay in Faizabad, after receiving Martin's report, Col Hunt first rushed to the tomb at Naka Muzaffara, where the treasures of the aged Begum Khursheed Mahal, mother of the late Nawab Asaf-ud-Daula, were stored. At this point, the octogenarian begum is said to have appealed in person to Col Hunt with folded hands and tears flowing down her cheeks, requesting him not to punish an old widow and deprive her of her possessions for crimes committed by native sepoys. She was, she said, an eighty-year-old and had only a few more years to live. She had had nothing to do with the revolt nor had she personally ever defied the

Company Raj. Col Hunt however, ignored her pleas and ordered his soldiers to use force if need be, and take away whatever items they found. Upon receiving such orders from their senior official, the soldiers broke in and forcibly carried away precious things worth several millions along with eight million gold coins that belonged to the begum. After the raid was complete, Col Hunt arranged to have the confiscated goods transported to Lucknow by bullock cart, accompanied by an armed escort.

While the cart was on its way, Begum Hazrat Mahal of Lucknow and Manvati, (one of the Hindu wives of the exiled Nawab Wajid Ali Shah and the sister of Raja Man Singh) declared war against the British. Both these royal wives came to Faizabad to seek help from the rebel forces that they heard had gathered there to chase away the British.

Their first encounter with Col Hunt's men took place near the village of Khojinipur. When news of Begum Khurshid Mahal's treasures being looted by the British spread to Faizabad, rumours also began to circulate that with their limitless lust for gold and cash, the British would soon be targeting the homes of various prosperous citizens in the city. A secret public meeting was hastily organized within the Jhau forests on the banks of the river Sarayu. This was attended by all the major native rebel leaders from the surrounding Baiswada region, such as Raja Devi Singh of Gonda, Raja Veni Madhav Singh of Rai Bareilly, Raja Lal Madhav Rao of Amethi (Sultanpur), and also prominent citizens of the Ayodhya area such as Baba Ram Charan Das, Acchan Khan, Shambhu Prasad Shukla and Amir Ali of Hasnu Katra (*not to be confused with jihadi leader Maulvi Amir Ali of Amethi, shot dead by the British in 1853. Translator*). All of them extended support unanimously to Begum Hazrat Mahal.

Meanwhile at Khojinipur, as rebel forces surrounded Col Hunt and his men from all sides, a group of native sepoys rushed to the government's Grass Farm located at Nirmali Kund near the cantonment area and set it on fire, even as desperate officers and their families tried in vain to escape by boats. As they reached the Jamthara Ghat, cannons began booming and all were killed by the soldiers of Raja Devi Baksh Singh who had lain there in ambush. Col Hunt's men were badly mauled in battle and he himself died at the hands of Raja Veni Madhav Singh. His ravaged body was hung upside down on a pole and paraded through the town by rebels to announce their victory.

On 13 November however, the euphoric rebels were taken by surprise when a larger contingent of the British army arrived in Faizabad and immediately mounted a strong attack against them. Among the leaders, some like Begum Hazrat Mahal, Manvati, Raja Devi Baksh Singh and Veni Madhav Singh managed to flee and disappeared in the forests of neighbouring Nepal along with Bujhawan Singh, Mangal Pande's nephew. But no such luck was in store for Baba Ram Charan Das, Acchan Khan, Amir Ali and Shambhu Prasad Shukla who were captured by the British forces.

Revenge was in the air. Shortly after their capture, Baba Ram Charan Das and Amir Ali were hanged publicly from a tamarind tree next to the birthplace of Lord Rama in Ayodhya. Meanwhile their supporters, Acchan Khan and Shambhu Nath were subjected to gruesome torture before having their skulls smashed.

Just like their native Hindu and Muslim supporters, the British behaved like animals during the violent reprisals at Faizabad. The reason for this ferocity was the realization that when faced with a sudden joint assault by native Hindus and Muslims, the Brits could be rendered totally powerless despite their superior weaponry. In order to prevent any future possibility of Hindus and Muslims attacking them together, the British unleashed the most brutal punishments against Baba Ram Charan Das and Amir Ali—two men who had successfully brought the erstwhile feuding religious sects together in Ayodhya.

Baba Ram Charan Das, the chief priest of Hanuman Gadhi was a highly respected member of the Hindu community in the area and was a close and trusted friend of Amir Ali, a respected Muslim leader from Hasnu Katra. Over the years, both these men had worked hard to promote communal harmony and goodwill in Faizabad district. Around the time of the breakout of violence, they were very close to solving the ancient problem of Ram Janma Bhoomi amicably. Both communities had a sense of ownership about this spot in Ayodhya and it had been a source of considerable friction for many years. The joint peace initiative of Baba and Amir Ali, that would have united native Hindus and Muslims, was looked upon with suspicion by British rulers. They preferred the two communities in opposing factions, so that they'd remain suspicious of each other.

As the events unfolded during the ghadar, the British were also forced to recall with some discomfiture what had happened at Ayodhya on 26 June 1853. In order to drum up support for the British rule, they had then encouraged a large Muslim rally called by a known British sympathizer, Mirza Ilahi Baksh. This gentleman was son-in-law to the last Mughal emperor Bahadur Shah Zafar of Delhi and care had been taken that at his public meeting at the Badshahi mosque in Faizabad, Husn Banu, the daughter of the emperor, was also present. Speaking to the local Muslims at the rally, the Mirza alleged that the country had been going downhill ever since Bahadur Shah Zafar had assumed charge in Delhi. He said he firmly believed that if the Company were to assume charge and govern the land, it would bring about revolutionary changes across the country.

As the Mirza spoke, Acchan Khan, the local hothead jumped to his feet and yelled at the audiences, 'My brothers, beware of this traitor! He has sold himself to the goras and now also wants to handover the entire country to them. A man who is disloyal to his own father-in-law, who lent him this aura of nobility, cannot be expected to be true to anyone!'

Enraged by Acchan Khan's words, the public tried to attack the Mirza, who had by then been swiftly escorted to safety. After the Mirza departed, Amir Ali took over and managed to pacify the crowds. He reminded the gathering that through all disturbances, both at Lucknow and Delhi, their brave Hindu brothers had chosen to lend their unstinting support to the Muslim rulers, thus strengthening their hands. For the Muslims, it was time to repay the Hindus for the trust and generosity they'd shown. One way, he said, of repaying them would be to hand over the Babri masjid that had been built during Babur's reign, by demolishing it for a temple for the Hindu brothers since they firmly believed that this was the holy spot where their revered Lord Rama was born. This single gesture could forge a bond of love between Hindus and Muslims throughout the land that even the father of these goras would be unable to destroy, he said.

Amir Ali's impassioned speech made a deep impression on the listeners and as they dispersed, they indicated that they might consent to his generous suggestion. But the spies planted by the British in the crowd had rushed to their masters and informed them of a possibility of forging of strong ties between the warring communities. The British were not pleased. This was why moments after capturing Baba Ram Charan Das and Amir Ali, they lost no time in pronouncing them guilty of sedition and hanged them in public. The people however, did not forget these leaders' words and the tamarind tree at Kuber Teela, where the rebel leaders were hanged, soon became a sort of pilgrimage spot for both Hindus and Muslims. They took to visiting the place and leaving little offerings at the base of the tree. Finally, the area Deputy Commissioner J.P. Nicholson chose to have the tree cut down and its roots gouged and destroyed.

How secular was Wajid Ali Shah?

The ousted Nawab Wajid Ali Shah was by no means a conservative follower of Islam. He liberally used Hindu phrases in his musicals—words such as *Ramchandra ki Jai!* (Victory to Lord Rama), and also wrote a dance drama called *Krishna Bhakt Jogin* (The Female Saint Follower of Lord Krishna). A story about the complex times he lived in was recounted to me by an old jeweller of Lucknow, Lala Moti Chandji Johari. According to this tale, in the present day Chowk (then known as Company Bagh, a rather crowded area), some officials of the nawab demolished a Hindu temple that belonged to the community of jewellers, who were greatly enraged by this act and went to the British to complain about the Nawab. Wajid Ali Shah was deeply distressed by the fact that instead of trusting him, the Hindu community chose to send one of their senior leaders to the bada sahib Sir Henry Lawrence. Some quick intervention and intelligent mediation by Mahtab Rai Johri, a senior Hindu jeweller attached to the Nawab's court, prevented anything untoward from happening and peace and trust were restored by mutual consent.

Another contemporary reference in the book *Savanhat-e-Salateen-e-Awadh* authored by Kamluddin Hyder refers to both the above incident and the troubled past of the Hanuman Gadhi in Ayodhya. Hyder writes:

'As trouble at Hanuman Gadhi began to grow, some senior followers of Islam viz. Maulvi Syed Amir Ali, grandson to Ali Bandagi Miyan of Amethi and brother Sheikh Husein Ali who worked for a major talukedar, Raja Nawab Ali Khan of Mehmoodabad, desired that a case of insulting Islam be registered. The leader of the Islamic group first discussed the matter with the Maulvis at Sandila and thought of declaring jihad (against the offenders). But several senior members of the community opposed this. They felt that an adversarial stand would ultimately pit the jihadis against the senior administration and officials of the Company. Nothing good could come out of it and Islam may be humiliated for no reason. This view was rejected but the Maulvi remained adamant.

'Finally the Nawab turned to the religious head Munshi Mutavassil Bashir-ud-Daula , and told him that he wished that a clash should be avoided at any cost. But many influential members of his kingdom—including Maulvi Amir Ali, who was close to Bashir-ud-Daula – opposed him. These people want to stoke the fires of anger among the public to increase the likelihood of communal clashes, he said, and so that Nawab Wajid Ali Shah's name gets tainted for no reason whatsoever.

'To probe the matter, Basheer-ud-Daula sent for the Maulvi to appear at the Imam Bara at his house and accompanied him to the Nawab and tried to make peace between them. The Nawab said that should the Maulvi drop the idea of storming Ayodhya, he would be honoured with a khillat from the Nawab. But the Maulvi did not change his mind and refused the khillat. Finally he was allowed to go and do as he pleased and the palace thought it was good riddance.'

Kamluddin Hyder, who wrote the above details, was known to be close to the British. But it is obvious from his description that Nawab Wajid Ali Shah did not encourage the Maulvi. The Nawab's opposition to the Maulvi's stand was not because of an ideological polarization between them, but because the Nawab, an aesthete, found the thought of any sort of violent confrontation rather distasteful.

Soon after the communal riots of 1853, the coming together of Hindus and Muslims during the ghadar further proves that the two communities were closer to each other, and disliked the British equally. This could explain why, when the British challenged the rebels in 1857, a Hindu and a Muslim leader: Baba Ram Charan Das and Miyan Amir Ali of Hasnu Katra, fought and died together.

Sultanpur

The district of Sultanpur is situated on the banks of the Gomti river and had been under Muslim rule since the twelfth century. When the Awadh Irregular Infantry posted at Dariyabad prevented the British from carting off a treasure to Lucknow, the detachment of the fifteenth Bengal Irregular Cavalry from Sultanpur also joined the uprising and murdered their commanding officer and other European

*officials stationed there. Then they proceeded to Salon, a nearby town
and released the prisoners from jail after looting the treasury there.
The old town had been destroyed by the British after the uprising was
quashed. Interestingly, the lands of the erstwhile landlords, known as
the Khanzadas of Amhat, were confiscated by the British to build an
airport. Even after Independence, the families were not compensated,
though the airport, known as the Amausi airport, has expanded
manifold since it was built. In the 1940s, the Khanzadas joined
Mahatma Gandhi's Quit India movement against British occupancy,
and one of them managed to foil a British attempt to delay a train
carrying Gandhiji for a public meeting, by urging fellow railway workers
to forego a proposed strike.*

Mrinal Pande

On 9 June, I set out on the third lap of my journey to Sultanpur.
The present day Sultanpur, rebuilt after the ghadar, stands at
the same location where the British cantonment once was. It
was late in the afternoon and as the train arrived at the station,
I could see the district information officer standing at the exit
gates station looking for his guest. As soon as I was near him,
I greeted him as though he was an old acquaintance, dodging
his query if I was Amritlal Nagar.

The ghadar broke out in the district of Sultanpur early on
the morning of 9 June 1857, exactly a hundred years ago. The
commanding officer Col Fisher, who was returning home from
the police lines, was shot in the back by rebels and killed. Two
other civic officials were killed in a similar fashion. Later after
they regained power, the British avenged these deaths by razing
the entire town to the ground. The ruins of that old Sultanpur
are still visible across the river.

Passing through the city in a government jeep, I kept imagining how all those who once peopled this area may have moved about. Native soldiers from the British army marching quietly, single file, their sahibs sitting astride horses and shouting orders as they led their troops, resplendent in their attire: starched white trousers, red jackets with gold braids, gleaming gold buttons and boots. Then there were the images from the *Faizabad Gazetteer*: dishevelled and dazed white officials on the run, attempting desperately to save themselves and their women and children from being butchered by lynch mobs of natives yelling revenge! The ghadar was a hellish time when an overriding desire for bloody revenge turned people on both sides into animals. Nothing mattered except drawing the enemy's blood!

Sultanpur is a small but prosperous town dotted with several modern-looking buildings. I learnt that the gentleman by the name Kisan-ji, who was supposed to have been my escort, had been in a bit of a quandary over my visit. His eldest son was getting married and the formal betrothal ceremony was to take place the next day. He said he could ask a friend of his to distribute the invitation cards for the ceremony and accompany me wherever I needed to go. But I insisted that he just let me use his jeep and the driver and carry on with his filial duties without a worry. I told him I was quite capable of navigating the area on my own. After a few moments of polite hesitation, he agreed and appeared to be much relieved. He said that a local teacher whom he knew, would accompany me to the Amhat village, where the local heroes of the ghadar, a band of men known as the Khanzadas, were believed to have fought against the British with admirable courage.

So I left for Amhat with a school teacher whose name I have forgotten. Amhat is situated close to the city and on the way I saw the old jail house and ruins of the bungalow where Col Fisher's assassination triggered off riots. In Amhat, we met a member of the Khanzada clan: Javvad Hussein Khan. After we apprised him of our mission, he called out for some chairs for us and sent for the village panchayat head, Inayat Hussein Khan. By now, a couple of elders and a few young men had gathered and conversation began, led for the most part by the loquacious duo of Javvad Hussein and Inayat Hussein. Others would just offer brief comments whenever they could.

Javvad Hussein told us that as per his information, when the British forces arrived in the village, his forefathers, the Khanzadas, had faced them bravely. Among them he named Fateh Khan, Dariyav Khan, Pir Khan, Fateh Bahadur Khan, Hussein Baksh Khan, Fenku Khan, Khatir Khan, Ghani Bahadur Khan and Raza Khan alias Raja Khan. These patriots fought a pitched battle against the gora paltan. Of their 1,800 supporters who fought alongside the Khanzadas, a few were killed and some ran away. Those who stayed on at Amhat after the battle, were forced out of their homes when the reprisals began. Much later (after the Royal Amnesty) they were provided with alternative accommodation, but their disloyalty was unforgotten and hence they were relocated to some far off burial grounds.

The old Amhat village where they once lived, was forcibly evacuated and their land was given to the people of Diyara. Forced to live in the burial grounds, the original inhabitants were reduced to the living dead. The slain British colonel's bungalow lies close by and it is believed that his evil spirit still haunts the area, riding a white horse.

But how come the villagers of Amhat got involved in a skirmish between officers and men at the army camp? It was due to a royal letter, I was told. A little before the altercation at the army camp, a secret missive had been received—on behalf of the infant prince Birjis Qadr Shah—by the Khanzadas, urging them and their loyal men to support the native armies when they rose in revolt against the enemies of faith.

'Do you still have it?'

'Yes, Khadim Hussein's brother has it.'

'Can I have a look at it?' I asked.

The Sarpanch Inayat Hussein Khan spoke up. 'Please come tomorrow and I shall have it ready for your eyes,' he said. He added that he had himself seen the letter. Written in Persian, it said that the British army accompanied by a few Sikh and Hindu regiments had been noticed surreptitiously entering and exiting the area between the rivers Ganga, Yamuna and Ghaghra. The villagers of Amhat were asked to follow them and capture the native soldiers, so that the rebels' ranks were strengthened and killing the goras became easier.

'Who was the recipient of this order?' I asked.

'Bakshi Khan, a much decorated landlord of Amhat. The order must have been addressed to either him, or his son Bakhtawar Khan, who followed it through. Bakhtawar died young during the ghadar and then Mehndi Hasan Khan, also known as Mindai Khan took over. The area ownership continued to be registered in the name of Bakshi Khan but there were many claimants to the ancestral land. My grandfather's sister was married to one such relative by the name of Raza Ali Khan, a high-ranking official who maintained an army of 10,000 men. Charges were framed against about twenty-two men from among the Khans. Some were sent to the prison and two men, Mindai Khan and Hussein Baksh Khan, were hanged despite fervent appeals from fifty-two landlords petitioning on their behalf.

The main charge against all these men was that they had not given a proper burial to the bodies of the British colonel and soldiers killed in battle. The second charge, was that we, the villagers of Amhat had captured the colonel's steed but killed the groom. There was also a third charge—the villagers had murdered Jay Lal of Paraupur Chhitauna, a native legal official employed by the Company at Girdaur village.'

'So poor Mandai Khan and Husein Ali Khan were finally hanged?

'Well, they were lucky. It was the year of Queen Victoria's coronation and their lives were saved by the royal pardon. However, they lost all their land and property,' the sarpanch replied.

An old man spoke up. 'There was this peepul tree near the police station on which the natives found guilty of supporting the rebels were hanged. Each day, the head of the police station would remind Mendu Khan that he too was headed for a similar gory end on the branches of that tree. And every time, Mendu Khan who had retained his native wit, would reply politely that it was not to be, and that he would finally get out of the jail house as a bee from a pot of honey. "You'll see, sir!" he said.'

I went back from Sultanpur to Amhat the next day, to see Begum Hazrat Mahal's firmaan. I found a large gathering of all the Khanzadas waiting for me. Some twenty-five or thirty of them began to fire questions back at us. 'Why are we being asked about all this? Will the facts be used to provide us some sort of relief? The British had grabbed large tracts of our agricultural land for allegedly making an airport. Are we going to get our land back? The British considered us rebels. Is our own government also going to treat us like the British or change our status...'

Finally the sarpanch shushed all of them into silence and began to speak. 'Babuji,' he said to me, 'we may be simple villagers, but we know the difference between the words baghi (rebels) and khairkhwah (well-wishers). The British labelled us as baghis, which means "the insubordinate ones". We had actually carried out the commands of our then royal masters and in the battle many of our brave men were martyred. How can we continue to be described as rebels?'

I replied, 'The British may have had their own reasons for using the word baghi for your forefathers, but surely you were well-wishers of the nation. This is evident from the letter Prince Birjis Qadr received from the government that you still have in your possession and which I have come back to see.'

Another wave of loud questions and complaints arose. But someone stopped it, calling for peace. He said he had the above mentioned letter in his house in Nihalgarh village. He was unwell and had to be brought for this meeting by relatives. He wished to inform me that the precious missive could only be viewed if I would do them a favour and visit their village after two or three days. I told him that it was not possible for me to prolong my trip any further. I would be obliged if they would forward me the letter through Kisan-ji. I would get it photocopied at Lucknow using special cameras and return the original to them. The sarpanch hesitated, adding as a cautionary note, 'After our lands were confiscated, those royal papers are all that we have been left with, as proof of our ownership,' he said.

Finally it was decided that I would have to take responsibility for the safe return of the letter, only if the villagers agreed. Khadim Hussein then dictated some facts loud enough for everyone to hear, asking them to correct him if they felt he was factually incorrect:

'We, the Khanzadas are originally Gajlauti Muslim Rajputs related to the Rajasthan royals by ties of blood. And our area of Amhat Tallukedari confiscated in connection with the 1857 uprising by the British, was well-known in the northern plains. I have myself seen both the royal firmaan as also sundry other official papers with my own eyes. I have also seen a royal summons in the Farsi language issued by the Nawab of Awadh for Raja Khan and Tasfiyar Khan. These were among a total of fifty-seven claimants to the land of whom fifty-six belonged to four clans of the Khans.

'Our ancestors who led the attack against the British, first drove them towards old Sultanpur, forced women and children to cross the Ghaghra river and then set violence upon the menfolk. Much blood was shed thereafter. A certain Englishman managed to cross the Gomti river from its eastern banks, helped by a boatman. The boatman also handed over a letter on his behalf to the Raja of Diyara, soliciting his help and protection. After the ghadar was suppressed by the British, their forces rushed to the area and they were livid when found the body of their colonel hanging from a tree. A second contingent was then sent for and the villagers were told they were guilty, not merely of killing an official, but also desecrating his body and denying him a proper burial.

'The second contingent entered Amhat firing shells all around to re-establish the suzerainty of the British. The shelling destroyed several grand mansions that stood by the roadside, forcing people to flee from their homes to save their lives. Those ruins still stand as reminders of the British backlash against the rebellious villagers of Amhat taluka. When the divisional commissioner arrived in the area, the clever Raja of Diyara showed him the letter from the British army official whose life he had saved during the ghadar. In return for his kindness to the angrez, he was handed the area of Amhat, confiscated from the Khanzadas. These details I got from my father's late elder brother Ghani Bahadur Khan. He also told us that after peace was re-established, the British sent word to the absconding villagers that they could now return without fear of any retaliation by the government. Not many trusted them, but about a dozen of them like Ghani Bahadur Khan, Mehndi Khan, Raja Khan, Jhau Khan and a few others whose names I do not now recall, went back and were promptly arrested and sentenced to death by hanging. They were however pardoned at the last minute by the judicial commissioner and were thus saved.

'We are confident that the gist of all these incidents that took place in this confiscated region, must have been published in the area gazette. A copy of that is available locally and may be perused. There should also be specific papers about Amhat in the official records of Diyara, since this area was originally not a part of the Diyara principality but an independent one. An airport was deliberately constructed over the land where the original village stood so that the people would be rendered homeless and never again be able to plan a rebellion.

'The seeds of rebellion against the British remained dormant. In 1919, when Muhammad Ali and Shaukat Ali from the area were members of the Congress, Gandhiji was to travel through this route on 24 December by train, for addressing a meeting at Amritsar. My cousin Hussein, employed with the Indian Railways at Saharanpur, was pressurized by his British superiors to go on strike along with his colleagues so that all trains on that route would be stalled. But Hussein saw to it that the strike was postponed by a day and Gandhiji's train passed without a hitch. When he was asked why the strike had been deferred, his reply was that the local boarding schools where the children of British officials were sent to study, routinely sent them home by train on 24 December so they could celebrate Christmas with their parents. Stalling the trains would have meant depriving those children and their parents of that pleasure. Hence the employees decided to defer the strike by a day. The British had no answer to his fine piece of logic and kept quiet thereafter.'

(Signed by Khadim Hussein Khan, sub-inspector Morraka, on behalf of the clans of the Khanzadas of Amhat on 10 June 1957)

P.S: 'After the regrettable act by the British government, the land of the rebels of Amhat was given to a co-operative for purposes of building an airport there. The magistrate in charge of the aerodrome had then ruled that in case the land is not utilized for the purpose allotted, it should be returned to its original owners. Since the aerodrome was never constructed, we should have rightfully got back our lands. But that hasn't happened. It has been two years since we brought this matter to the government's attention through a signed request, but it has been neglected. We request a review and appropriate action so the area can regain its original liveliness. This may be read as a post script to our description of the ghadar days as the villagers of Amhat experienced it then, and remember it now.'

Khadim Hussein Khan

As the villagers of Amhat also acknowledged, it is undeniable that Indians were often quite cruel towards their British victims and indeed were so carried away by Nawab Birjis Qadr's orders to chase out the invaders, that they occasionally victimized women and children unnecessarily, something that is unforgivable in any age. The government headed by Begum Hazrat Mahal on behalf of the infant prince Birjis Qadr had not ordered these pogroms. They had, as a matter of fact, intervened on several occasions on behalf of enemy women and children taken prisoners by the rebels and having rescued them from death and torture, refused to hand them back to the rebel forces.

Later, I met Babu Ganpati Sahay, a local lawyer. He said he did not know too much about the incidents during the ghadar but the people of Amhat village were certainly in the forefront of rebel forces in the area. The battle between the British and the natives was fought at old Sultanpur, across the river at a place known as Kadu Ka Nullah. A certain General Bakht Khan Ruhella made it big during the ghadar, but that entire village was bombed by the British to avenge the deaths of their officials and soldiers. The area where present day Sultanpur is located, was earlier the site of a British army camp, and is locally still known as Kampu. The remains of the village where the ruins of a mosque and temple still exist adjacent to each other are proof that back in the day, Hindus and Muslims had lived in perfect peace and harmony with each other.

During the violence, several local British officials and their families found a saviour in the Raja of Diyara, Babu Rustam

Sahi. He managed to send them to safety to the city of Jaunpur nearby, in covered palanquins. When the British regained their hold, the raja was decorated and also rewarded with the Amhat village as a jagir. The land of the rebels was confiscated and hundreds of them were hanged publicly on the branches of a neem tree near Sitakund.

The imam of the local Bibi Ki Masjid also told me that during the ghadar years, a Sufi saint named Hazrat Abdul Shah Latif had suddenly arrived here and stayed on till his last days. He was rumoured to be a son or a grandson of the last Mughal emperor, Bahadur Shah Zafar.

Apart from these few worthies, I was given the names and addresses of a few other men who I was told, were the district intellectuals. I was told that they would be gracing the engagement ceremony of my local host Kisan-ji and I could try and interview them. But the way they had avoided meeting me when I went calling at their homes, and the hyped up descriptions of their erudition brought to me formally by their hangers-on, put me off completely. If they are the district intellectuals, I am a national intellectual, I thought to myself. The very thought was so ridiculous, that I burst out laughing. Of course, I made no efforts to meet them.

Gonda

This district, part of the Baiswada region of Awadh, had several Rajput talukedars from clans such as Bais, Janwar, Raikwar, Gahlot and Gautam. With grants of land from either the local Muslim authorities or the Delhi emperor, by the eighteenth century, they had established sizeable assets for themselves in return for military or political service.

Gradually, a form of Rajput federalism like that in Rajputana grew in the area and among its various members, the King of Gonda, Raja Devi Baksh Singh enjoyed the status of a leader.

The ghadar first broke out in Sekora, near Gonda, in early June after which the commissioner of the division Wingfield, Lieutenant Boileau rode towards Gonda quietly without leaving any instructions. The rest of the European officials followed the next day upon being told by native sepoys that they were going to revolt soon. Baiswada offered a stiff resistance to the British, with Raja Devi Baksh Singh and Rana Beni Madho intermittently threatening the enemy and also holding a dialogue. Even after a few rajas surrendered, their soldiers went and joined the arch-rebels Devi Baksh Singh and Veni Madhav, who had acquired the status of local heroes. After a week-long chase across Baiswada, the rebel forces were defeated and forced to run towards the Nepal Terai region. Raja Devi Baksh and one of his two wives went to Nepal while Rana Veni Madhav, the Rani of Tulsipur and half a dozen other talukedars remained outlaws and died of disease or exposure while wandering in the forests at the foothills of Nepal.

Mrinal Pande

Jiya Lal of Gonda is a poor brahmin who earns a living carrying goods on his pushcart to various areas in Lucknow. He occasionally drops by my house to exchange pleasantries or to get my help in composing a letter. One day, I asked him if he had heard the name of Raja Devi Baksh Singh of Gonda who had fought on the side of the native rebels during the ghadar. 'Of course I have,' he said. 'Raja Devi Singh's name is famous in all four corners of the district and every child in the area is familiar with his illustrious name.' Jiya Lal then cupped his hand upon his ear and broke into a sonorous Alha in Awadhi.

Raja Devi Baksh was a man of steel no doubt,
Tales of his fame were drummed from here to there.
When the raja ruled, everyone was happy,
Paddy, millets, wheat, all sold cheap.
The men dressed in good fabrics woven by weavers for them,
The women wore cottons and silks,
One could get a padded jacket stitched cheap and keep his dignity.
Raja Devi Baksh was a handsome man
He wore a bracelet with gold bells on it,
In front of him all others looked like moles.

The raja's kingdom ran full eighty-four kosa.
When his cannons boomed, the earth cracked.
Thousands of goras rushed back, yelling Oh my Bappa,
oh my Mother!
Oh my Mem, lets run back to London away from this super man.
A hundred were men the raja tied up.

The kingdom of Raja Devi Baksh Singh, as Jiya Lal explained after he finished reciting the lines, extended to the area between Chowk to Lohiya Ka Pul (the iron bridge) in Lucknow.

These songs are proof that no matter how historians feel about him, Raja Devi Baksh Singh of Gonda lives on in public memory. On 15 June, I arrived at Gonda to learn more about him. I was also keen to visit Tulsipur, as the brave queen from that village was one of the native heroines of the ghadar. It is believed, that just like the Rani of Jhansi and Begum Hazrat Mahal, she too gave up the veil when the time came to take on the British army.

While the scholars may debate endlessly whether 1857 was a revolution or a mere sepoy uprising, what often goes unnoticed is the greater social revolution it unleashed among women from various tribes, castes and social backgrounds including queens, princesses, concubines and dancing girls who came out openly in defiance of the mighty British empire.

However, the additional district information officer Shri Singh who met me at the railway station, informed me solemnly that since the driver of the official car was away on leave, they would be unable to provide me with a vehicle for further travel. I realized with a jolt that I was short of cash for hiring a taxi and my luggage would now become an additional burden if I were to lug it around on public transport. My visit to the nearby village of Tulsipur was therefore definitely out.

Of all the districts I had visited so far, Gonda appeared to be the poorest. The area is known for a high incidence of criminal cases and most of the houses here looked dilapidated. It is an ancient area inhabited by various tribes like Gond, Tharu, Bhar, Passi, and Kurmi. It is said that these tribals are so poor that they will even rob temples and shrines unhesitatingly. The only two holy shrines even they don't touch, are the temple of Lord Jagannath and the grave of Syed Salar of Bahraich. Colonel Sleeman, who wiped off gangs of thugs in the north, also refers to Faizal Ali, a well-known killer dacoit from this area.

As we moved towards the city, the additional information officer talked to me about Raja Devi Baksh Singh. The raja had two wives, one of whom committed suicide by swallowing a diamond when her husband was defeated in battle and chose to flee to Nepal with other rebel leaders. The other wife, who belonged to an area known as Payagpur, accompanied the raja to Nepal and after he fell ill and died there, came back to her maternal home where she continued to live till her recent death.

In the city, we first arrived at the imposing home of Thakur

Naurang Singh, a respected citizen and currently an old and committed member of the Congress Party. I was told that he also headed the District Board and is always surrounded by a crowd of petitioners of various kinds. We found that it was indeed so. An old visitor told us that thakur sahib was related to the family of Raja Devi Baksh Singh and commanded much respect in the area.

After Thakur Naurang Singh was told about my mission, he dismissed the waiting crowds and welcomed us with a smile and spoke:

'My ancestor Raja Devi Baksh Singh belonged to the famous Kshatriya clan of Bisens who also find a mention in the area gazetteer as a martial clan. He owned one-third of the area known as Baddiha (about twelve kilometres from Gonda), and the rest was owned under the local custom of Pancha Dua, by the rest of the members of the clan. After the ghadar, the British confiscated the entire area including the land owned by the raja's clansmen.

'At present, the area belongs to someone from a brahmin clan of Pandeys. Their ancestors had been serving as the head of the royal granaries for Raja Devi Baksh Singh, but one of them had betrayed him and joined the British without letting anybody know. During battle, he saw to it that rations did not reach the raja's armies. More than his defeat, such betrayal distressed the raja deeply and he swore that henceforth he would not drink water from a land polluted by the British and their deceitful native henchmen. After the raja left for Nepal, the British confiscated his kingdom. They divided the entire area into three portions and gave away a portion each as reward to three local chiefs who had turned against the raja and become British loyalists during the ghadar. One of these loyalists was the

Pandey of Gonda. The remaining two portions were awarded by the British to the Raja of Ayodhya and the Raja of Balrampur in return for their support during the ghadar.

'Pandey had played a double game. He was aware that our ancestors, who had been chased away by the British, were hiding in forests. He would visit them periodically to make sure they stayed in the forests and would tell them that the British were still looking for them. When he returned, he would tell the British that the villagers were planning sedition from within their forest hideout. After the ghadar was suppressed and the British administration restored, he managed to convince the British that resettling the original inhabitants would not be prudent. The British then decided to confiscate the entire Baddiha area and hand it to loyal outsiders. It was only after Queen Victoria (in her jubilee year) announced amnesty that our ancestors were able to meet her representatives. When they apprised them of the real facts of the case, the British told them that they would compensate them for their loss by helping them acquire upto 2400 bighas (acres) of land wherever they could get it. The only condition was that the owners would have to pay taxes regularly to the government. Earlier, Pandey-ji paid the taxes but later when the Raja of Balrampur bought the area off him, it was he who began to pay them. Even today, the original fruit orchards can still be seen in the area. Now we all pay taxes to the Congress government.

'As the Raja of Gonda, Devi Baksh Singh lived in a large palace. The palace had a secret tunnel inside that led to a little island in the middle of a man-made lake. The lake and the island, with a little temple for the family goddess, were created by Raja Ram Sevak Singh, a previous ruler and an ancestor of Devi Baksh Singh. He was a great devotee of Lord Krishna and had gone to live in Mathura. He was persuaded to return only after the queen assured him that she would get Lord Krishna's area recreated around the palace for his pleasure. The areas were thus named after various villages associated with Lord Krishna.

'Raja Devi Baksh is said to have been a tall man with exceptionally long arms. His queen, who was from Payagpur, had fled with him only to return to her family after he died in Nepal. Before he left his kingdom, his other queen is said to have committed suicide by swallowing a diamond. Some say that he had joined the rebel forces, when requested for help by Begum Hazrat Mahal. As for the Muslim rulers' participation in the ghadar from this area, Raja Ashraf Baksh, from a small principality known as Kasbah, and the queen of Tulsipur had also fought in the ghadar against the British. Their kingdoms were confiscated after the ghadar. Tulsipur was awarded later to the ruler of the state of Balrampur.'

We learnt later that Thakur Naurang Singh and the erstwhile Raja of Mankapur had jointly constructed a memorial to Raja Devi Baksh Singh at Gonda which cost Rs 25,000. The site also houses the offices of the district Congress committee.

Before I left Lucknow, Ram Ujagar Dubey, a friend, advised me to make sure I called on eminent local lawyer Shanti Prasad Shukla while I was visiting Gonda. Shukla-ji turned out to be a man in his early fifties, frail of frame, with a butterfly moustache on his thin dark face, greying hair and very endearing mannerisms. He also turned out to be a great storyteller. He was thrilled when I told him about the royal firmaan still preserved at Amhat village. He fished out an old copy of the area gazette and poring over it, insisted that I note down all the trivia he was going to recount to me.

'Raja Devi Baksh Singh was a man with an imposing personality and a superbly maintained physique. His hands were so powerful that they say he could easily fold a silver coin in two. He was also a very good equestrian. The family had come into prominence when one of his ancestors by the name of Man Singh, gifted Prince Salim (Emperor Akbar's son and successor to his throne as Emperor Jehangir), a rare pair of white elephants from Nepal. The prince remembered his friendly gesture and when he became emperor, presented his friend with vast tracts of land in this area. From then on, the family of Bisen Thakurs went from strength to strength. Villages of the area bearing the Bisen name such as Imrati Bisen and Dutt Nagar Bisen, are mentioned in local court documents dating back to the Mughals.

'When he was around twelve years old, Raja Devi Baksh got married to a girl from Bansi, an area across the Gonda district boundaries. Around the same time, the then Delhi emperor Bahadur Shah sent for him, after hearing of this brave and handsome young lad and his potential as a future member of the nobility. At the Mughal durbar, as a test of his prowess, Raja Devi Baksh was ordered to handle a notorious horse from the imperial stables that had earlier caused grievous injuries to several young men who had tried to mount him. Raja Devi Baksh however mounted the unbridled horse quite easily. The horse bucked hard, trying to overthrow him, but failed. Once he was under control, the raja rode him so hard that when he came back and dismounted before his royal audience, the once uncontrollable horse stood meekly, totally exhausted and panting. Several of the begums had been watching this handsome and fearless lad from the roof of the palace, anxious about his fate. The empress Hazrat Mahal was deeply moved, and addressing him as beta (son), is said to have seated him on her lap. Devi Baksh addressed her as ma (mother), and from then onwards, became her devout follower. When the ghadar happened and his ma asked him to support the uprising against the British, Raja Devi Baksh obliged immediately and took an oath to support the emperor's armies even though he knew the consequences of his defiance quite well. Legend has it that while he was camping this side of the river, the British sent an emissary to him. The emissary told the raja that he would be pardoned and his properties would remain intact if he were to side with the British. Devi Baksh refused saying that as long as he was alive, he would not betray his oath of loyalty to his mother.

'After a couple of battles fought at various spots at Gonda, it became evident that the British were winning. The raja then left for the nearby state of Balrampur with his two wives and after leaving them under the local ruler Digvijay Singh's care, left for Nepal with the rest of the rebel leaders. However, as soon as he left, Digvijay Singh betrayed his trust and offered to hand over Devi Baksh Singh's wives to the British. As soon as they got wind of it, the queens too departed for Nepal in covered palanquins. One fell into the hands of the British and committed suicide by swallowing a diamond, while the other reached Nepal and returned after the raja's demise there. It is said that just before she died, the queen cursed the Raja of Balrampur, stating that he would die childless, and he did.

'Raja Devi Baksh was a proud, secular and just ruler. He never discriminated between his Hindu and Muslim subjects and resented the hegemony of the British. Long before the ghadar, he had ruled that when the Shia Muslims of Gonda went to immerse their tazias at the end of the Mohurram festival, they must first halt briefly at the palace gates where the holy tazia would be honoured by the raja personally. The Muslims considered this a great honour and routinely brought their tazias to the royal palace each year. Even today, although the palace gates lie in ruins, the local Muslims will not pass it by without first halting there awhile to pay homage to a just and wise ruler. They offer so many flowers and pots of water at the ruins that the earth remains wet for several days. The sight of the once grand palace of this popular ruler lying in ruins brought tears to eyes. The grand durbar hall lies dilapidated today and the roof of the inner room may collapse any day. Only one large well in the courtyard still stands.

'There are many stories about the principality of Bansi as well. The raja's first wife, who later killed herself, hailed from this place. It is said that once a *bhat* (local balladeer) from Raja Devi Baksh's durbar visited the Raja of Bansi and saluted him with his left hand, a gesture that was against royal etiquette, and said that his right hand would only rise in salute for Raja Devi Baksh Singh. The Raja of Bansi ordered that bangles be forced upon the wrist of the poet's right hand as challenge to the Raja of Gonda, saying that he'd now like to see who proves himself to be stronger. The bhat went back and showed Raja Devi Baksh the bangles upon his wrist at which the raja announced war against Bansi. Not only did he lead from the front and defeat the Raja of Bansi, but also removed the vast gates to his palace and carried them back to Gonda with him, to be placed next to his. Ruins of those famous gates are still there. However, now that Chandra Bhanu Dutt of Dhanipur owns the area and is said to have sold part of it for residential constructions, this piece of history might soon be lost to encroachment by the newly prosperous groups of realtors.'

I requested Shukla-ji to tell me whatever he knew about the brave Queen of Tulsipur and her contribution to the cause of the rebels during ghadar. He confessed that he knew very little about her. Hearsay has it that she was a strong-willed and proud woman, and for some reason her arch-rival and enemy, the Raja of Balrampur had sent his general Veni Madhav Baksh to raid and demolish her humble mud fortress at Tulsipur. By now, I had some idea of the brittle egos and petty rivalries that prevailed among local chieftains ruling over small principalities in the nineteenth century. What I needed to know was how and why exactly did the Rani of Tulsipur join the ranks of the rebels? Shukla-ji smiled. 'My mother was the grand daughter of the general (Veni Madhav Baksh) sent to raid Tulsipur,' he said. 'I had heard it said that the general had defeated the queen in battle, after which she either died due to injuries, or killed herself. I should ask you not to mention this fact, but knowing writers, I am sure you will mention it in your book.'

So much for our discretion!

It was a pleasure to come across an intelligent and innately honest man like Shukla-ji in the hinterland. As I was leaving, he let it be known, that he did not care what use the notes I had been taking would eventually be put to, but said that he would appreciate it if I would at some point, write about the grand and tragic life of Raja Devi Baksh Singh. I promised him that I would, but added that as a creative writer, my gestation period for mulling over facts and arranging and rearranging them into fiction, was rather long and unpredictable. What I could do, however, was that if I ever wrote a novel about that great uprising in Awadh, Raja Devi Baksh would definitely figure in it as a great hero.

Time, I told Shukla-ji, keeps us all in its grasp, whether we are writers of creative fiction or a lowly clerk outside a district court typing out letters for clients. Time, Shukla-ji agreed, is all there is to it.

5

BAHRAICH

The district of Bahraich is located in the trans-Ghaghra region towards the north-eastern part of Awadh, bordering Nepal. Part of this district (Tulsipur Dang) was presented to Nepal Durbar by the British in exchange for help and friendship extended during the ghadar. Sikrora, located here was a major military station garrisoned by the first regiment of Oudh Irregular Infantry, commanded by Captain Daly, second Irregular Oudh Infantry under Captain Boileau and a local horse battery under Lt Bonham.

In Bahraich, division proprietary communities had never been too numerous or strong. But when Charles Wingfield, the commissioner of the region further reduced the number of talukedari villages and targeted two estates of Bondi and Tulsipur for default and contumacy, disaffection grew among the rajas. The Raja of Gonda, the Raja of Bondi and the Queen of Tulsipur came out early in support of the rebels led by Begum Hazrat Mahal. After being chased out of Lucknow, the Begum was holed up in the fort at Bondi where she called a famous conclave of native rajas to enlist their support in the fight against the British, and urged them to plunder the British loyalist traitors.

Mrinal Pande

The original name of this town was Bharaich, the abode of the Bhars. The origin of this community remains a mystery. According to late Dr Kashi Prasad Jaiswal, one of the few scholars who tried to solve this puzzle, the Bhars were perhaps the same as the ancient tribe of Shiva worshippers, the Bharshaivas. It is also possible that they were tribals who were the original inhabitants of the area, and gave the town its name Bharaich, later christened to Bahraich. During the thirteenth and fourteenth centuries, when Muslim invaders stormed Awadh, Bahraich became a nodal point for many martial groups who fought the invaders unitedly. The Bhars were finally crushed by Syed Salar Masud and later, his grave became a revered shrine, now worshipped by all communities.

According to local lore, the shrine to Syed Salar stands where a temple to the Sun god and a small pond dedicated to the celestial deity once stood. In fact, several other dargahs are also said to have been built in the area where a bunch of ancient Hindu temples stood around the Sun temple, each devoted to one of the nine celestial star signs (nava graha). One such dargah, said to have replaced the temple of the headstrong star Mars, is known as the Dargah of Hatheele (strong-willed) Pir. Another shrine, which supposedly replaced a temple to Venus (Shukra), is referred to as the Dargah of the Sukru Pir. The day I reached Bahraich, it was the last day of the Urs and the streets were milling with thousands of villagers from many of the neighbouring villages. At this point, the district official accompanying me announced suddenly that he must depart by the evening each day since he was scheduled to tour some nearby areas and halt there at night. This meant that if I wished for him to be my guide, I would have to pursue my mission in the first half of the day and visits to nearby villages would also have to be limited to areas that lay close to the town. Since I had no other option, I accepted whatever help was available under the circumstances and re-configured my itinerary accordingly and left for the nearby villages of Bondi, Chahlari and Murauvadeeh on 17 June.

In 1857, the small principality of Bondi was being ruled by Raja Haridutt of the clan of Raikwar Kshatriyas. Just like his friend, the raja of the neighbouring state of Charda, he was also a close friend of Begum Hazrat Mahal and his entire clan supported the rebel forces led by the Begum of Awadh during the ghadar. The British considered Raja Haridutt as a friend and expressed great surprise at how he and several other local rulers and landlords, all erstwhile friends of theirs, chose to turn against them suddenly during the ghadar. Perhaps they did not realize that no matter the occasional bad blood, familial friendships and loyalty to the nawabs of Lucknow actually mattered for the rulers of these tiny principalities in Awadh. The British forces, miffed by this reaction, retaliated sharply after they had put down their revolt and confiscated about 1858 villages.

As listed in the area gazette, among the rulers punished by the British for sedition were Thakur Balbhadra Singh of Nawabgunj in Barabanki (owner of thirty-three villages), Raja of Dhaurhara (twenty-six villages), Raja of Bondi (305 villages), Raja Charda (428), Rani of Tulsipur (313), Raja of Akauna (506), Raja of Rehua (14), Raja of Bhinaga (138), and Tiphara state (nineteen villages). The state of Bondi was where Begum Hazrat Mahal had stayed for several months during the ghadar and her historic reply to Queen Victoria's official communication to the natives was also sent from here.

Among local rulers who stood by the native rebel armies, the Raja of Balrampur, a Janawar Kshatriya by caste, was a notable exception. The British gazetteer praised his unwavering loyalty during the uprising and how he helped the British in various ways during the mutiny. He was later handsomely rewarded by the grateful British with several prestigious titles and gifts of fertile land confiscated from his rebel brethren.

The district information officer accompanying me, a member of the Janawar Kshatriya caste himself, said he felt stigmatized by the betrayal of one of its members during the ghadar. He told me several times that it disturbed him greatly that while fellow Raikwar Rajputs and Bais Rajputs had behaved like true Kshatriyas and supported the local cause during the ghadar, the Janawar Kshatriyas were let down by their leader, the Raja of Balrampur. I tried to console him by pointing out that the brave Raja of Charda was also a Janawar Kshatriya and his sacrifice proves that not all leaders from that clan were turncoats. I do not know if it calmed him. The thought remained with me however, that those we regard as martyrs today, may have been considered somewhat dangerously foolhardy by many of their contemporaries, especially the ones who chose to be loyal to the British and outshone the rebel princes by witnessing a meteoric rise in their fortunes in the post-ghadar years.

The road to Bondi was green, flanked on both sides by mahua trees. Men and women were spreading mahua seeds out to dry in the shade. As we passed, the young women stood up, a few of them chose to dart suddenly across the road as we approached and giggled when the driver honked the horn angrily. As the vehicle screeched to a halt, the young women crossed the road again, hand in hand, laughing and swinging their youthful hips. Who wouldn't get mad at such beauty? We drove off smiling at their audacity.

A hot 'loo' was blowing as we arrived at the village of Sai near Bondi. We stopped to ask for directions to Murauvadeeh where we had decided to halt on our return journey. Our throats were parched, and although we carried a clay pot with our drinking water, we decided to save that for later and asked for a drink. The villagers brought us a large brass lota filled with sherbet sweetened by jaggery. Along with the lota, Parasdeen Baba also made an appearance, a man who we were told was the village elder and well-versed in the history of the area. While we sipped on our drink, Baba began to speak:

'After Begum Hazrat Mahal escaped from the siege of Lucknow, she camped briefly at a place known as Bhanwari that lay on the other side of the river Ghaghra from Bondi. At this point, Raja Hardutt Singh, who accompanied the Begum, sent a message for the ruler of Bondi that told him that if he helped the Begum regain her throne, she would reward him suitably. The raja agreed. He then sent for other princes and landlords from nearby areas like Gonda, Charda, Pyagpur, Rehua, Nanpara, Tapraha, Mallapur and Ramnagar. The princes then gathered at Bondi, and having agreed to help the Begum, battled the British at Chinhat. Raja Hardutt was killed.'

'Was he killed in battle or later?' I asked.

'God only knows. They say he died somewhere up north, in the hills. Later Raja Mahesh Baksh and Hardutt's son Mahavir Singh are said to have received the royal pardon and grants of land. That's all I know,' Baba replied.

The Begum of Awadh must have been an intelligent and gutsy woman. She appears to have travelled constantly to seek the necessary help from her contemporaries. I had heard several stories by now about her meetings with the princes. No one knows about her background, but what is known is that she had been kidnapped as a child by two notorious procuresses, Amman and Amaman. They taught her to dance and sing before introducing her as Mahak Pari to the harem of the Lucknow Nawab Wajid Ali Shah, known as Parikhana or 'the abode of fairies'. The pleasure-loving Nawab was always surrounded by pretty young women who danced and sang to please him. Even after he was captured and sent into exile by the British, his lifestyle did not change. It's nothing short of a miracle that the same Begum Hazrat Mahal, a minor wife and erstwhile courtesan, managed to grow into a towering army leader, leaving behind those infantile, scheming and high-born begums of the nawab's harem.

Nankau Singh, author of the famous Jangnama

We arrived at Murauvadeeh, where the grandson of Thakur Balbhadra Singh's only daughter and the head of the local panchayat stays. We were told that he had just returned to his village by the same road we had taken. We asked a young man near Pipri village for specific directions to his house. He told us that if we went a little further we would see the house of the gaddar (traitor) and see a small lane next to it that would lead us straight to Girija Shankar-ji's house. I was a bit taken aback by the use of the word gaddar and asked him about the turncoats who had lived there. He said he did not know any names, but their home was referred to by villagers as the house of the gaddars.

Soon we arrived at Murauvadeeh, the village of Raja
Balbhadra Singh. He was born here in a small fort (Kote). The
river Ghaghra flows to the north-west of the village and the gate
to the fort opens towards the north side. There were ruins of a
dome close to a mango tree nearby. The fort is built on a high
mound. To the north, where the gates once stood, there was
a small pond. It held very little water and looked dilapidated.
Some people stood in the knee-deep water, fishing. Traces of a
moat existed all around the fort. We were told that when the
fort was intact, the moat was filled with water and at night,
after the removal of the wooden planks that bridged it, no one
could enter the fort. The family of Chahlari Raja's daughter
still lives here. There was a small house to the right, with a
tiled roof, part of which had collapsed. Four other smaller
houses with thatched roofs stood adjacent to it, one of which
had collapsed. Peacocks could be heard from the trees growing
all around. We were told that the royal forces used to parade
up and down the stretch of the river in preparation for battle
against the British in 1857.

We could not meet Girija Shankar-ji, but his cousin Shri
Babu Ram Singh showed us an ancient map of the fort that
had been handed down over generations in the family. He
told us that Balbhadra Singh had an only child, a daughter,
who was married to Kunwar Gajraj Singh of Jevan village of
Shahjehanpur district. They had four sons—Munua Shiv Dan
Singh, Devi Baksh Singh, Raj Bahadur Singh and Hanuman
Singh.

Munua Shiv Dan Singh and Devi Baksh Singh had later
settled down in Murauva. The other two brothers continued
to live at Jevan, their father's village. Munua Shiv Dan Singh
had two sons, Girija Shankar Singh and Shankar Baksh Singh.

His brother Devi Baksh also had two sons, the late Ganesh Singh and Babu Ram Singh. Ganesh Singh had three children, and he, Babu Ram Singh was one of them.

I asked him why his father and uncle had chosen to leave their father's village and settle in Murauva even after their grandfather's lands had been confiscated. Babu Ram Singh told us that they settled down here because 250 bighas of good arable land had been donated to the family of the erstwhile rulers by a Punjabi gentleman, who was the new owner. They wanted to manage the land locally, hence migrating to this village was considered the best option.

By now, another elderly villager Ashirwadi Pandey, made his appearance. He told us that while Balbhadra Singh was fighting the British troops, his wife was being terrorized by his men who told her that the area was unsafe for her and her young daughter, her only child. She finally decided to go to her father's house and died there without ever asking for compensation like many others. Her daughter, however, later applied to the government to regain some of her family's lost properties. It was as a result of this that she was granted a monthly pension of Rs 200 along with 250 bighas of land that included the villages of Chahlari, Than, Gangapurwa, Bachhmaria, Bhaisi, Rajapur Kalan, Baijwari and Munjauna. After the daughter died, the pension was discontinued and after Independence, when the zamindari system was abolished, most of the village land was also lost to the family.

'If Raja Balbhadra Singh stayed in the village of Murauva, why was he referred to as the Raja of Chahlari?' I asked.

'Well, he may have lived in Murauva, but since his royal treasuries and granaries lay in Chahlari, his name got officially associated with that area,' Pandey-ji replied.

As our conversation continued, gradually men, women and children began gathering around us. Names of all those that had fought in the battle of Chahlari began to be hurled at us with such speed that I had to stop noting them all. I then requested them to calm down and allow me to record properly what was being said. Making note of my concern, Pandey-ji said that all the names were listed in the book *Jangnama* (The History of the Battle) by Nankau Singh, a local poet. Before I could say another word, Pandey-ji began reciting lines from what seemed to be a very popular ballad in Awadhi:

> *All those that were riff-raff, they ran away first*
> *Then all the riders of elephants too ran away*
> *Only Hardutt says, I shall fight the angrez to death*
> *And lay in wait among the reeds by the river side.*
> *Another brave one was Balbhadra Singh*
> *He leapt upon the angrez, killing them all.*

As he finished, a young man stood up and recited some more:

> *The Raja of Bondi became a lap boy and slave to the angrez*
> *Long live the Raja of Chahlari!*

The last words were pure folk expletives. Pandey-ji yelled at him angrily and recited to us what he said was the correct version:

> *Long live the raja of Chahlari who killed the angrez.*

At this point, a local brahmin, Pandit Jagannath Prasad made an appearance sporting a long white beard and wooden slippers on his feet. He was older than Pandey-ji, around seventy-five years of age, we were told. Jagannath-ji told us that his grandfather had accompanied the Raja of Chahlari on his last journey. It seemed that the raja had gone to fetch his young bride with the usual entourage of drummers and liveried servants and friends. He was not a rebel, though he had been the recipient of royal largesse from the Begum of Awadh in the past. So this procession, that included Jagannath-ji's late grandfather, began moving towards the bride's village firing their guns in the air. At the temple of Lodhesur Mahadev, the raja told his grandfather to stay there. The rest, as they say, was history, something that we could read in Nankau's *Jangnama*.

By then, I was getting more and more eager to lay my hands on this legendary epic about the ghadar. I was told that Nankau Singh, now about a hundred years old, was actually Raja Balbhadra Singh's nephew and lived in Tikuri village, just a mile away.

Excited at the prospect of meeting the old poet, I left for Tikuri immediately with Shri Babu Ram Singh. It was a blazing summer afternoon and as soon as our car arrived in the village, some children sitting under a tree raised an alarm and followed it to the door of Nankau Singh's house. We were told that he was unwell and was therefore resting. I told Babu Ram Singh that we should wait quietly till he was awake and was ready to receive us. But there was no holding back a government servant. He rushed inside, and in a short while I heard his loud voice announcing that someone had arrived from Lucknow, a government official who wished to hear the *Jangnama*. Obviously Nankau Singh's hearing was not what it used to be and a raised voice was required to direct any queries to him. After a while, I was ushered into a large sitting room, followed by a crowd of locals. I missed not having a camera with me.

Thakur Nankau Singh was a slender man. His sight and hearing had faded substantially, but he still had all his teeth and his voice was still powerful. I was told by various people how Thakur Nankau Singh was well known for his love for two things: the written word and weaponry, and had a large stash of both. He maintained a register in which he meticulously recorded all the births and deaths in the area. Now those records are updated by his son. The register also records all the quarrels and litigations he has had with various clans over the years.

'This Aghan (early winter month of Agrahayan), I lost my eyes to some infection. Let's see what happens now. I was born the year my uncle (Balbhadra Singh) had fought the British. I am now almost a hundred years old,' Nankau sahib said to me.

I requested him to show me a copy of *Jangnama*. As his son handed him the bound volume, the old man first ran his fingertips over its contours and then said in a satisfied tone that this indeed was it. Then he began reciting the poem himself. As I had feared, he was very loud and recited too fast. My polite requests for slowing down fell on deaf ears. I eventually stopped trying to take notes and requested that the edition be loaned to me for a short period. I would have a copy made as soon as possible and return the original.

As soon as I said so, I noticed a quick exchange of glances between him and his son. There was obviously a certain unwillingness in handing over the precious manuscript to an outsider. But having seen it, I would not let go of the treasure either. So I finally went close to Nankau Singh's ear and repeated my request loudly. He asked would it not be possible to have the manuscript copied locally within four or five days? I found that a somewhat dicey proposition. In my experience, relegating a vital task to others within a given time span seldom yielded results. So I repeated that I had to return the very same day and if he loaned the manuscript to me, I promised to guard it with my life until it was copied and returned safely to him.

Nankau Singh-ji nodded. He said I could take the precious manuscript of *Jangnama* with me but I must take care to send the original back safely as soon as I had made a copy. By doing this, he hoped his words would be able to reach far and wide and his brave uncle's name would be remembered amongst all the martyrs of the ghadar. 'All I want,' he told me, 'is a signed request and receipt from me with my permanent address duly noted on it.'

I readily gave him what was required and felt rejuvenated holding the precious pages of *Jangnama*.

As I left, the noble poet humbly requested me to correct any grammatical or other errors that may exist in the original, and then to have as many copies of *Jangnama* published and circulated as possible.

Nankau Singh's *Jangnama* itself has a history, which is recorded at the end of the book. According to the facts recorded, the first draft was completed by Beniram Misra of Bhadeva village in district Sitapur on the fifth day of the dark fortnight (Krishna Paksh) in the month of Margsheersh. The year was 1941 of the Vikrami Samvat (1885). He writes:

'The present copy of *Jangnama* has been respectfully prepared with insertions of various details that had inadvertently been left out in the original draft. These facts are beyond doubt since they were supplied by one who had participated in the battle at the behest of his raja and who, after returning wounded from the battlefield, had later met Hallen sahib, the British civil administrator in Lucknow in the year 1889. He told us how when he went to meet the sahib, he saw an aged pensioned-off soldier wearing a sword with a golden hilt. After the talks were over, he asked me where I was from. When I said Bahraich, he said the Raja of Bahraich, Balbhadra Singh was indeed a brave king among kings. At this, I burst into tears. When he asked me the reason for my tears, I told him young Balbhadra Singh who died in the battle at Barabanki on Sunday in the Vikrami year 1913 (1857) at the raw age of eighteen years and three days, was my uncle, and that my grandfather Ganga Singh and the raja's father Sripal Singh were brothers.'

Jangnama may not be great literature, but it provides several valuable historical details. It states that Raja Balbhadra Singh faced the British armies when he was escorting his brother Chhatrpal Singh's marriage procession, not his own. This contradicts several stories and songs I had heard in the neighbouring Barabanki district, about a just-married Raja Balbhadra Singh fighting the British army while still dressed in the traditional gear of a bridegroom.

The book also claims that Begum Hazrat Mahal of Lucknow was then camping at the nearby principality of Bondi, where she had called a meeting of all the community leaders of the Baiswada region and asked for their help. She had heard much about the brave young raja's valiant deeds and so she sent him a handwritten invitation through a special messenger.

The messenger first went to Chahlari, where he was told that Balbhadra Singh had gone with his brother's marriage procession to Shivpur. The messenger did catch up with the procession as it was returning and handed the Begum's letter to Raja Balbhadra Singh. The raja instructed the marriage party and the groom to proceed to Chahlari as planned, and he himself left for Bondi, where he was greeted warmly by the Begum. According to Nankau Singh, she hugged the brave young lad and said that he was as dear to her as her own son and went on to present him with the royal khillat consisting of an elephant, jewels for his wife, and royal robes for both of them. As he departed to fight the British army along with drummers and pipes playing martial tunes, the Begum bade him farewell by putting a traditional tilak with saffron on Balbhadra Singh's forehead and asked her son Birjis Qadr and her trusted Mammu Khan to do likewise.

The *Jangnama* also records the actual names of over ninety brave men who were among some that were killed in battle along with the brave raja. The names make it amply clear that not only the nobles but common farmers and artisans, palanquin bearers (*kahar*) even barbers (*nau*) from all castes and communities had chosen to join the Begum's armies in the fight against the British.

Singh sahib had carried a home-cooked lunch for us that we ate sitting under a gigantic neem tree. As we ate, we also discussed various issues with Ashirwadi Pande and Pandit Jagannath. It turned out that the lack of facilities for education for the youth in the area had long been a source of concern to the elders. Jagannath-ji expressed satisfaction at the opening of new schools and the spread of education after Independence but felt that mere literacy and ability to spell was not enough.

While at school, the young must also acquire learning and that was mostly lacking in classrooms.

As we were eating, I soon became aware that chatting with people while sitting on a string cot and having a meal out in the open was contrary to established caste traditions and might be taboo to most families in the region.

'Tell me, Pandit-ji,' I asked Jagnnath-ji, 'how do you feel when you see me breaking the usual taboos on eating lunch under a tree? Isn't it offensive?'

Pandey-ji piped up before Pandit-ji could speak, 'Well, that's the way things are today, so we'll just overlook it.'

'He is right,' Jagannath-ji agreed. 'In this age, that is acceptable as a new kind of dharma. What is important is that you are observing your basic dharma by going from door to door in search of new information and knowledge despite your various other preoccupations. That kind of core dharma cannot be maintained by sticking to old rules and traditions. I see this happening in my own house. My grandson, a school dropout, does not observe the same traditional disciplines as me. So I tell my family, let him follow the new dharma. Although, I must add here—personally, to me the old way of life still feels the best.'

After lunch, we left for Bondi by a road that ran along the canal. I was handicapped by lack of time and proper travel facilities and had to cancel a visit to Chahlari, where I could have perhaps got access to more trivia and information about Raja Balbhadra Singh. But I had to satisfy myself with the good stories Murauva and Tikuri villages had provided me with. Someday, maybe someone else will fill in the gaps that remain.

Bondi and Ikauna

How fourteen villages in Ikauna came to be owned by the
Kapurthala state in Punjab

After a long journey, we finally arrived at the citadel of the
Raikwar prince Raja Hari Dutt Singh at Bondi, the site of
a historic meet of the native rebel leaders in 1857. The area
the building occupied—despite being mostly rubble now—was
certainly two to three times larger than the one covered by the
fort at Murauva. As you entered the premises, on the right-hand
side you saw an office of the Kapurthala state, while a printing
press stood on the other side. To the left was a school building
that faced the ruins of Raja Haridutt's fort. Of the old structure,
only the walls remain.

A farmer now owns the lands behind the school. He told
us that he had heard from his family elders that this spot
where their fields lay, was once a royal abode. Even now, each
time they dug deep, they unearth several old Lakhauri bricks.
It is said that the fort that stood here used to be surrounded
by a bamboo forest. It had four large gates and four domes
mounted with cannons. But now no one knows much about
Raja Haridutt here. They have only heard stories about how
once upon a time the Begum of Awadh had graced the area to
meet the Raja of Bondi. After they lost a battle, the raja had
escaped with her and her fleet, somewhere up north in the hills.
They never returned because once defeated, they all perished
one after another in exile.

The next morning we left for Ikauna where the ruler Raja
Udit Prakash had also been associated with the ghadar. We were
told that the principal of the local intermediate college and his

lawyer brother Shyam Lal knew quite a bit about the history of the area. But when we went to meet the man, we were told he had gone to visit his brother in Bahraich.

The next name on our list was Shri Ramkumar, son of the late Lala Saligram, one of whose ancestors Lala Kishun Persad had served as a legal advisor to the government of Wajid Ali Shah at Lucknow. Ramkumar-ji told us that the Raja of Ikauna, Udit Prakash had disappeared after being defeated by the British and was never seen again. Ramkumar also solved for me the mystery of Kapurthala state offices in both Bondi and Ikauna. It seems that for some reason in the past, fourteen villages from Ikauna and several others from the area had been presented by the landlords to the state of Kapurthala in Punjab. In return, the erstwhile owners were given the status of specially honourable nobles (Ji Izzat) in Kapurthala state. They received a monthly rental of forty rupees as well, an amount that had lately been reduced to thirty. The legal papers regarding this exchange were still extant.

To learn more about Ikauna we decided to go to Bahraich and meet the lawyer Shyam Lal. On our way, we saw the ruins of the great Buddhist city of Shravasti that lay barely four miles away from Ikauna. It is said that the land for building a garden was bought from the ruling prince by a rich Buddhist Anathpindak in gold coins that were enough to pave the entire area. Jetvan, Buddha's favourite forest lay here once. The little stone mound on which he sat under a tree and spoke to his followers still exists.

In the evening we visited lawyer Shyam Lal-ji. He told us that Nana Saheb Peshwa had visited the area when he was organizing an army against the British. Nana Saheb also attended the princes' conclave at Bondi. There was a sadhu in Ikauna who resembled the Nana and whom the British arrested after the ghadar, only to be released later. There was another mentally deranged man, Patandin, in Ikauna, of whom it was said that he had lost his mind after the rebel army—in which he was something of a hero—lost out to the British forces.

The Raja Udit Singh of Ikauna had participated in the uprising, but never returned from the battlefield. He belonged to the clan of Janawar Rajputs.

There was a local tale about the curse of a Brahmin whom the Raja of Ikauna had insulted publicly and driven to suicide by hanging from a bargad tree in front of the palace. The raja tried to expiate for his sin of killing a Brahmin (Brahm Hatya) by building a memorial there, but that did not help—the raja died intestate. An annual fair is still held at the samadhi of the dead Bechu Maharaj though.

Shyam Lal-ji also took us to meet his neighbour, Kunwar Indra Pratap Narayan, successor to the princely houses of both Rehua and Bondi. It was somewhat ironic that the two houses that had fought bitter battles against each other in the past should now have one descendant straddling both families. Kunwar Indra Pratap confirmed that the Begum of Awadh and her son Birjis Qadr had briefly sought shelter in their family house during the ghadar.

'Our family belonged to the Raikwar clan of Kshatriyas whose origins can be traced to Raka Dev Rathore of Rajasthan who once ruled in Kashmir. In Awadh, their line was traced to two brothers Saldev and Baldev who were the lords of the principality of Ramnagar Dhameri. Later, Saldev gave charge of Dhameri to his brother after he conquered an area known as Bambhnauti on the other side of the river Boodhi Saryu.

According to a book *Nagkoshlottar* by Babu Gorakh
Prasad (also known as Musho Babu), during the reign of the
Mughal emperor Jehangir, one of the royal wives arrived at
one of Bahraich's shrines on a pilgrimage. At that time, two
descendants of Saldev and Baldev, Harihar Dev and Gajpati
Dev controlled the lands along both banks of the river Saryu
and asked the begum to pay a tax for being allowed into the
area. When the begum protested, her retinue was held back
till she presented the landlords with an elephant and other
expensive gifts. Upon completion of her *ziarat* (pilgrimage),
on her return to Delhi, the begum complained to the emperor
about the unbecoming conduct of the brothers towards a
queen. Around the same time, a Brahmin at the court of the
brothers advised them that before the Mughal armies hit back
in retaliation, they should go to the badshah and clarify that
they meant no disrespect. As controllers of the royal lands in the
area, the brothers were fully entitled to ask all pilgrims to pay
tax. The brothers agreed and as Harihar Dev left for Delhi with
his brother, he installed his son Prasanna Dev as his successor.

When Harihar Dev arrived at the durbar of the Mughal
king, two other princes from this area, Raja of Basti and Raja
of Majhauli, Devariya were also present. The emperor asked
which one of the three was considered the most important.
The other two remained quiet and Harihar Dev said he was
the bravest. The emperor then asked him to go and capture the
Raja of Chunar and bring him to the durbar as proof of his
bravery. The brothers left, accompanied by their own men and
a few Rajputs from the Mughal army. Near Chunar, they hid
in a nearby forest and entered the city dressed as sadhus, their
weapons concealed in their saffron robes. After arriving at the
fort they sent word to the raja that two sadhus wished to see

him. The Raja of Chunar had just finished his ablutions and was sitting down for a meal but nevertheless he sent for these two. As soon as they saw an opportune time, the brothers drew out their swords. While one held the raja hostage, the other stood guard. When the guards came running, the brothers announced that they'd kill the raja in case they tried to pull any smart moves. As the soldiers withdrew, the brothers announced that they were no assassins but had been sent by the Badshah of Delhi to capture the Raja of Chunar. Their armies had surrounded the fort and would attack if the raja resisted them.

The Raja of Chunar said that he had no objection in accompanying the brothers who were also fellow Kshatriyas. But the badshah was an old enemy and was bound to humiliate him if they took him to the durbar as a captive. The brothers promised him that before presenting him to the emperor, they would make him promise that no ill treatment would be meted out to the captive raja, or else they would do unto him what they had done to the raja. After this assurance, the raja agreed to go to Delhi with them.

The fearless brothers, as promised, made the mighty badshah give his word, and presented the Raja of Chunar in the durbar, as proof of their bravery. The badshah kept his word and honoured the Raja of Chunar with a khillat (royal robes). As a mark of his appreciation for the bravery of the two brothers, he awarded them with fertile land in an area close to the Baunha hills at the edge of the Shivalik mountains. The area is now in Nepal.

After their return to Rehua, Harihar Dev handed the principality to his brother Gajpati Singh, and to his own son —already crowned as prince regent—he gave the newly awarded area of Baunha to rule, with its headquarters at Harharpur near

Chilvaria railway station. After moving to the newly acquired Baunha area, Harihar Dev remarried, this time a girl from the local Muravani community. A son was born of this union, but the Kshatriya community refused to recognize the newborn as a pure Raikwar Rajput. The descendants of Harihar Dev from the Muravani wife eventually came to be known as the Raikwars of Raikwari.

In time, Gajpati Singh also shifted his headquarters to Rehua, located at a distance of a mile to the south of Bondi. Sometime in the mid-nineteenth century, the relations between Rehua and Bondi soured. Despite belonging to the same clan (Gotra), Raja Dhuankal Singh of Rehua was killed by Raja Mandhata Singh of Bondi, who performed a ranpooja by chopping off his rival's head and planting his own flag over it before offering it for the ceremony. His court poet Ishwari Brahma Bhatt tried to stop him from killing his own clansmen, but Mandhata Singh paid him no heed. A cousin of the slain Dhuankal Singh, Raja Raghunath Singh then swore revenge upon the killer. Not only did he chase the Raja of Bondi out of Rehua, but also witnessed the cowardly raja go and hide himself in the home of his mistress. The cousin dragged them both out and since he did not wish to sully his hands by murdering a clansman, simply removed Raja Mandhata Singh's headgear signalling his humiliation. To complete his vow though, he chopped off one of the breasts of Mandhata Singh's courtesan mistress and performed the gory ritual of ranpooja over it. This signalled an end to the clan war and his son Haridutt made peace with Raja Raghunath Singh.

Begum Hazrat Mahal and her son Birjis Qadr had spent a few days in the Bondi fort as honoured guests of the maharaja. Nana Saheb Peshwa also spent three days at Bondi during the same period. The Raja of Bondi hosted both without fearing the wrath of the British and made arrangements to provide them with vital military support. The Raja of Rehua, Haridutt Singh was helpful too, but he was somewhat handicapped by his chronic asthma and one of his brothers being mentally challenged. He however, did send another brother Hari Sharan as a commanding officer to the begum's forces. Hari Sharan was shot in the leg during battle and came back to Bondi after their defeat.

While the Begum was camping as an honoured guest of Raja Haridutt at Rehua, Nana Saheb Peshwa also paid a three-day visit. Prince Birjis Qadr was about the same age as Raja Haridutt Singh's elder son Mahesh Baksh Singh and he became good friends with him, and his younger brother Mahavir Baksh.

After they lost the battle, Raja Haridutt along with Begum Hazrat Mahal and some other major rebel leaders fled towards the hills into Nepal. But defeating the rebels only energized the British as they struck back hard at the native rebel leaders. Their principalities were confiscated and the fort at Rehua along with its famous moat and turrets, where no less than 152 cannons were placed, was razed to the ground. Raja Raghunath Singh of Rehua had already died in battle and no sooner than that came the news that Raja Haridutt too had died in exile somewhere among the hills in the north.'

At this point I chose to intervene in the narrative and ask Kunwar sahib a crucial question: If Raja Haridutt did indeed escape to Nepal with the begum and other rebel leaders, why does the *Awadh Gazetteer* claim that he was captured by the British, tried and sentenced to life imprisonment in Port Blair?

'That is all wrong,' Kunwar sahib said. 'How could they capture a man who was just not available? The fact remains that the trial was held in absentia and the absconding Raja Haridutt was sentenced to life imprisonment in the Andamans. His principality was of course, confiscated by the British government.'

'What became of Haridutt's two sons?'

'Both princes had been sent to live under the protection of a fellow Rajput, Raja Man Singh of Ayodhya. They stayed at Bijulia Deeh at one of the palaces of the raja for about thirteen to fourteen years. Apart from Raja Man Singh, the kings of Rampur Dhameri and Rehua also helped out. In fact, Raja of Ramnagar Dhameri later handed over the area of Sardaha to Prince Mahesh Baksh Singh for himself and his family. After his death, we inherited the village and his other properties from his widow. But since the current raja of the area wanted his area back, we have returned it to him. We do not wish to create bad blood among our own clansmen.

'Our own father, Raja Vijay Bahadur Singh was the son of the martyred Raja of Rehua, Raghunath Singh. He was a learned man and known as an excellent wrestler. It is said that he even offered to wrestle a tiger owned by the Raja of Nanpara but his friends like Justice Piggett and Raja Ranjit Singh of Nava Nagar talked him out of it. Our father died young, leaving behind two sons: myself, Kunwar Indra Pratap Narayan, and my elder brother Raja Rudranath Pratap Narayan Singh who passed away on 30 September 1953. My brother left behind three daughters and a son. I have a son and a daughter. They are all pursuing their studies at the moment. Let's see what the future holds for them. That, in short, is our family history.'

Nepal

The Raja of Charda and how the Begum finally bought peace

On 19 June, having met with members of almost all the prominent princely families of Bahraich connected to the ghadar, we set out to meet the descendants of the Raja of Charda. A local worker of the Congress Party, Maheshwar Baksh Singh of Bhavania village, had very kindly agreed to be our guide and take us to Dhaudhey village of Nepalgunj district across the Indo-Nepal border. On the way, when we arrived at Kevalpur village, Mahesh Baksh-ji said we may like to meet Rasheeduddeen Kidwai, a man whose ancestors had fled with Begum Hazrat Mahal into Nepal and who often talked about the ghadar days.

Shri Kidwai was a polite, cultured man who spoke a beautiful courtly Urdu: 'The Begum had found refuge in Charda village in India, but the British forces arrived there looking for her. After they had laid siege to the area, Begum Hazrat Mahal escaped to the fort at Masjidia through a secret underground tunnel. The fort was at a distance of some eight miles from Kevalpur.'

'Did such long tunnels actually exist in those days?'

'As far as underground tunnels are concerned,' Kidwai-ji replied, 'when I go hunting in the interiors, I can make out the remnants of the historic tunnel that stretches from Masjidia fort to the Maan rivulet. It was common in those days to build long secret tunnels for a quick escape to a safe haven within palaces and forts. When the British forces chasing the Begum arrived at Masjidia, she chose to escape arrest by leaving through the tunnel leading to the Maan rivulet in the Mahadev hills. After crossing the rivulet, she passed quite easily through Sotar into the territory of mainland Nepal. The locals still point out various signs of her long journey along this route. There are stones marking areas where she had halted and buried her treasure in a piecemeal manner. Places like Mahadeva, Sonar, Charda, Masjidia and Angurkot (ruled by the Raja of Tulsipur) that lay in her path, are all believed to have marked spots where parts of her royal treasure lie buried. I have come across one such spot in the Angurkote forests where I had gone hunting. I was told some manual labourers had found a couple of pots of gold and gems while digging there. The soil still showed marks of rounded bottoms of heavy pots.'

I said I was sorry but I couldn't believe this story because it seemed rather improbable that all those spots, so conveniently marked, would have escaped the hawk-eyed and rapacious British forces chasing the begum along the same route. A couple of years ago there was an effort made in Lucknow by some members of the erstwhile royal family to locate old buried treasures at considerable expense. Even various kinds of secret magic rituals were performed by practitioners of black arts, and finally a police posse was posted at the site indicated by the priests, but when it was dug, nothing was found.

'You may be right,' Kidwai sahib agreed, 'but there still are stones at these spots, with something carved upon each in Arabic. And there is no doubt the begum was carrying a treasure. It is said that she had presented the Maharaja of Nepal with two priceless necklaces by way of thanks for giving her shelter. But coming back to the subject of my family members who had accompanied the begum from Barabanki—they included several men who chose to settle here. There is one lawyer in Barabanki by the name of Mukhtar Ahmed whose grandfather was also part of the team of men that had come here as part of the Begum's royal escorts and stayed on till her death.'

Just before he left, quoting a Nepalese noble who was a close friend of his, Kidwai sahib hinted that the begum and the king of Nepal had developed some kind of intimate relationship. I found his remarks and the tone they were delivered in, somewhat distasteful. Had the Begum agreed to become one of the wives or mistresses of the king, she would have had a very comfortable life. But all available facts show that the Begum was too proud to use her sex as a means to ease her way into the royal society of Nepal. She chose, instead, to spend her remaining days in penury in Nepal and devoted herself entirely to religious activities. It is noteworthy that she never abandoned her family and got her son married to Mukhtarunnisa, the daughter of Prince Daud Beg of Delhi, living likewise, in exile in Nepal.

It is true that given the debauched atmosphere of the closely guarded nawabi harem in nineteenth century Awadh, it would be rare to find a royal who had not indulged in some form of deviant behaviour. Many of the glorified princes who were martyred during the ghadar may also have had questionable personal morals. But only because Begum Hazrat Mahal was brought up by courtesans and was later sold into the infamous Parikhana (abode of fairies) owned by the Prince Wajid Ali Shah, gossip about her becoming the Nepal king's mistress does not become credible. She was given the title of Iftekharunnisa Begum and her newborn son was named Birjis Qadr. After Wajid Ali bypassed his elder brother Mustafa Ali Khan in 1847 (Hijri year 1263) and became the Shah-e-Awadh, he rechristened his favorite Begum Iftekharunnisa as Hazrat Mahal. Wajid Ali Shah's autobiography *Huzn-e-Akhtar* makes it clear that at the time of the ghadar, his son Prince Birjis Qadr

was fourteen years old. Hazrat Mahal bore him when she herself
was no more than fifteen or sixteen years old, which makes her
around twenty-seven to twenty-eight years old in 1857. Had she
been the kind of flirtatious woman, gossip makes her out to be,
she would certainly not have received the respect and attention
from her contemporaries that she did, and be accepted as the
supreme commander of Awadh's rebel army after her husband
was exiled in captivity.

As we entered the Nepalese border, a Gurkha policeman tried
to stop us. As soon as we told him we were pilgrims on our
way to the temple of the goddess Bageeshwari, we were allowed
in. The topography and faces across the border seemed no
different. There was a large pond within the premises of the
temple guarded by a life-sized marble statue of Lord Shiva. I was
told that the idol of the goddess is installed inside a room across
a paved courtyard but one could go in only after one collected
some traditional gifts to offer her during pooja: red fabric,
vermilion, and several such items including cash. I decided
to close my eyes and see the goddess through my mind's eye.
To me it seemed senseless to enter a holy place where one is
expected to first strike a barter of sorts with a priest. We decided
to walk towards the village to treat ourselves to some of the milk
sweets the area was famous for. Our companion Maheshwar
Baksh Singh shared his rich collection of local ghadar stories
with us on the way.

'I belong to the family of Bisen Thakurs of village Lodhiya
Ghata in Gonda district. The mother of Raja Jot Singh, of
the Janvar Thakur clan, belonged to our village. During every

festival, she was treated like a daughter of the family. During the monsoon festival of Teej, when my ancestors Thakur Munnu Singh and his two brothers Prakash Singh and Chandan Singh went to Charda bearing the usual Teej gifts for the queen mother, the raja requested them to guard the Masjidia fort on the Nepal border against an imminent attack by the British. They accepted, and all three were later killed trying to defend the fort battling the British forces that had arrived there chasing the rebel Begum of Awadh.

'After beating down the rebels at Masjidia, on their return journey, the jubilant British cracked down on all those who had had the temerity to challenge them. Charda's Raja Jot Singh was jailed under charges of sedition. Then there was an inhuman massacre at Bankuti village in which the whole family of Rafi Khan, the naib tehsildar (a block level revenue official) of the raja was butchered. Even the women and children in his family were not spared. Their graves still serve as reminders of those terrible reprisals.

'When Raja Jot Singh was released from jail and some of his properties were restored under the Queen's Amnesty Scheme, he sent for the fatherless children of the three martyred brothers from our village, who had died defending the Masjidia fort. He awarded a village each to the three bereaved families. Since then the three villages Tikuri, Bhavanipur and Bijli have been with our families. Over the years, our Kshatriya clansmen, the rajas of Charda and Balrampur, who prospered after the ghadar, have extended considerable help to our families.'

In the erstwhile principality of Tulsipur Dang towards
Dhaundhey Gaon, Nepalgunj in Nepal, to meet the grandson of
Jagjot Singh of Charda

Shiv Raj Singh, the eighty-year-old son of Jet Singh, the late Raja of Charda, lives in Dhaundhey Gaon across the border in Nepal. India has had an open border with Nepal and as we moved towards the village, the faces, the language, clothes, the foliage, and fields—some bearing green crops and others dug up and awaiting the monsoon rains like large round platters—all seemed so familiar. Only a few faces here had the Mongolian gurkha features.

The roads in the area are uniformly uneven and can barely be negotiated in a moving vehicle. After a long and bumpy ride, we finally arrived at the village where we were told that if we went ahead and took a turn to the left, we would face the raja's abode.

We followed the instructions but faced a brick house which turned out to belong to a Muslim farmer. To our right, there was a long row of mango trees, where the road turned to the left along a slight incline. We continued to follow the road and finally arrived at a simple double-storeyed structure with a tiled roof. This was the palace! The boundary wall for the ground floor was long and covered a large area. Two baby goats lay asleep at the door, next to a square wooden seat. We entered the brick house through a very large open square with a tamarind tree on one side, and a couple of mud huts with thatched roofs on the other. One of those looked brand new. Two bullocks and a goat stood tethered on either side of the gate that led into the courtyard and several cows and colts were being fed by servants. A few bullock carts and push-carts stood stacked against the wall. Outside, where the boundary wall ended, lay a large open maidan and beyond that, the forest. It was initially sparse, but grew dense gradually and was said to be home to a variety of wildlife.

Could this be the abode of the descendants of the Raja Sahib Charda, asked one of our team members. Were the villagers pulling a prank on us when they referred to this mud building as the Raja Sahib's palace? But it did not seem that any sarcasm was implied. The people of the village seemed to hold the raja in high esteem. He was a regent who may have fallen into bad times, but a king would always remain a king. As a matter of fact, we who live in urban areas need to be somewhat disillusioned. We are somehow misled by the opulent and glamourous lifestyles of a few members of major royal families and believe that all erstwhile rajas live lavishly in ornate palaces. In reality, most princes those days chose to live among their people in largely rural neighbourhoods. They were wary of displaying their wealth and considered it public property, to be used only for public purposes. Their houses were simple brick and mud structures and they lived and ate just a shade better than their cultivators.

The raja, we learnt, had gone to Duvidhapur across the border. In his absence, we ended up meeting his young grandson, Kunwar Harnam Singh, a young man in his early twenties, who turned out to be a really cordial host. He insisted on treating us to a hot lunch with freshly cooked rice and would not hear of our making do with the simple home-made fare—the chapatis and pickles that Mukhtar Singh carried. I realized then, that in traditional homes, rice is normally not to be eaten outside the kitchen where it is cooked. But with the passing of time, such taboos are now becoming less binding. We told him that we would be happy to sit and eat out in the open, under the tamarind tree. The brahmin cook brought out platters of steaming hot food. I asked him if he felt uncomfortable about breaking the kitchen rules to serve us a meal in this manner.

'Half the world now eats their meals this way,' he told me good-naturedly.

'You are not alone. Even the officials of the government of India observe no taboos now.'

While we were enjoying our meal, the young Kunwar, who was supervising the arrangements, asked if after lunch we'd like to see some family papers about the ghadar. As soon as he said this, I almost jumped in joy. Our long and tedious journey would not be a waste after all.

After lunch, a bundle of rolled up and somewhat torn family papers were brought to us. They were handwritten in pen and ink by the old raja. The style of writing was reminiscent of *Bharat Mein Angrezi Raj*. The paper was hand-made and hand-polished, similar to the scrolls frequently used by traditional astrologers for making horoscopes. Kunwar-ji told us that he had brought out only the scrolls that covered the story of their family with reference to the 1857 ghadar. This is what the scroll said:

'In the year 1847, after Raja Mahipat Singh passed away, the brave Raja Jagjot Singh ascended the throne of Charda. He had been a raja for over a decade when the mutiny broke out simultaneously all over Awadh. Jagjot Singh felt compelled to participate in it because the British were continuously insulting our emperor at Delhi, our fellow rajas, nawabs and landowners. As soon he joined the the revolt in 1857, he was declared a rebel. When the honourable rebel leader (from Bithur) Nana Saheb Peshwa sought shelter in his fort, the raja gave him complete protection. The British tried to tempt him into giving up his guest. They told him that if he turned the Nana over to them, they would reward him with a sizeable portion of fertile land in the district of Bahraich. But the raja turned down the request.

'Enraged by his obstinacy, the British attacked his fort at Charda. By then, Jagjot Singh had already smuggled Nana out of their reach to the Nepal border, under the protection of guards led by his brother-in-law, Raja Devi Baksh Singh. With just a handful of soldiers and one cannon, he staved off the British forces for three days. On the fourth day, the British sprinkled vast quantities of country liquor all around Charda fort and set it on fire. Using the same tunnel, the raja escaped with his family and most of his belongings to his forest fort at Masjidia in the foothills of Nepal. As he left, he vowed that he would not re-enter Charda until he had avenged his defeat. He never returned.

'The British chased the raja again and he had to leave Masjidia. This time he escaped to his fort in Bargdaha at the western edge of the forests in Nanpara tehsil. He was not allowed to live in peace even there, so he finally left it and sought shelter in Nepal. As a fellow Kshatriya, the Maharaja of Nepal not only took him in and awarded him a couple of villages towards his maintenance, but also wrote to the British and requested an amnesty for the brave raja who had followed the tenets of his dharma in sheltering Nana Saheb. This was around the time of the Delhi durbar. When the then Viceroy, Lord Curzon heard that one royal rebel, the Raja of Charda had survived the ghadar and was living in Nepal, he was curious to meet him. He urged the Maharaja of Nepal, who was invited to the Delhi durbar conclave with other native rajas, to bring along Raja Jagjot Singh as well. Thus the brave Raja Jagjot Singh was finally rid of the stigma of being dubbed a rebel on the run from the government.

'In Delhi, the raja was welcomed warmly but his estates had already been awarded to the loyal Raja of Balrampur who had helped the British quell the revolt. The Raja of Charda was given permission, however, to go to his fort and dig out whatever treasures he had buried there. The proud raja refused to do this and said that he had vowed not to step into his fort at Charda till his honour had been avenged. But unfortunately his honesty and unbending pride made the British Viceroy somewhat wary of the raja and told him that he could not travel with more than ten men, nor halt at any place for longer than three days. He was, however, given Rampur Malawan, one block of villages in the district of Bahraich by way of pardon and compensation.'

Soon we left for Duvidhapur, accompanied by Kunwar, to meet the aged former raja camping there.

Duvidhapur

At Duvidhapur, we re-entered Indian territory and following a long meandering road along the fields, arrived at a modest brick house with a kuchcha mud interior, even less impressive than the one at Dhaundhey Gaon. The inner courtyard was under repair and the raja, son of the great Raja Jagjot Singh, and his son Maharaj Singh were sitting in the veranda, watching the men at work. The old raja seemed to be in his late seventies, his hands and face, a nest of wrinkles, but his proud grey moustache was still rounded at the ends.

I told the raja that I had heard that his father had fought the British at Chahlari in Nawabgunj Barabanki along with Raja Balbhadra Singh.

'No,' he replied in a tired voice, 'our battle was fought here itself in Bahraich.'

The son began to speak:

'The conference at Barabanki was held after the Kanpur massacre. My grandfather, a good commander of armies, told the princes that if they fought separately, our side would never win. At the behest of Nana Saheb Peshwa, the rajas (under the command of the Rajas of Charda and Gonda) had jointly mounted two attacks on the British Residency at Lucknow. But these attacks failed as Nana Saheb-ji was not a very trusting man. His people kept poisoning his ears and told him that the princes of Awadh may later begin to think of replacing him as the leader of the rebels. So he let the Rajas of Chahlari, Charda, Bondi and Gonda return to their principalities.

'As they were crossing the river Ghaghra, somebody alerted the British and the rajas had to fight a pitched battle, which they lost and ran helter-skelter to save their lives. After this debacle, they decided to never mount a joint attack.

'Raja Jagjot Singh meanwhile managed to escape the British spies and returned to Charda. When the rebel forces were defeated by the British at Lucknow, Nana Saheb Peshwa, Balaji Rao and Tatya Tope came to us again. But the British found out about this and immediately wrote to my grandfather stating that all would be forgiven only if he would hand over the other rebel leaders to them. My grandfather refused saying that he would do no such thing, since it would mean betraying their trust. At this, the British suggested that he should ask them to leave Charda, at which grandfather said that he couldn't do that either, because as a Kshatriya it was his dharma to give refuge to those that came to him. Frustrated by now, the British sent a troop of 40,000 soldiers to smoke out the leaders. When their army reached Nanpara, the rebel leaders escaped from Charda to Masjidia, where a pitched battle was fought.

Raja Jagjot Singh had attended a major conclave of princes at Barabanki that was held after the fall of Lucknow. The Rajas of Chahlari, Charda, Gonda, Balrampur and Ikona had all gathered there at the invitation of Begum Hazrat Mahal. The objective of their coming together was to strategize about their future course of action. It was decided that protection of all families involved was crucial and so one of the rajas had to remain non-partisan. In case of the rebel leaders' defeat, or death in battle, that raja had to be a guardian to all bereaved families and provide them with shelter and means of sustenance. Digvijay Singh, the raja of the small principality of Balrampur was chosen for this task and he wrote a formal letter declaring that he would continue to support the British, so that in case the native army lost, or some of the princes were killed in battle, he would be there to take care of their families and bring up their children. We had handed this paper to Raja Digvijay Singh's British tutor and received an increase in our compensation in exchange.'

'But we were told that first they fought the British forces in Charda?' quipped Maheshwar Singh.

'No,' said Maharaj Singh, the battle took place in Masjidia.

The old raja sahib spoke up now:

'Nothing happened in Charda. What could happen here anyway, since the rebel leaders had already escaped by the time the British forces reached here. We do not remember though if they razed the fort upon reaching Charda, or later, on their way back from Masjidia.'

Maharaj Singh elaborated further, describing the battle at Masjidia:

'The British chased the rebel leaders till the forest fortress of Charda's raja at Masjidia. They lay siege to the fort and kept firing. When they had ensured that those inside the fort were running out of rations and ammunition, they raided the fort. But it was too late, because the men they wanted had already escaped into the hills of Nepal. The Maharaja of Nepal treated these fellow princes with warmth and generosity and gave Raja Jagjot Singh some land. He also pressurized the British into pardoning him. After that he was given some land in India as well.'

I asked the old raja sahib if he could tell us about Begum Hazrat Mahal's visit to Charda. 'She did visit Charda but did not stay here. The Maratha leaders Nana Saheb, Bala-ji and Tatya Tope had stayed at Charda. As a note of thanks, the Begum offered Raja Jagjot Singh a bag of diamonds, but he refused them stating that they were all travelling by the same boat and it was his dharma as a Kshatriya to extend protection to whoever came asking for refuge.'

At this point we were served the traditional sherbet and betel leaves. After thanking them for their hospitality, I picked up the lost threads of the story again. I asked the raja sahib about his lineage.

'Our lineage?' he asked, and quoted a couplet about the Janwar Kshtriyas:

King Janmejaya, the grandson of the Pandavas created three houses
The world knows his gotra as that of the ancient sage, Atri.

'Originally,' he continued, 'our clan of Janawar Rajputs had been invited from Pavagarh, Gujarat by the Mughal king at

Delhi and Bariyar Shah. They were asked to go north as military representatives of the badshah and bring the ever-rebellious Bhars under control. The Janawar leaders defeated the Bhars comprehensively and were given rich agricultural lands here. Initially, the principality was headquartered at Ikona, but it was later sub-divided to form the estates of Balrampur, Gangwal and Charda, all a part of the principality of Payagpur in their early days. Thus the area became a cluster of principalities, all ruled by Janawar Rajputs.'

As we were leaving, the old raja put his trembling, withered hand on my shoulder and said, 'What we earn from our lands—some two hundred bighas—mostly goes towards meeting our daily expenses. The taxes are high. Our properties in Nepalgunj are all heavily forested and yield us practically nothing. Our income has shrunk to a mere thousand rupees per year. This is where the first battle for independence was fought, but see what we have been reduced to. We do not have much time left, but there should be some way of sustaining ourselves with dignity. We need to be looked after.'

I asked Maharaj Singh about the kind of grants his father Raja Jagjot Singh received from various sources.

'Raja Jagjot Singh received 300 rupees per annum from Nanpara, 500 rupees per annum from Payagpur, 1200 rupees per annum from Balrampur along with five villages, and the earnings from one village from Bhinaga. The British had (after Amnesty) also given him the zamindari of Rampur Malawan area and the Maharaja of Nepal had given him 600 bighas of revenue-free land and one village.'

The Kshatriya princes had obviously kept their word to help their rebel clansmen cope with bad times. Clan ties had remained strong among the erstwhile rulers even after the ghadar, and they did what they could, to help those among them who had fallen on bad times. Another fact I learnt was how, on the eve of a battle, native leaders would collectively decide to dissociate one clansman (the Raja of Balrampur, for example) from warfare and make him promise that he would help their wives and children. In this way, they tried to ensure that their families could live and have a future, even if they didn't.

I left for Lucknow by train the same night.

6

SITAPUR

When news of the insurrection reached Sitapur, a native sepoy shot dead his commanding office Colonel Birch (of the forty-first native infantry), a man who firmly believed in the unswerving loyalty of his native soldiers. This stunned the thirty-odd Brits posted in the area. Even as they were recovering from the shock, the military police of Sitapur also joined the rebels and together, they lynched six other officers, a white woman and her child to death. The mob then proceeded to attack the divisional commissioner's house which had sheltered all Europeans in the area. Twenty of these, including the commissioner were killed.

The Sitapur rebels also incited the natives in the nearby district of Kheri. Together, they allowed the survivors of the Sitapur carnage to escape, but as the collective rage grew, the survivors were eventually chased and killed. Only one of them survived and reached Lucknow, with the help of a few kind-hearted sepoys.

After the recapture of the capital of Awadh by the British, the native rebel leaders and their armies once again headed towards the Baiswada region where the rebel talukedars and most of the soldiers were confident of getting local support. Mehmudabad in Sitapur and Mitauli in nearby Kheri district became the refuge for the rebels to lodge themselves to fight another day. *The Raja of Mitauli though, remained a vacillating rebel who first protected the British, but when great public pressure mounted to throw them to the wolves, he sent them off to Lucknow where they were killed by rebels. Later, he surrendered to the British hoping he could cash in on his earlier support to them, but one of the survivors, a woman, alerted the British about his treachery, for which he was sentenced to life imprisonment at the Andaman jail. He died alone, embittered, and both his people and the Brits did not forgive him. Local sources reveal that the female informant received a reward of 700 villages, but she sold them all at a premium to local talukedars, and proceeded to England as a rich woman.*

Mrinal Pande

26 June 1957

I boarded an early train and arrived at the town of Sitapur around ten in the morning. There was initially some apprehension that the heavy downpour outside may hamper our mobility. But as it turned out, Indra, the Lord of Rains, had done us a favour by restricting us to the waiting room for some time. As we waited for the downpour to stop, Vasant Kumar Verma, the district information officer who had come to receive me, regaled us with several interesting tales about the ghadar years at Sitapur. Sweet tea was served while we learnt that the great sixteenth century saint poet Tulsidas Goswami, the creator of *Ramcharit Manas*, had once visited Sitapur and halted at the palace of the raja during his trip here.

During the ghadar, Verma said, Sitapur's residents were split between British loyalists and supporters of the native rebels. After the united native forces lost the battle, the jubilant British unleashed a chain of vicious reprisals against those natives who sided with the rebels. Fellow natives start baying for each other's blood and ended up creating an atmosphere of animosity and hatred. The residents of Kaziara locality helped the British locate those rebels who had gone into hiding. After the British traced them, they were lined up and crushed to death with road rollers.

In many ways, the life and death of Lone Singh, the Raja of Mitauli in the nearby Lakhimpur Khiri district, represents the violent and complex era. Deemed to be a loyalist, later events proved that the raja acted as a friend of the rebel forces. After the ghadar, when charges of betraying the British were levelled against him, he was put under house arrest at Sitapur palace.

The story, as I pieced it together, ran like this:

In the initial days of the ghadar, the wily Lone Singh chose to support the British and sheltered a few British officials and their families when they sought refuge at his palace in Mitauli. Later, as the rebels swelled in numbers and Lucknow fell briefly into their hands, the raja pretended that he was sending the Brits to safety at Lucknow under an armed escort, but instead laid an ambush and turned them over to the rebel forces in Lucknow. All but two of the British officials were killed, and of the two that escaped death, one was the daughter of the commissioner of Sitapur Division who revealed the truth about Lone Singh and had him arrested when he arrived to claim a reward for being a loyalist.

George Christian, the police commissioner of Lakhimpur Khiri had sensed the imminent violence but decided to move with caution. He gathered all the British men, women and children from their camp bungalows and moved them into his own house. In addition, he recruited some more native men in his police ranks and had four cannons installed outside to defend his turf. But with tempers running high and news about bloody skirmishes pouring in from all around, the atmosphere inside the house kept getting increasingly tense. On 2 June, the young mercenaries recruited hastily by Mr Christian to swell the numbers of his troops, began hollering about some bags of flour supplied to them. They alleged that the flour (meant for their chapatis) had been adulterated with finely powdered bones of animals, and if they ingested such a polluted meal, they could lose their caste and the Jesuit priests would then force them to become Christians.

To appease the jawans, those bags of flour were thrown into the river, but that did nothing to quell their anger. Later, the same day, the men went on a rampage in the orchards at Civil Lines, a British residential area. They were brought under control with great effort only after extra forces were deployed from nearby villages such as Muhammadi Mallavan.

On 3 June, a company of native jawans again went on a rampage. They looted the district treasury and shot dead several officials. Among those killed were the police commissioner, George Christian, his wife, his youngest child and the nanny. They were all slaughtered while trying to escape. Many other British officials were also killed on that day. Some lucky ones managed to slip away and find shelter at the palace of the Janawar Rajput Raja of Ramkot and finally reached Lucknow in a few weeks. Another party of men and women ran off to a nearby village where they hid for ten months, and eventually made their way to Lucknow somehow.

During the ghadar, barring a few like the Raja of Ramkot, the Kayastha families at Biswan and some local moneylenders, the entire population of Sitapur had risen in revolt against the British and helped push them out of the area. Bande Hassan of

Tambor emerged as a leader to reckon with in the rural areas of Sitapur, while the village of Maholi became a stronghold of anti-British forces. Nawab Ali Khan, the Raja of Mehmoodabad, who was initially friendly towards the British, also decided to throw in his lot with the native rebels. Martial clans of Raikwar Rajputs from Chahlari to Bhitauli and Bondi, all chose to join the rebel forces, and after the British were pushed out of the area, Nazim Bakshi Har Prasad of Khairabad took over the reins of administration in the area. After the fall of Lucknow in March 1858, the British forces re-entered Sitapur (from the Badi area) on 11 April. During the ghadar, this area was largely controlled by the rebel forces of Maulvi Ahmedullah Shah about whom I've written earlier.

The British commander, Sir Hope Grant was initially successful in pushing the rebels down and pressing ahead. But he was quite put off, wrote the gazetteer, because he discovered that as soon as his back was turned, two major leaders of the rebels in the area: the Maulvi and his accomplice, the Raja of Mehmoodabad, gave him the slip. They finally managed to escape, unpunished. Soon, the Maulvi and his forces relocated to Shahjehanpur and tried to keep the fires of revolt burning in Awadh, from their new perch. The rebel district of Sitapur held its head high for quite some time, even after the shameful assassination of the Maulvi by the Raja of Puvayan's men for a cash reward from the British.

After the fall of Lucknow, the principality of Bondi in Bahraich district became another major military camp for all rebel forces of Awadh. It was here that Begum Hazrat Mahal met the rebels and guided them. The local rulers like Narpat Singh, Feroz Shah and Hardutt came for the conclave at Bondi and stayed on, while several other rebel leaders like Rana Veni

Madhav Baksh Singh, Raja Devi Baksh Singh, Nana Saheb
Peshwa and Bala Saheb visited the area from time to time for
consultations and help.

In October 1858, Hari Chand, with an army of 6,000 left
Sitapur for Sandila and defeated General Barker's forces. Sir
Thomas Seaton was meanwhile camping at Shahjehanpur
awaiting an opportune moment for entering Sitapur from the
north-western side. Following a two-pronged strategy, Lord
Clyde, the chief commander of the British forces ordered his
men to cross the villages of Muhammadi and Aurangabad,
and after reaching Sitapur, push the rebel armies into crossing
the Ghaghra river, where Lord Clyde and his men awaited
them. The British forces crushed Mitauli and a lack of arms,
ammunition and cohesion resulted in the fall of the rebellious
Sitapur in November 1858.

Deputy Commissioner Santosh Kumar Chaudhary told me
that the well-known Sitapur Plywood factory now stands on
very ground where the battle for Sitapur was fought in 1858.
He also instructed Verma-ji, his talkative district information
officer, to accompany me to Mitauli in Khiri district after I'd
finished my interviews in Sitapur.

*Tales of loyalty and betrayal as the ghadar is quashed in Sitapur
and the fleeing Begum is ushered to safety in Nepal*

I asked Verma ji to first take me to meet Dr Naval Bihari Mishra,
a close friend's uncle teaching at Lucknow University. He was
a well-known physician and apparently a scholar of Hindi
with a sizeable collection of antiques and local lore in Awadhi.
Dr Mishra received us with the warmth of a family member.

Guru Prasad Dixit, who had come to visit the doctor from Pandariya village revealed that Major Jodha Singh of the Dhanapur Pandariya village had received orders stamped with the royal seal of the Nawab of Awadh, instructing him to go and face the British in Butwal.

'As the battle was raging,' said Dixit-ji, 'just when soldiers on both sides began feeling exhausted, extra British forces arrived and Jodha Singh was hit by a bullet on his thigh. The Begum of Awadh asked Jodha Singh's elder brother to escort her to Nepal. Her feet were also bleeding as she carried her son Birjis Qadr in her arms. She did arrive at Pandariya, but fled when she heard that the British officials had arrived. On her way to Nepal, she halted at Chahlari. She had heard about its brave ruler Raja Balbhadra Singh whom she asked for help. The raja agreed.

The son of Ram Charan, a favourite royal barber of the Raja of Chahlari, had initially run away but returned to join the royal team escorting the Begum to Nepal. He died on the way, fighting the British forces which came chasing the begum. After the Begum reached Nepal, Havaldar Ganga Baksh Singh of our village received a letter of commendation, a special spear and some cash from the begum for helping her.'

I was delighted when the good doctor also agreed to accompany me to Mitauli.

The Raja of Mitauli who wanted to run with the hares and hunt with the hounds

The block development officer at Mitauli had collected several knowledgeable people at the village's Panchayat Bhavan so I could hear some more local stories about the controversial Raja Lone Singh of Mitauli, who I learnt, had initially earned the goodwill of the British when he gave shelter to some British families. But he later chose to betray them. When contrary to most predictions, the British managed to quell the ghadar and resumed their rule, Raja Lone Singh came forward to claim a reward for having sheltered a posse of British officials during the violence. He would have received it but for one young lady who had survived the brutal massacre at Lucknow who acted as a whistleblower. His duplicity exposed, the raja was arrested and sentenced to imprisonment in the Andamans. He however died on the way.

Muhammad Saklain of Mitauli village had this version to share about the incidents that led up to the arrest of the raja:

'Before the ghadar, the British had planted two spies in the court of Mitauli. One was Syed Miranjaan of Khiri, who enjoyed very good ties with several local rulers. The other was Munshi Zahurul Hasan, a lawyer. Raja Lone Singh had awarded a village and a house to my ancestors in the summer of 1249 of the Fasli calendar. The raja was reputed to be somewhat tight-fisted and cowardly, but was not an evil man at heart.

'The rebels and the British forces first clashed in Aurangabad village. The graves of the British soldiers that were killed exist there even to this day. About five or six British officials and a woman, said to be the wife of Captain Ore, had sought shelter at Raja Lone Singh's palace after they escaped from Aurangabad to Mitauli. The raja looked after them well. In the meanwhile, his trusted courtier Munshi Zahurul Hasan told the raja that the British Raj was over and therefore it was not prudent to be found sheltering some British officials. He suggested that the raja send them to Lucknow without delay, and let the native forces in control of the city deal with them as they saw fit. The raja agreed. He saw them off, not as prisoners though. He sent them riding one of his own elephants, like special guests.

'Soon after the British guests had left Mitauli, word arrived that the British had managed to turn the tide in their favour and re-established their Raj. But by then, it was too late for the raja's guests. They'd been led like lambs to slaughter, because as soon as they arrived in Lucknow, except for the lone woman, they were all killed by rebels lusting for revenge. After peace was restored in the area, it was she who eventually testified against the raja, who by then had managed to convince the British of his loyalty and obtained a twenty-two page letter of thanks from the them. The letter promised him half the district of Aurangabad in lieu of services rendered to the British officials during the ghadar. But after the testimony of the survivor of the Lucknow massacre, this offer was cancelled, Mitauli was raided and Raja Lone Singh was arrested and sent to trial.

'When the British took him captive, Raja Lone Singh had expected that his friends and relatives in the nearby villages of Rampur, Oyal, Mudwara, Jalalpur, and Kotwara would understand his plight and come forward to help. But even his own brother Madho Singh refused to have anything to do with him. The reality was that the reprisals against the rebels were so swift and so severe that people were afraid to stand by the raja.

'When the British forces attacked Mitauli, the raja's soldiers ran away as soon as they began shelling the fort. It didn't take long to capture the raja and take him to Calcutta. It is said that after his arrest, he stopped eating or even brushing his teeth. By the time the city police arrived for him, he was dead.

'The fort of Mitauli was completely destroyed. But two solitary graves that were once housed within, still exist there. No one knows who is buried there. Some people say they contain the mortal remains of two Sufi saints that Raja Lone Singh revered. Some say they belong to two famed Syed brothers who had helped the raja's ancestors establish their rule in Mitauli. The raja died childless and thus his family has no successors.'

Another man now stood up to share some more stories about the Raja of Mitauli. As he began to speak, he insisted that I note down details of his own lineage.

'My name is Awadhesh Baksh Singh. We are Gauda Kshatriyas of the Bharadwaj gotra. Our ancestors studied the Vedas under Rigveda scholars of the Katyayani branch. We originally belong to Kachura village in Sitapur district. Our ancestors hailed from Gazni and after halting at Ajmer, finally landed at the village Peeer Gaon, Dakhlaur in district Sitapur. Now write down what I know about Raja Lone Singh.

'Raja Lone Singh's sister was married to Thakur Barwand Singh, who belonged to a Kshatriya family of Kachura, the same village to which I belong. When the fort at Mitauli was destroyed and looted, some ancestral relics were collected by villagers and sent to Kachura. Among these were several pairs of wooden clubs made of precious khair wood. My family still has some precious pearls which Raja Lone Singh had presented to them. The raja was not arrested at Mitauli as is believed. He was taken captive at Sitapur by Thompson sahib. His photo is framed on a wall at Calcutta museum.'

Indupal Shukla spoke of the raja's family and some hitherto unknown aspects of his complex personality:

'Raja Lone Singh's kingdom lay in the area between the Sharada river in the north and Maholi village to the south. In the west, it extended up to the spot where the junior school of Muhammadi village stands now. They were four brothers in all: Khanjan Singh, Lone Singh, Bhagwant Singh and Madho Singh. Bhagwant Singh's family still lives in the Lilsi village. He had two sons. The other brothers were childless.

'Raja Lone Singh built a public guest house and a charity centre and mess (Bardashtkhana) in Gola Gokaran Nath. The latter provided food for the poor and also free blankets during winter. Today the buildings are owned by the government. To the east, he also built a bridge and people in those areas still sing songs in praise of him. The thakur at Puwayan had some old royal robes that belonged to Raja Lone Singh that he'd brought to our village during the recent centenary year celebrations of the ghadar.'

The clothes were sent for. A coat was brought. The size denoted that Raja Lone Singh was not too tall, but he probably had a large girth.

Soon after, I visited the ruins of Mitauli fort. A large area was pointed out as the erstwhile puja room of the royals. A small spring-fed pond that was once inside the fort can still be seen in the fields surrounding the fort. A tamarind tree stood looking forlorn near old graves made with medieval bricks.

At Semranvan village we met Thakur Shiv Baksh Singh who, we were told belonged to Raja Lone Singh's family. He spoke to us in Awadhi highlighting the role played by old enmities rooted in issues of land, jealous relatives and devious lawyers in the story of the rise and fall of the hapless Raja of Mitauli:

'Nawab Wajid Ali Shah of Lucknow had appointed Syed Mir Jan as Chakledar at Muhammadi village. A few Company officials were also posted there along with Zahurul Hasan, a lawyer representing British interests. My grandfather had challenged a forced occupation of village Mohkamsingh by Raja Lone Singh of Bada Gaon, in the local court. His stand was that he'd inherited the village, since he was a younger brother to Raja Lone Singh. The raja objected to this and sent Zahur Hasan to Muhammadi to plead the case on his behalf. While this litigation was going on, word came in about the outbreak of the mutiny in Awadh. Soon after this, Zahurul Hasan brought Captain Ore and his friends (who were trying to flee from native rebels) to Mitauli and some bungalows of the raja, who was keen to win the case in their court. The Brits found a safe haven in his bungalows while violence wrecked the countryside. But when the fires of the ghadar reached Mitauli, the raja decided to send the British to Lucknow.

'Actually Zahurul Hasan wanted to embezzle 1500 gold sovereigns that the British had given him for safekeeping. So he misled the raja by instilling a fear of reprisals by the rebels. He managed to convince the raja that it would be better to hand over his British guests to the rebels in Lucknow. He did not mention that in case the rebels were defeated, the reprisals would be harsh and as a disloyal man, the raja may end up losing his kingdom. Egged on by the cunning lawyer, the raja sent the British to Lucknow, accompanied by a posse of 200 men and two cannons. When this group arrived at the Lohiya bridge in Lucknow, the rebels began killing the British prisoners. One lady managed to escape along with a fellow firangee. Later the mem told the British about the raja's treachery. The British then crossed the river, entered Mitauli and wreaked havoc here.

'At the time of the ghadar, all the rebel leaders had gathered at Mitauli. Raja Narpat Singh of Ruia, Ferozshah of Najibabad were all here when Begum Hazrat Mahal and the prince Birjis Qadr arrived with the Nepali Begum.'

'Who was the Nepali Begum?' My curiosity arose.

'Ah! Wajid Ali Shah had a large harem full of women he'd collected from here and there. Among them there was this one begum from Nepal. When the British attacked the palace at Lucknow, she requested Begum Hazrat Mahal to take her along and get her to Nepal somehow. When the British mounted an attack on Mitauli fort with twenty-two cannons and began hurling grenades, Raja Lone Singh told everyone to carry on the fight while he accompanied the Begum, her son and the Nepali begum in crossing the Kaudiyala river on elephant back. On his way back, he met the Raja of Oyal, who was also on the run, and was informed by him of the fall of Mitauli and asked to halt in his tracks. Raja Lone Singh also learnt from him that British troops were stationed at Sitapur and one Walmeen (sic) Sahib was their commander. As soon as he heard this, the raja went to Sitapur and told the sahib how he had helped many British escape and requested a ceasefire. Although his request was granted, he was made to stay in a tent outside the palace at Sitapur.

'The next day Raja Lone Singh was arrested, tried and sentenced to be jailed at Kalapani (the infamous jail at Port Blair in the Andamans), thanks to the testimony of the lone woman who had escaped the massacre in Lucknow. Lone Singh's wife too was sent for, but she refused to go. Instead of her, Sita, one of her maids, was sent dressed in the queen's garments. The queen was later sanctioned a pension of 150 rupees per month towards maintenance.

'Raja Lone Singh was carried in a palanquin upto Allahabad. Budhua, the royal cook also went with him. From Allahabad, the raja was sent by river to Calcutta in a fire boat. After that, the British confiscated Mitauli. Kusail village has a stash of the initial Bandobast records (Ibtidai Missil Bandobast) wherein file number 82/83 has all these facts duly noted in it.

'The memsahib who testified against Raja Lone Singh was awarded all the 700 villages that constituted the principality of Mitauli. She later sold them for three or four lakh rupees to the Raja Sahib of Mahmudabad and left for England.'

Whatever happened to the laudatory poems about Raja Lone Singh that had been composed by the villagers? Could someone recite them to us, I wondered.

Shiv Baksh Singh took a long drag of his hookah and said, 'There are no poems. Raja Lone Singh did not fight in the battle of Mitauli, so why would there be poems about his valour?'

Lone Singh remains an ambivalent and sad figure. Even his own relatives harboured a deep dislike for him. It was his own sadhu bhai (wife's sister's husband) Jagannath Singh, the Raja of Puvayan who had persuaded Lone Singh to give himself up. Raja Jagannath Singh had supported the British side during the ghadar to the extent of inviting that brave British baiter Maulvi Ahmedullah Shah to Puvayan only to get him murdered. He must have known well how the British would treat the Raja of Mitauli once he gave himself up. It was such malice between rajas like Lone Singh and Jagannath Singh that made it easy for the British to quell the revolt and regain their Raj.

Raja Lone Singh failed to get help locally, because he had rubbed most of his neighbouring rulers the wrong way, grabbing and amalgamating their lands. I recalled reading an article about him by Shriram Sevak Pande in a Lucknow daily *Swatantra Bharat* which described him as an aggressive bully who was constantly trying to grab neighbouring rulers' lands to add to his own. He had acquired 117 villages from the principality of Maheva, the villages of Atwapur and Shankarpur from the Raja of Oyal and the entire area belonging to Munnu Singh. He also mounted an attack and wrested away the Kukera Mailani area from its owners. According to British records too, Lone Singh gave shelter to the beleaguered British rather grudgingly and offloaded them as soon as Munshi Zahurul Hasan warned him about the dangers of sheltering the Brits.

From all these stories, Lone Singh emerges as a venal but cowardly and foolish man. Unable to foresee which side would ultimately win, he chose to play both sides, and as often happens, lost everything in the end.

I learnt that Ramsevak Singh, the writer of that article on Lone Singh, lived in the Bada Gaon village nearby. We decided to head there next.

Bada Gaon is a large kasbah, really. There was a wedding going on and the lane was aflutter with colourful paper buntings. A loudspeaker belted out Hindi film songs without which no Indian wedding is considered complete. Ramsevak Singh turned out to be a slender, sophisticated looking man in his seventies with a soft voice. He asked me if I had read his article on the Raja of Mitauli published in *Swatantra Bharat* and offered to give me a copy. I told him that I had seen the article already but would be grateful for any other details he might be able to give us. Ramsevak began:

'Raja Lone Singh initially helped the Begum in a major way. At one point, Mitauli had even become the hub of activities for the rebels. Apart from Begum Hazrat Mahal and her son

Birjis Qadr, various other rebel leaders from Dhaurhara, Ruiya and Najibabad also came here for consultations. The raja even saw to it that the British were not neglected. Captain Hearsay of the third regiment at Sitapur had halted at Mitauli while on the run, and taken refuge there for two days because his elephant had been left behind. Lone Singh's army commander Sardar Khanna Singh, who belonged to Bada Gaon, was sent to Lucknow to help the Begum. He died fighting the British forces.'

The Timeless Tale of Bakhat Lodh
How a Dalit landless farmer outsmarted the killers and escorted
some British children to safety

Ramsevak's testimony further convinced me, that, like many others in Awadh of those days, Raja Lone Singh was an opportunist. He took advantage of the fact that moral lines were increasingly getting obliterated by immediate incidents and old rivalries in small principalities, and tried to grab land and influence people. Ramsevak-ji put it succinctly when he said that there were many who played the game. Some succeeded, some did not. Lone Singh was perhaps one of the unlucky ones.

'Who were the lucky ones?' I asked him.

'There was this Lodh (an untouchable) by the name of Bakhat Lodh, who used to till the lands of upper-caste thakurs in the village of Daraura. When violence broke out, he took in some children from the beleaguered British camp and saved them from certain death by hiding them in a curtained cart.

He pretended that he was taking his own children to the holy river side at Naimisharanya to perform a ceremony that's part of the religious ritual of tonsuring boys. He even asked some of his relatives to follow them in a procession beating drums, brass pots and blowing conch shells to distract onlookers. The children were safely deposited, and after the ghadar, Bakhat was amply rewarded by the British in the form of many villages like Kunwarpur, Lachha, Madhiya and Barbatapur. However, the powerful thakurs of Daraura took exception to this reward to an untouchable. They swore at the poor man saying, "So you think you are going to be our equal?" and snatched away half of those lands from him.'

There is a certain poignancy in these stories of loyalty and betrayal, cowardice and revenge, confiscations and rewards. They bring home to us the disturbing fact that during strange times with no visible moral boundaries, the rules of niti and dharma may go for a toss, both among the rulers and the ruled.

The East India Company's army that invaded Awadh after the battle of Buxar in Bengal, brought in a host of their traders, keen to sell British or Bengal-manufactured goods and buy saltpetre (potassium nitrate) from Awadh. With them came Bengali Gumashtas, representing their British employers, to whom the Wazir Nawab was pressurized into giving special papers that exempted them from paying local duties. The Bengali Gumashta as a trade representative and interpreter for the Brits became associated in the public mind with exploitative trader practices and redundancy among local weavers. The word Bengali thus became something of a pejorative denoting cunning and underhanded practices.

Another pejorative the ghadar generated was the word 'nakki'. This referred to the devious role played by Naqui Khan, vizier to Wajid Ali Shah, in the dethroning of the regent and his subsequent signing of a humiliating treaty that gave him a small pension provided that he never returned to Lucknow or claimed his throne again.

Mrinal Pande

I remembered reading in Shri Sundarlal's account of the British Raj (*Bharat Mein Angrezi Raj*), how during the ghadar the village of Ambarpur in Awadh had been the scene of a major confrontation between a handful of native rebels and Nepali soldiers in the British army, in which all thirty-four natives were killed but not before they had badly wounded twenty-three of the enemy's men.

Another link I had with this village, was my long-time friend Balbhadra Dixit. Between 1936 and 1939, Dixit, better known as the poet 'Nirala', and the renowned Hindi scholar Ramvilas Sharma were regular visitors to my house. Of these, the soft-spoken and self-effacing Dixit—he sported a rather awesome moustache—was a man of many hidden talents. Despite a comprehensive knowledge of Hindi, Urdu and Persian, he chose to write in his native Awadhi dialect and his idealism drove him into resigning from several lucrative jobs in the city and made him come back to his village. He wanted to till the soil with his own hands and teach the children of the untouchables, he said. He knew though, how both these forbidden acts would enrage his caste brethren in the village. In 1941, barely two years later, he died thanks to an infected wound from the tip of his own plow.

Dixit had then spoken to us frequently about *Manva Ka Kote*, a historic fort near his village where ancient ruins and sculptures dating back to the Gupta period could still be seen. But now, after a taking a round of the ruins, when I quizzed two elderly locals about the famous clash that had taken place there between native rebels and Nepali soldiers of the British army, we drew a blank. They said that no such battle was fought there. They had, however, heard that at the time of the 1857 ghadar, there was a lot of panic and many villagers had fled to the forests for safety. Also, before fleeing, the villagers had dropped all their tools of trade in a well and closed its mouth.

Upon probing further, I was told that a Muslim rebel leader Maulvi did pass through the village with his men, but the petrified villagers refused to help him. Later they heard that a clash had taken place between the Maulvi and the angrez army, near a lake at a distance of about two miles. The British overpowered the Maulvi and his men, and they ran for their lives. The lake was then known as Fateh Ali Ka Tal, but over a period of time the locals began calling it, Teli Ka Tal (the oil extractor's lake). It was obvious that the battle between the natives and Nepalis did not take place at that fort.

We returned to Ambarpur. It was noon and several men were resting under the shade of a large tree near the village well. We were provided with string cots to rest on and as word spread about our arrival, a crowd of curious onlookers began to grow. One of them, Pandit Ram Sevak Shukla, a man in his mid-seventies, had this to say:

'Our elders used to say that near the lake a battle did take place between the Maulvi's men and the British. The Maulvi wore a holy amulet on his upper arm that was believed to have made him invincible. He was killed later, after he lost that magical amulet during battle. This led to panic among the rebels and the native soldiers ran away. The villagers had already gone and hidden in the forest near the Gomti river, carrying their gold, silver and other precious goods.

Ghanshyam Das, a man from our village who owned nothing except for a few cracked pots and a broken griddle, looked very happy as he bundled those precious belongings, saying, 'Ah! You friends of this poor man, thank you for giving me the status of an owner at last!'

Ghanshyam Das's century old merry musings in the midst of a gory battle made my day! The pandit's brother Ram Sukh Shukla capped this with another riveting tale of death and survival:

'The Maulvi was enraged by the duplicity of the villagers who first offered him help but later declined it. It is believed that he put a curse on them that would ruin everything they owned. But by then the villagers, busy bundling their belongings and planning to escape in the forest, did not care who cursed them and why. All families left the village, but for two: one was a barber, Kesri Das, and the other was his neighbour Ganga Pasi whose young wife had just had a baby. She was in no condition to be moved. Ganga sought help from his neighbour Kesri Das who assured them that so long as he was alive no one would be able to harm the mother and infant. Fortunately after the Maulvi had been killed, the British army did not come back to this village and Ganga Pasi and his family lived to tell the tale.'

I learnt now that there was another village here by the name of Ambarpur that was located in the then principality of Puvayan, in Mahmudabad. This was perhaps the same Ambarpur where the famous freedom fighter Maulvi Ahmedullah Shah had gone after losing the battle at Teli ka Tal. He arrived in Mahmudabad in March 1858 with about 3,000 of his men, after defeating Sir Hope Grant's forces at Lucknow. He had passed through Manva

Ka Kot area and briefly held the British forces at bay there, by occupying the fort and shelling the British from the turrets. Later, after he arrived in the other Ambarpur, the treacherous Raja of Puvayan, now a friend of the British, assassinated the Maulvi and received 50,000 rupees as reward.

From Ambarpur, we left for Atariya where Prayag Dutt Shukla, who was over a hundred years old, seemed quite knowledgeable about the various battles that had taken place in the area during the ghadar years. It did not take us too long to get to his house located near a Shiva temple. Meeting a man who has lived for over a century is strangely exciting. You can actually see history come alive as he speaks. However, we found that age had affected Prayag Dutt far more than the two other centenarians we had met: Sahibdeen of Barabanki and Thakur Nanku Singh of Bahraich. Their memory and voice had remained strong despite poor hearing and eyesight. Not so in Prayag Dutt-ji's case. His son had to shout in his ear and tell him about who we were, and why we had sought him out. As the words sank in, the old man stirred, sat up slowly and began to speak in Awadhi. His disjointed memories scurried on, one merging with another, with many gaps:

'I know about the ghadar. I was born two years after it. First there was one angrez who came here to see the countryside. Then word arrived to meet more of them on the banks of the river Ganga. Six angrez, who were going by fire boat, were stopped and mowed down by Rao Ram Baksh at Buxar Ghat during the ghadar. There was also one Nawab Nakki who betrayed the Begum and joined the British.

Balbhadra Singh fought (the British forces) in Nawabgunj. Over 300 white men were killed at Umariya. There was also a battle at Teli Ka Tal. The Maulvi had mounted cannons on the parapet of Manva Ka Kot. The Begum fled. Raja Man Singh accompanied her right up to the kingdom of the Raja of Nepal, across the river. The Maulvi that fought at Teli Ka Tal, was a supporter of the badshah (by the mid-nineteenth century, a near independent Nawab of Awadh had acquired this nomenclature that the wily British supported) and he was killed somewhere close to that spot.'

Here Prayag Dutt-ji stopped to take deep breaths. I told his son to ask him if the battle between the rebels and the Nepalese soldiers was fought here or elsewhere.

The son hollered the question in his ear. Dutt-ji replied:

'(After the initial victory) Begum Hazrat Mahal had said that dark times had descended upon the countryside, and requested everyone to gather at the Machhi Bhawan (the Imambara residence bearing the coat of arms of Awadh, depicting three swimming fish). Then a new group of about 500 British soldiers came and attacked viciously, forcing the begum to run. It is true that the Nepali army helped the British. They came during the battle at Lucknow. After winning (the first round), the men at Lucknow began to raid and loot homes and that is why they lost the final battle. Nawab Nakki (vizier to Wajid Ali Shah) also joined the British side. The British army followed (the Begum) right upto the border (of Nepal) moving through Itaunja, Mahauna and Manva, creating mayhem in the countryside.'

Another long pause. I now told the son to ask him, who in his view, did the ordinary folk actually support during those times?

'Basically we all agreed that the British were more powerful, but the Begum commanded more respect,' Dutt-ji replied.

I was beginning to see by now how in the public domain in India, historical fact and fictional embellishments get inseparably interwoven over time. According to Prayag Dutt-ji, the first angrez who came to see the country and reported back to his superiors in Britain, may have been Colonel Sleeman, who had toured Awadh extensively three or four years prior to the ghadar. The incident involving the killing of the British travelling in a boat down the river Ganga occurred in Kanpur long after that. As for the Begum escaping to Nepal with Raja Man Singh, it confirms that the raja was no turncoat. He did help the Begum.

Prayag Dutt-ji's narrative also confirmed reports about the merciless acts of looting and arson by tilangas (notorious armed bands of local ruffians who entered the rebel forces, and together with the native soldiers terrorized the city until put down severely by the British forces) in Lucknow during the short period when the British were reeling under the sudden eruption of violence. His account also supported my friend Dixit's assertion that Maulvi Ahmedullah Shah and his men rode into the heart of Awadh after losing in Lucknow and mounted cannons at Manva Ka Kote on the way and then waged a pitched battle against the British forces. Later the Maulvi was betrayed by the Raja of Puvayan and killed. This also made it clear how the simple folk of rural India would never forget an act of betrayal against one's own, nor forgive a gaddar (traitor), no matter what the reason for his becoming so.

Later that evening, as we sat swapping various tales about betrayals and treachery during the ghadar, I recounted how in rural Bahraich the villagers had directed us to the family house of an erstwhile traitor and kept referring to it as 'Gaddaran ka Ghar', meaning 'the abode of the traitors'. Dr Naval Bihari told us that ever since the infamous betrayal of Nawab Wajid Ali Shah by his vizier Ali Naqui Khan of Machharhatta, the word Nakki in Awadhi, had become synonymous with the word 'turncoat'. 'I can give you another instance of how pejoratives were derived from names associated with betrayal of one's people. When we were children, one of my brothers had developed a habit of carrying tales to the elders to win favours from them. One of my uncles would pull a sour face when referring to him in Awadhi, like an ever hungry Bengali,' he said.

My writerly instincts were immediately aroused. I had frequently come across the pejorative bhookha Bangali (hungry Bengali) in Hindi, usually referring to a predilection for using one's official position to make a quick buck. The British, then headquartered in Calcutta, had sent bands of rapacious officials of the East India Company to Awadh to carry out administrative work for the government. They were invariably accompanied by trained Bengali clerks who also functioned as their sole intermediaries with the common folk of Awadh, who came to regard them as controllers of their fate. In his novel *Shrikant*, the well-known Bengali writer Sarat Chandra Chattopadhyay has also described how the typical Bengali babu, employee of the British sahibs at Calcutta, would treat even his own fellow Bengalis with disdain. One such babu makes the young ones in a boat take off their coats so he may wrap them around his own shoulders, and orders the grown-ups to step into the freezing waters of the Hooghly to push his boat. One can easily imagine how such babus would treat humble and poor farmers and citizens in the far-off northern plains of Awadh, Agra, Punjab or Delhi. I had heard a friend, Dr Satya Narayan Dubey, a professor at the Agra College, quote a proverb from his native Manipuri district. It said that the man with the hat earns and the man in a dhoti, loots (*Kamaye topi wallah, lootey dhoti wallah*). The man in the hat is an obvious reference to the British official and the rapacious man in dhoti is the typical Bengali babu clad in his traditional muslin cloth. Dr R.C. Majumdar quotes from the diaries maintained by several Bengali babus. It is true that during hard times, other men from east (Purabiyas) may also have been unkind to the citizens of the Hindi belt, but the Bengalis, who referred to them constantly as *sala chhatukhor* (the miserable sattu eaters) with an air of superiority, wounded them much more.

Khairabad

How the rebel leader Maulvi Fazal-ul-Haq managed to write and smuggle out his Surat-ul-Hind *while serving a prison sentence in the Andamans*

Before the ghadar, Khairabad division, named after Khairu Pasi, was the district capital. The last time I'd come here was as a guest at a friend's wedding about a quarter of a century ago.

According to the district gazette, Khairabad has a long history that stretches as far back as the legendary King Vikramaditya. It acquired its present day name much later, after it came to be ruled by Muslim Nawabs of Awadh. Under them, Khairabad became a major centre for Arabic and Persian scholars. Today, this little kasbah is full of ruins and little houses made of ancient Lakhauri bricks, but during the ghadar it was known as the native land of two major rebel leaders: Munshi Harprasad Nazim and Maulvi Fazal-ul-Haq.

The Maulvi, himself a renowned academic of Arabic and Persian, belonged to a long line of scholars. We told Verma-ji that we would like to call upon his grandson Maulvi Hakeem Zafar-ul-Haq at his home in the Miyan Ki Sarai area.

Verma-ji had taken us there to meet the chairman of the
Khairabad municipality and our host sent for Maulvi Zafar-ul
Haq immediately. Upon arrival, the Maulvi told us that several
ulemas in the area had participated in the ghadar in support
of the natives.

'My grandfather was among those who were sentenced to
prison in the Andamans when the British later cracked down
on the rebels. Once there, my grandfather wrote his memoir
which was published later as *Surat-ul-Hind*. Since the prisoners
had no access to paper, grandfather wrote it out in a piecemeal
manner upon bits of torn cloth, leaves or even pieces of leather.
Good-hearted samaritans returning to the mainland kept
smuggling these out of the prison and forwarding them to my
father. After the book was complete, it was put together and
a copy was painstakingly prepared. There was no question of
it being published during the British Raj, but it has now been
published in the original (Arabic) along with Urdu translation
on facing pages. But when my father managed to get a reprieve
for his scholarly father, he was told on arrival at the jail that
his father had died and his body had been taken to the local
graveyard for burial.'

That, the Maulvi said, was all he had learnt from the family
elders about his late grandfather. However, an article published
by Ratanlal Bansal in a local Urdu daily *Quami Awaz* offered a
few more details, he said, including the fact that as a Maulvi,
his grandfather had announced a fatwa and declared this war
against the British to be a holy jihad. He had urged all Muslims
to participate in it as their religious duty. This, the article stated,
was the main reason why he was sent to jail.

'Are those bits and pieces of cloth, leather and those leaves
which formed the original manuscript, still with your family?'
I asked. The answer was in the negative.

I had read that article which the Maulvi had referred to. It also mentions how as a precocious child, Maulvi Fazal-ul-Haq was already teaching his father's students by the time he entered his teens. An elder Maulvi was appointed as a tutor for him at this point, but teacher and student did not get along from day one. The miffed student threw away the books, stating that this teacher could not help him and should therefore stop coming for his lessons. When the father learnt of the situation, he called his son and slapped him hard, saying, 'How could you expect an ordinary teacher to have a brain such as yours? As the son of a prosperous man, you've lived and dressed well since your birth, and have been taught lovingly by whosoever you chose to go to for lessons. How could a common teacher have such exposure to learning?'

The learned Maulvi went to meet the British Resident with his relatives. Badshah Akbar Shah and the Resident had a deep respect for him and in 1828, he was appointed a Mufti. The trouble started soon thereafter, as the British officials loved flattery and expected all natives they elevated to positions of authority, to remain servile and grateful.

As a proud and learned man, the Maulvi refused to stoop so low and was soon transferred to the court at Allahabad as a government lawyer. He worked there for a while and then resigned. After quitting government service, Maulvi Fazal-ul-Haq roamed around visiting various princely states, spending time at places like Jhajjar, Tonk, Alwar, Lucknow and Rampur. During the early days of the ghadar, he worked hard helping the leadership in Delhi contact the princes of Awadh.

Ruhela's General Bakht Khan had enormous respect for this learned man, who declared a fatwa stating that it was the religious duty of every Muslim to take up arms against the British colonizers. This helped stir up the conscience of the Muslims and got them to support the badshah's royal armies. After the ghadar, he was captured by the British near Khairabad. The local British judge, who had once been taught by the Maulvi, waived off the death penalty and sentenced him to lifelong imprisonment at the Andaman jail instead. Maulvi Fazal-ul-Haq died there in 1861.

I failed to get much information about Munshi Harprasad Nazim. An old resident, Chaudhary Achal Bihari Lal who belonged to a family of zamindars told us that the Raja of Khairabad, Harprasad did not live there. He and his successors lived at Naseerabad near Jayaz. His father-in-law, Ram Narayan Rai, who was also Achal Bihari's great-grandfather, had looked after the state on his son-in-law's behalf. After the ghadar, he was sued for keeping a cannon.

Although there was little information about Munshi Harprasad, my queries about him yielded some valuable information about the lives, loves and rivalries among the nobility of the day. I learnt that the landlords of Awadh seldom, if ever, paid their annual taxes to the royal exchequers of Awadh. When the irate rulers sent armed men led by their revenue officials, the landlords would go underground until they were gone. At times when they didn't, the defaulters were arrested and humiliated in horrific ways, either by having their hands nailed, or by getting their legs chained with barbed wire before they were forced on a run. At times, they had bags full of human excreta wrapped around their faces. But despite all this, the rajas continued to cheat and avoid paying taxes.

It seems those so-called 'good old days' were actually days of barbaric forms of justice. In the absence of real laws, the laws of the jungle had taken over, and be it government official or tyrannical landlord, none would let go of a chance to humiliate and terrorize those weaker than themselves. This, they were convinced, was the purpose of power.

Naimisharanya

The site of the great brahminical conclave, Pandit Ballu Prasad's story of the mysterious Kailasan Baba, believed to be Nana Saheb Peshwa in disguise

Early next morning I left for Naimisharanya. It has long been a holy spot for pilgrims from all a parts of India. Those who have heard the story of Lord Satyanarayana being recited in their homes, would remember how every chapter begins with the words: *Ekda Naimisharanye* (Once upon a time in Naimisharanya). It is said that once, 88,000 rishis had gathered here for a religious conference.

I may be a gatherer of historical stories and proud of our great religious and philosophical heritage, but I have often been peeved by the repeated misuse of religion to justify inhuman treatment of women, untouchable castes and those that belong to other sects. I am therefore quite averse to a purely religious interpretation of religious myths. I prefer a more detached and secular understanding and recounting of historical events.

The fabled Naimisharanya meet held sometime after the Buddhist Kushana kings had been dethroned, was not an ordinary religious gathering. After the Kushanas, Buddhism lost its state patronage and its influence began to fade. The gathering of thousands of learned men at Naimisharanya may have thus marked the social, political and moral reassertion of Brahminical values in the north. The Brahmins, eager to

be the power behind the throne, may have collectively urged
various rulers to arrange for a large (and undoubtedly expensive)
gathering for their brahmin gurus, to discuss and ponder over
various matters related to both religion and politics. A fringe
benefit of this conclave was the recitation of traditional myths
and stories from the Puranas. Telling of these stories since then
has become an inalienable part of various Brahminical rituals,
including the Satya Narayan Katha Vachan and fasts observed
on holy days like Hartalika Teej, Rishi Panchami, and Vinayak
Chaturthi.

As we drove towards the town, my driver began pointing
out various *teerth sthan* (holy spots) to me. I asked him why he
thought each such spot was located near a source of water. His
answer confirmed that in the eyes of the local folk, like most
of our Tamil brethren, the word teerth denotes a place 'for
crossing over'. Chakra Teerth, Charan Kund, Godavari Kund,
Seeta Kund and Dadheech Kund are all water bodies that were
declared a holy teerth. Chakra Teerth is easily the most famous
of them all, and a temple of Goddess Lalita Devi stands by a
natural lake. As we passed by, Chakra Teerth was milling with
pilgrims from the southern states and Gujarat. The neat marble
paving and benches dotting the temple premises were proof
that human hands had renovated the spot not too long ago.

An old priest, who later identified himself as Pandit Ballu
Prasad, moved towards me as I got off the government vehicle.
I asked him my usual questions about the ghadar and the
involvement of locals in the rebellion. The sum total of what
Ballu Prasad-ji told me in his Awadhi dialect was that the
elite living in the area had had a bad time during the mutiny.
Munshi Chandi Sahay Gurusahay, chief administrator to the
Raja of Kotra Kamalpur had built himself a palatial house here

and was killed. Another victim of violence was Gulab Singh, the brave Kshatriya chief of Raja Saheb of Birua's army. The cowardly raja, when he saw the violence all around him, donned a woman's attire and ran away to save his life. But not Gulab Singh. He fought the brave the British bravely. It is believed that he came to the Chakra Teerth, held the sword aloft in his hand, and took a dip in the holy pond there. He was never seen again after that. They say he disappeared somewhere in Nepal.

'Is it true,' I asked him, 'that the locals believe Nana Saheb Peshwa returned from Nepal and lived incognito at Naimisharanya as a saint for several years?'

'It is true,' Ballu Prasad-ji replied. 'Apparently, two mysterious sadhus came here sometime after the ghadar. One was called Brahmanand Brahmchari, while the other one was called Baba of Kailasan. From his appearance the Baba, looked like a man from the south of the Vindhyas who was living under an false name. Some said that he spent a lot of money each time he came visiting from Kailasan. Not only did he distribute fruits and sweets among children, but also got the Lalita Devi temple covered in marble. He always moved about with a large band of his close followers, carrying a walking stick studded with many precious gems. Periodically he would remove one of them from his stick and sell it to a jeweller. The handsome price that it fetched ended up covering all his immediate expenses.'

'How long did he stay here?' I asked.

'Many days,' he replied, 'until a quarrel broke out between him and some locals. After that, he went back to Kailasan, never to return.'

'What caused the quarrel?' I asked.

The pandit confessed he did not know more details about it. If we wished to know more, he asked us to meet Mathura, an eighty-year-old gardener with a sharp memory, who worked at Lalita Devi temple

Where had I heard about Baba of Kailasan before? I suddenly recalled Mishra-ji, a friend of mine telling me about one sadhu called the Baba of Kailasan, who'd come to reside at a local inn called Mira Ki Saray in Kannauj. It was said that he'd arrived there from Naimisharanya. But despite all these stories about him, it seemed unlikely that a careful and shrewd rebel leader like Nana Saheb Dhondu Pant Peshwa would risk attracting public attention and being taken captive, by living a lavish life in close proximity to Kanpur, a town where he was very well known. Would he, after the quarrel, look no further than Kailasan to settle in with his men?

The story about Nana Saheb living incognito in Kannauj that Mishra-ji had heard from his grandfather and recounted to me, ran thus:

There is a small hillock at Kannauj known as Vishwa Nath Ka Tila (the mound of Shiva). Apparently, this was the site of a major massacre by the British forces and many natives had been butchered there mercilessly by soldiers seeking revenge. Since then, it was said that the area was haunted. The locals avoided going there, even during the day. One day, a tall sadhu in white robes arrived at Kannauj and went up to the hillock. He had the look of a man from the south, and asked about some thakurs who had supported rebel forces during the ghadar. The locals, mostly farmers who had tilled the land for the thakurs for generations, received him with great honour and guided him. He then enquired about the history of Vishwa Nath Ka

Tila and asked the thakurs if they would like to accompany him there. This absurd request led to some hesitation. Did he not know that the spot was haunted, they asked him. The sadhu did not pay any heed to their doubts and fears, and left for the hillock accompanied by a young man who was moved by this strange sadhu's persistence and courage.

The two of them went up and saw the dilapidated state of the Shiva temple that had lent the mound its name but now stood looking derelict and full of trash. Shocked at the squalor all around, the sadhu could not contain himself and began to sweep the premises. He then looked for a water source and was told that there was a well that required cleaning but was still usable. Reassured, the sadhu announced that he would sit and fast at the mound till the temple was cleared of the trash and the well was made usable. Those were the days when a sadhu's words were respected. Soon the well and the temple premises were cleaned up and the sadhu got the temple renovated and decorated, using expensive marble. Where he procured the money to purchase all that, still remains a mystery. The only time he came down the hillock was to have a bath. He spoke to no one. According to Mishra-ji's grandfather, a devotee of Lord Shiva and a frequent visitor to the temple, the sadhu would decorate the Shiva Lingam himself, using all sorts of expensive essential oils. The locals believed that the sadhu had miraculous powers and was actually the famous Nana Saheb Peshwa of Bithur (Kanpur) in disguise.

There is another story about a mysterious sadhu. Once, two brothers in the area had a bitter quarrel. One of them had killed the other's son and dumped his body into a well. After the murder, the repentant man came to the sadhu, confessed and begged for his protection. The sadhu heard him out and remained silent for some time and then said, 'You have indeed committed a heinous crime, but since you asked for my protection, I will try to save you.'

The next day, the missing child's father arrived at the sadhu's abode and asked if he could use his astrological powers to locate the boy. The sadhu told him the truth, and added that the murderer was genuinely sorry for his crime. Since there had been enough violence already, it would be best to declare truce and not drag the sordid matter to court. The man didn't pay any heed to his advice and petitioned the courts to punish his brother for the murder of his child. Since the whole case rested on the sadhu's testimony, he had to appear in court. Under oath, he gave the accused an alibi by saying that he had been with the sadhu at the time of murder. Left with no choice, the court then acquitted the accused. Soon thereafter, the sadhu, rumoured to be Nana Saheb Peshwa, left town. While leaving, he told one of his devotees, who incidentally happened to be Mishra-ji's grandfather, 'My conscience is burdened. I do not know what price I will have to pay for this lie.'

He was thereafter believed to have moved to Kailasan and became known as Kailasan Baba. At Naimisharanya, he had also had the Lalita Devi temple renovated.

Nana Saheb Peshwa's mysterious disappearance has generated several myths all over the north. One would recall how Deen Dayal Dixit of Barabanki had also given me some handwritten papers that recounted, among other things, a chance encounter his grandfather had had with a man he believed to have been Nana Saheb Peshwa. But in my opinion, the Kailasan Baba of Mishra-ji's tale could not possibly have been Nana Saheb. Perhaps Kailasan Baba was just a kind samaritan with a noble mind, sick of the bloodshed he may have witnessed in the region during the ghadar. When they summoned him to court, neither the murdered boy's family or the area police or the magistrates were aware of massive scale of search operations launched by the British to capture Nana Saheb Peshwa and the handsome reward his arrest would provide.

Truth be told, public memory in India generally refuses to let go of a noble myth. About twenty years ago, I recalled seeing a news item about the death of a mysterious sadhu in Naimisharanya, which the locals believed to have been the reclusive Nana Saheb Peshwa. I also came across a hand-painted photograph of Nana Saheb on a carved wooden seat at the Koteshwar temple in Mount Abu in Rajasthan, where he had apparently meditated. A young man from Jaunpur district in eastern Uttar Pradesh had also written to me once, stating that he was Nana's descendant from a local woman of the Ahir (cowherd) caste, that Nana had married after the ghadar, in exile. However, when I asked him for proof, he never came back.

Nevertheless, I did call upon the octogenarian gardener Mathura at the Lalita Devi temple and asked him about the ghadar and the mysterious sadhu believed to have been Nana Saheb Peshwa.

'I am all of eighty years, and I was around ten years old when Nana Saheb arrived here as a sadhu. He lived near the tamarind tree and regularly offered lavish teasts to brahmins.'

'Did he claim that he was indeed Nana Saheb?' I asked.

'He said nothing of that sort, but his servants and various men in his entourage told the locals that indeed it was him.'

'What was he like to look at?' I probed further.

'Well, he was very fair and his body seemed completely sun-burnt. He stayed here for a little over a year and then left for Kailasan, where he lived for a long time.'

'Did he ever get involved in some sort of a quarrel with the locals?'

'Why should he get involved in local affairs? He kept to himself, walked alone using his favourite walking stick and rarely spoke to anyone. It was his servants who did all the work, welcoming and feeding the devotees.'

'But surely,' I continued, 'all that feasting and renovation work must have cost him a substantial amount. Did he have a secret treasure?'

'That, I would not know of, sir.'

7

RAE BAREILLY

In 1857, Rae Bareilly was just a village west of the Ghaghra river. The district of the same name was created only after the ghadar around this village. According to local lore, the community here was established by Tilok Chand following the downfall of the Jaunpur dynasty in the fifteenth century and its name was inspired by its increasingly prosperous Kayasth landowners who held the honorific of Rae Bareilly. The second half of the name was derived from the tribe of Bhars who were the original inhabitants of the area before the Muslims. Initially referred to as Bharauli, it was later changed to Bareilly.

The term 'raja' here does not always denote a major landlord. After they acquired the title of raja, several landowners in the area saw to it that the title was handed down over generations, even after some of the families lost most of their land. Thus by 1857, the original Tilok Chandi estate shrank to the small village of Murarmau but its ruler was still called raja. Similarly, the Raja of Chanda estate had inherited only a few cannons that were never used but the name of the estate was carved with a coat of arms. When the guns got the raja in trouble, he did not hesitate to have them buried in a field.

Despite its poverty, the ethos in the area remained proudly martial and the sepoys and talukedars believed in the Rajput concept of honour.

The districts of Rae Bareilly and Unnao alone accounted for about
40,000 native sepoys in the Bengal army. Their concern for their
overtaxed families and local rajas, humiliated, bullied and penalized by
the British out of suspicion, lent a sharper edge to their acts of defiance
during the ghadar. The great folk hero Rana Veni Madhav Baksh of the
Bais clan emerged in 1857 as one of the major rebel leaders and many
songs record the pitched battle fought from his fort at Shankargarh.

Mrinal Pande

It was five minutes past seven when I finally arrived in this town
on the morning of 11 July. Harishchandra Mehrotra, the district
information officer at Rae Bareilly, was an old schoolmate
and lived in a house close to the railway station. This proved
to be rather valuable for reworking my travel itinerary. After
returning to Lucknow from Naimisharanya, I had to extend
my stay at home for some personal reasons. My trip to Rae
Bareilly had thus got somewhat delayed, and required me to
skip visiting a few important villages and families of martyrs.
Originally I had planned a visit to a place called Shankarpur,
but I was told that Jitendra Singh, a descendant of Raja Shankar
Singh of Chandapur, lived close by and was likely to go out of
town quite soon. It was therefore better to postpone the visit
to Shankarpur and meet Jitendra Singh instead.

I had heard that Raja Shankar Singh was a selfish and
treacherous turncoat who had betrayed the native rebels during
the ghadar. An article written by Anjani Kumar in *Swatantra*
Bharat claimed that the raja was earlier a member of the rebel
leader Raja Veni Madhav Baksh Singh's group, but had later
gone rogue and sided with the Company's men.

I must quote a song here by Shri Ram Dularey, a local poet,
which refers sneeringly to Raja Shankar Singh as 'Sudershan

Kana' (a one-eyed good looker) and has immortalized the last farewells of the public hero, Rana Veni Madhav Baksh Singh of Rae Bareilly:

A manly battle was fought at Awadh, my brothers,
The first clash came in Buxar at the Semri maidan.
As our Rana moved eastwards, angrez laat (the governor) panicked
And Nakki, Man Singh and Sudershan, the one-eyed
(Shankar Singh),
All joined the laat, but not the Rana.

Let the world learn that all Kshatriyas are not the same,
Said the Rana saluting his kinsmen and family for the last time,
'They may have betrayed us to the British,
But my god will not abandon my side.'
Thus said 'Dularey', spear in hand, riding his horse jauntily,
Did the brave Rana Veni Madhav leave for the battlefield.

Jitendra Singh was an adopted son in the family of Raja Shankar Singh of Chandapur. Both he and his adoptive father, Chandra Lochan Singh, continued to be referred to as the raja, locally. I recalled Jitendra Singh meeting me earlier at Lucknow. A polite young man and a student of the Colvin Taluqdars' College in Lucknow, he had come with my old friend and classmate Om Prakash Khunkhun-ji to invite me to some literary gathering.

Speaking in Awadhi, Chandra Lochan Singh, the adoptive father of Jitendra Singh said that there were no articles or papers available with the family. However he did have an old published genealogy, *Kanpuria Bans* (The Eminent Families of Kanpur) that referred to his ancestor, Raja Shiv Darshan of Chandapur.

'He was always known as a hothead,' said Chandra Lochan Singh. 'Even when Wajid Ali Shah was the ruler of Awadh, he had had several clashes with his representatives who came to collect taxes periodically. Once, he killed one of them in a fit of rage. He paid taxes neither to the Nawab's men nor to the British revenue officials later. During the ghadar years he had had several clashes with the British about this. Physically he was said to have been very strong and it was said of him, that he could bend a silver rupee coin with his fingers. He was also reputed to be the best rider in the region between the Ghaghra and the Ganga rivers. Across the Ghaghra, only Munna, the Raja of Ikauna, and Digvijay Singh of Balrampur surpassed his prowess. These two were called full riders (Poora Savaar) whereas Raja Shiv Darshan was referred to as half a rider (Adha Savaar). The trio was known as the "Two and a Half Riders" (Adhai Savaar).

'In 1857, Raja Shiv Prasad joined the rebel Rana Veni Madhav and his men. But he panicked when the British confiscated one of his cannons. Discreet efforts were made to scratch off the inscription of the state of Chandapur carved upon it. In fact, when the British asked him if he was the owner of the cannon, he feigned ignorance and said that it did not belong to him. A rival landlord from Tiloi, Babu Thakur was then called and asked to judge whose cannon it actually was. Since the lords of Chandapur and Tiloi had had several differences in the past, as expected, Babu Thakur declared the cannon to be the property of Chandapur. The British then ordered that half the Raja's lands be confiscated if he failed to pay the fine of one lakh rupees slapped on him. As he was a stubborn man, the raja paid no heed to advice from his well-wishers and refused to pay the fine even at the risk of having his lands confiscated. He felt that after the British had exacted fines from various princes in Awadh, they would surely pocket the money and return to England. At that point it would be easy to take possession his confiscated property. He was then asked to choose which fifty villages (out of a total of hundred that he owned) he would like to part with. The raja agreed to handover only those villages where the relatively docile lower castes lived. He was sure that later, after the British departed for England, he could regain them with a little help from the aggressively armed militias of the upper-caste landowners from villages that he owned.

'Raja Shiv Prasad had no children of his own and had adopted his brother's son who had also died young, after fathering a son, Jag Mohan Singh. After the British declared him a rebel, Raja Shiv Prasad decided to step aside and bequeath the throne of Chandapur to Jag Mohan Singh. Meanwhile, since a single cannon alone had created so many problems for him, another cannon that the raja owned was hastily hauled on to a bullock cart and sent to a relative, Thakur Raj Baksh of Atara. However, news leaked out that the raja's second cannon had been hastily buried in a field after the cart carrying it had broken down. Once again the raja was asked to confess to being the owner of a hidden cannon. But Shiv Prasad Singh insisted that he wasn't; the cannon belonged to his cousin in Atara. So the wily British arrested his cousin's family members, including their women, who were then hung from trees and tortured in every possible way. Despite the atrocities inflicted on his near and dear ones, the raja remained unmoved. Even when his grandson Raja Jag Mohan begged his grandfather's permission to accept the ownership of the wretched cannon so that one could put an end to the brutal torture, the old man refused.

'Up until the time of Commissioner McDonald, the Raja of Chandapur was listed as a rebel, but later in view of the loyalty Raja Shiv Prasad had shown during the ghadar, the family managed to win a pardon. Additionally, two of the confiscated areas of Japalmau and Rajapur were returned to them. They could not, however, get back the remaining forty-nine villages that the British had already given away to various loyalists and local rulers like the rajas of Diyara and Mauravan. The lawyer Sarvar Miyan's grandfather was given one village and Chaudhary of Subeha was given four villages and Agha Ahmed Jan Punjabi also got one.'

Another interesting story Shri Chandra Lochan Singh recounted to us about the royal house of Chandapur, dates back to the days of Nawab Naseer-ud-Din Hyder (1827-37). Daljit Singh, a man from a village near Chandapur, and his mistress called Dhaniya Mahari, were said to be very close to the nawab. Over the years, together they fleeced the gullible nawab in various ways and amassed a fortune. The nawab suffered from syphilis, but one evening, ignoring the fact that the royal hakim had forbidden his patient from eating brinjals, Daljit Singh fed him the vegetable. The nawab passed away that night. Following this incident, Daljit's residence was raided by soldiers sent by the nawab's family from Lucknow. When the Raja of Chandapur heard of this raid at the house of Daljit Singh, he sent a posse of his own men instructing them to grab whatever valuables they could from the petrified women while they were being raided by the Lucknow soldiers. It is believed that his men brought back a big part of the stolen goods to Chandapur. Among the items acquired, were a priceless shawl and a navlakha necklace that Daljit Singh and his mistress had stolen from the palace of Nawab Naseer-ud-Din.

'The soldiers from Lucknow gave the raja's gang a swift chase but when they arrived at Chandapur, they found that Raja Shiv Darshan Singh had already forwarded the booty to his relatives at Suryapur Bahrela in Barabanki district for safekeeping. Shortly after this, Raja Man Singh of Ayodhya heard about the episode and raided Raja Chandapur's relatives at Suryapur Bahrela. He is believed to have carried the nawab's priceless shawl and the navlakha necklace with him to Ayodhya. These two items remained with his family for many years. But later, the personal secretary of the queen of Ayodhya once borrowed the necklace along with some other court jewels for a family wedding. Despite repeated reminders from the palace, the man never returned it.

The once powerful Daljit Singh spent his last days in penury. Chandra Lochan Singh said he had seen him on the streets as an old man hawking medicinal balm for a living.

This unforgettable tale of the navlakha necklace, more than anything else, symbolized the inner decadence of the entire feudal era.

Very little exists now of Chandapur fort after being destroyed by the victorious British, after the ghadar. Raja Shiv Darshan Singh's descendant, Raja Jag Mohan soon shifted to another large house that he built for himself and that's where his family now resides.

The head of the family, Shri Chandra Lochan Singh had already told us that there were no ghadar-related records available in his house. His son Jitendra Singh took us on a tour of the premises and it was soon quite clear that they did not have any papers dating back to those days, and even if they did, they must all have been carefully destroyed by now. Raja Jag Mohan had shown great loyalty and not only been rewarded with the Medal of Honour and a grade two magistracy, but also appointed as a CIE (Companion of The Most Eminent Order of The Indian Empire). How could a British loyalist like him risk having any questionable documents in his house?

References to the family line or participation of family members in the ghadar could perhaps have been traceable to a few handwritten books within the household. But after the demise of Raja Chandrachud Singh, a man who was quite fond of keeping a well-stocked library, those books had been donated by the royals to the Sharada Sadan Public Library at Rae Bareilly. However, all that remained of the old library at Chandapur was a bunch of moth-eaten and dusty volumes of ancient epics and some philosophical treatises, lying derelict in broken almirahs in a small godown within the raja's home. Obviously no one was interested in them. Among the dusty volumes within the almirahs, beyond the maze of cobwebs, I spotted a few English novels and two copies of the rarely seen English-Sanskrit dictionary by V.H. Apte. I was so delighted, I couldn't help myself but ask my host if I could have one of them. Jitendra Singh, looking somewhat embarrassed, said I could take whichever books caught my fancy. Along with the dictionary, I also picked up *The Golden Book of India* (1893 edition) published by Macmillan. The book lists all the kings and princes in the British colonies of India, Burma and Sri Lanka that the British had chosen for pompous and meaningless titles such as His Highness, Raja Bahadur, Rai Bahadur, etc. It provides brief but basic information about them, describing their exact role during the ghadar. Raja Jitendra Singh also presented me with two walking sticks, one of which, he said belonged to Raja Shiv Darshan Singh.

The Kanhpuria Rajput rulers of Nain were prime examples of freebooters who thrived around 1856. Like many others, the ruler would not pay taxes to the increasingly weak government at Lucknow, and the tale of the chakledar (revenue official) Jang Bahadur is illustrative of the crude methods adopted by emissaries from Lucknow to make defaulters pay their dues to the Crown. Just like the Raja of Mahona, the association of Bhagwan Baksh of Nain with the rebel forces remained tenuous and his lust for plunder had been an embarrassment even to the rebel leaders.

Mrinal Pande

Next, we left for the nearby village of Janai. Like many other villages in the area, Janai too had several ancient ruins, including an old well that had a snakeskin floating in its waters. Our young companion, a thakur, kept us amused with stories about local history all of which ended with *Ramji ki ichha* (as desired by god). It turned out that god had desired that the thakur go to jail and participate in a political sit-in and demand that all relics of the British Raj be removed. Once in jail, thakur felt that god again desired that he should ask for pardon and come out of jail and resume his religious duties. This he did, and thereafter, since he was of a marriageable age, god once again willed that he deliver a moving speech at a caste gathering and forcefully demand a vote in favour of certain reforms including all outdated marriage customs and rituals. This ruined his chances of finding a bride in his own caste and therefore he remained a bachelor. Such, he repeated, was *Ramji ki ichha*.

By evening we arrived at Nain, where we met Shri Shiv Dularey who belonged to the erstwhile royal family of the village. From his family, Bhagwan Baksh Singh had participated in the ghadar. Chandra Lochan Singh had told me a rather amusing story about the eccentricities of this family. It seems that during the nawabi rule, non-payment of dues to Lucknow was common among the royal families. The royal house of Nain was no exception to this. This had caused much turbulence between Khan Ali, the royal chakledar, and the local ruler. It is said that once, Khan Ali declared his intention to raze the fort of Nayangarh and build a pond at the site. He urged his armies to dig up the Nayan fort and create a pond for which they would be paid enough to feast on meat and chicken curries:

> *Maro murga khao kaliya*
> *Nain khuday karo talaiya.*

When word reached Nain's rulers, they made a counter offer to their own army, promising them similar treats for ensuring that the great Khan did not exact a single paisa as tax from the Nain estates:

> *Maro bakra khao kaliya*
> *Taka na pai Khan alia.*

Coming back to the ghadar, according to Shri Shiv Dularey, Bhagwan Baksh of Nain was suddenly caught in the cross-currents of the uprising. This is how it happened:

An army camp was located at Keshavapur, the location of the British headquarters within the principality of Nain. As rioting broke out at the camp and the outnumbered British fled to save their lives, Nain natives stormed into the empty officers' quarters and robbed them of their belongings. Several rioters returned to Nain carrying, among other things, a large bundle of legal stamp papers. These were put to use later for making handwritten copies of Goswami Tulsidas's great poetic work *Vinay Patrika*, a humble prayer to Lord Rama.

It was ironical, I thought, that a humble prayer to Rama, that paragon of virtue, should be inscribed upon stolen stamp paper from the British camp!

After the British regained the upper hand, the large ruling clan of Nain came together to decide that one elderly member of the family should be made the proverbial scapegoat and identified as a rebel. This way, the rest of the clan and their family property would be saved. After this was agreed upon, Bhagwan Baksh, the oldest member of the clan found himself declared a rebel and after he had 'confessed' to his participation in the ghadar at the court of the British, he lost his entire property but for one village. A deeply-shaken Bhagwan Baksh tried hard to forget the stigma, but could not regain his confiscated lands. According to Shiv Dularey, the rest of the nobles of Nain family were forgiven after being declared a misguided bunch of men who were protégés of the Lucknow nawab, and had inadvertently set the army camp on fire.

A book in Jitendra Singh's possession, *Kanpuria Kshatriya Vansh Parichay* (An Introduction to the Kshatriya Clans of the Kanpur area), also talked of two more princes from Tiloi Tikari and Man Singh clans who had helped the East India Company during the ghadar, and were subsequently rewarded with lands and titles by their grateful British friends. Thus the Raja of Tiloi was awarded lands confiscated from the rebel Ramgulam Singh of Kanpur. The Raja of Tiloi, Babu Sarvjit Singh, who had given refuge to several panicky Britons and sent them safely to Allahabad, was rewarded with Bhagwan Baksh Singh's lands along with four more tax-exempt villages confiscated from Ramgulam Singh. He was thereafter known as the owner of Tikari taluka.

At this point, I heard yet another interesting story about the principality of Tikari relating to Babu Jang Bahadur. He was born in 1762 (Vikrami year 1818) and was said to have commanded great respect even at the durbar of the badshah of Lucknow for his unusual administrative skills. In those days the tedious task of collecting revenues from the zamindars on behalf of the state was outsourced to contractors known as chakledars. Most zamindars, who had come to enjoy a near-independent stature, thanks to a succession of weak nawabs, were defiant about paying their dues. They would hide or attack the soldiers sent from Lucknow for forcible collection. When ultimately arrested, they were severely punished by the chakledars who had targets to meet and were at liberty to make defaulters cough up their dues by all possible means. To drive the fear of god into the perennially defiant landlords, the chakledars had developed some terrible punishments to make the tax defaulters comply. Their men would drive sharp bamboo stakes into the nails of their victims, or tie a bag of excreta on their mouths, hog-tie some of them and hang them upside down from trees, and spank their bodies with red-hot iron. When other zamindars realized that a particular chakledar meant business and would not hesitate to mete out such hellish punishments, they quietly paid up.

Babu Jang Bahadur was one such successful chakledar and was held in great awe for the barbaric and novel methods his law enforcers employed. A devout Hindu who conversed only in chaste Hindi, he totally rejected the use of words he considered 'foreign'. Even commonly used Arabic or Persian words were taboo in his vocabulary and he firmly believed that a Hindu's mouth would be defiled by pronouncing the language of the casteless 'yavans'. When stories about his rejection of the court language of the Muslim rulers reached the government officials in Lucknow, they called him and asked him to give the Hindi equivalent of a word like Asp (horse). Prompt came the answer, Ashwa.

'And feelvaan (mahout)?'

Jang Bhadur replied, 'Mahaavat.'

Those who were envious of Babu Jang Bahadur's clout, poisoned the ears of Banu Begum, one of the wives of the badshah of Awadh, who resided at Faizabad, having been awarded the talukas of Salone and Athehar. The begum was told that this particular chakledar who refused to speak Arabic or Persian, was a great baiter of Islam and was heard referring to her not as Begum Sahiba, as others did, but as Turkin Rani (the queen of the Turks). The begum was greatly upset and looked for a suitable opportunity to retaliate. Soon, an opportunity presented itself when Babu Jang Bahadur failed to exact the expected amount in annual revenues from the territories under his charge, and was arrested. The opponents of Jang Bahadur immediately rushed to the begum and asked her to test his refusal to utter Persian or English words.

The begum pointed at a tent at a distance and asked Babu Jang Bahadur what he would call it.

Babu replied, 'That is a textile fort (kapde ka kot).'

The begum then pointed at a water carrier (bhishti) carrying an animal skin (mashak) of water, and asked, 'What is he carrying?'

Babu replied, 'That is a bag of water (pani ka mote)'

When the begum did not know what else to say, Babu Jang Bahadur was allowed to go. The begum, however, continued to hold a grudge against this defiant kaffir who hated their language.

Soon thereafter, the begum's forces attacked Bhagirathpur, Jang Bahadur's native village. His eldest son and ruler of the village, Babu Vindhya Sevak Singh was beheaded and his severed head was sent to the begum, who in turn ordered that it be shown to Jang Bahadur himself.

When the severed head was taken to him and he was asked if he recognized whom it belonged to, he said, 'A brave man.' He added, 'This family has seen a martyr in the form of Thakur Balbhadra Singh who died in battle like a real Kshatriya. Here is another martyr. He died happy. The smile on his face, is evidence of that.'

The strange tale of chakledar Thakur Ramgulam Singh from Kanpuria Kshatriya Vansh Parichay

Among the Kshatriyas of Kanpur, Thakur Ramgulam Singh from Raja Man Singh's family is listed as another local rebel leader who lost his land because he chose to openly support the natives led by Raja Veni Madhav Baksh Singh of Rae Bareilly. After the ghadar, his principality was taken away from him and given to the Raja of Tiloi, leaving him with only four villages. Later, these too were confiscated and given to the new talukedar of Tikari. Thus an old principality ceased to be. *Kanpuria Kshatriya Vansh Parichay* further reports:

Whatever is known about Thakur Ramgulam Singh is through word of mouth. There are no written documents available. It is said that Thakur Ramgulam was the chakledar for the badshah of Lucknow, when a major controversy erupted in the British army camps regarding some new cartridges provided to natives in the British army. These were allegedly laced with lard and cow fat. Many of the local zamindars got together and prepared a representation (*ahednaamaa*) wherein they made a fervent appeal to all fellow landlords to support the forces of Prince Birjis Qadr of Lucknow against the British. When one of their young men, Lalata Prasad, son of Raja Hanumant Singh of Kalakankar was killed in battle at Chandapur at Pratapgarh district, his father and Thakur Prasad Singh of Tiloi wrote to Ramgulam Singh saying that it was time they dissociated themselves from the native army. Ramgulam refused to oblige and thus incurred the wrath of many of his fellow Kshatriya brethren.

When Thakur sahib visited Atheha village, he also sent for Thakur Ramgulam and talked of peace. Thakur Ramgulam said, 'We have chosen to side with the natives. If we back out now, they will kill us.'

This was indeed a point worth pondering. Ramgulam then decided to help the British without making it obvious and Thakur sahib sent him a letter detailing a strategy for his protection through his trusted courier Bhagwan Das. The letter somehow never reached Thakur Ramgulam, who in the meantime befriended General Beru (sic) and sent him along with an escort to his brother-in-law Hanumant Singh, requesting that the general be provided a safe passage to the British headquarters at Allahabad.

This gave Raja Hanumant Singh a good opportunity to gain the trust of the British government. He decided not to share the glory and managed to incite Beru Sahib against Ramgulam and got him to mount an attack on the poor man. The battle lasted for a day. Two British officials and 950 soldiers were killed. Ramgulam was forced to run to Veni Madhav Baksh Singh for protection and eventually escape with him to Nepal. Later when Thakur sahib realized how Ramgulam had actually helped General Beru, he granted him amnesty and recalled him from Nepal. Thakur Ramgulam was rewarded with four villages, but he didn't get back his entire principality that was already confiscated and given to the talukedar of Tiloi.

Given below are a few letters addressed to Thakur Ramgulam Singh handed over by his family members. Some of the names were illegible.

Letter 1

From C. Wingfield in Lucknow, dated 28 February 1866

This letter is addressed to the former talukedar of Rampur Khajuriha, Thakur Ramgulam Singh. Towards the end of 1858 our army had bombarded his fort and considering himself unforgiven he had been forced to run away to Nepal. But by the end of 1859, he had surrendered. Since he was not found guilty and his argument about being misguided into expressing animosity towards the government, I have managed to get Lord Canning (ex-governor general and the then viceroy) to grant him lease of a small principality to live by. Ever since, his behaviour has been beyond reproach.

Letter 2

From M. Ferar (sic) A.N.O. Camp Kudhiya, dated 9 March 1869

I was happy to meet Thakur Ramgulam Singh several times during my visits to various areas in the district. Once upon a time he was the owner of the Atheha taluka in Pratapgarh district, but lost that principality after the mutiny of 1857 due to some unfortunate association with the other side. I had the occasion to examine several cases in the area he had previously ruled over and never heard any words of criticism about his behaviour as ruler. His conduct is above reproach and he has quite a collection of letters of recommendation from various British officials, including one from the ex-chief commissioner Mr Wingfield. From the eminent position of a prince of a specific area he has now come down to being a mere owner of a village. But this dwindling of his fortunes was a result not of any ill will he bore our government, but of poor advice given to him by others. He therefore merits special attention from us. I have always known him to be a thorough gentleman.

(A limited edition of 600 copies of the *Kanpuria Bans Parichay* was published purely for distribution, in 1930. It was authored by Pandit Chandra Mauli Sukul, MA, LT, and commissioned by a wealthy local citizen, Babu Ran Bahadur Singh.)

Poor Thakur Ramgulam Singh! He became an unwilling martyr, and as they say, could reach neither god nor his beloved. The last lines from the poem about Rana Veni Madhav Baksh Singh, come to mind:

> *I salute my brethren and my clan.*
> *You have all joined the angrez,*
> *As for me, my god will keep me company!*

Dalmau

Tales about the battle of Bhira Govindpur where Rana Veni Madhav fought the enemy; memories of Latifan, the last courtesan in the now derelict village of fabric dyers and folk singers

Dalmau was originally inhabited by seven brave Bhar brothers, whom the villagers still remember by holding individual fairs for each of the seven.

The fair for the twin brothers Daal and Baal takes place in the area between Dalmau and Pakhrauli village. It is said that both of them were beheaded during the battle against the invaders. Miraculously, their headless bodies refused to fall off their horses and rode to that spot and asked a paanwallah (betel leaf seller) for a paan. It was only when the petrified shopkeeper asked, 'But you have no heads, sirs! How will you swallow them?' that the corpses fell down lifeless.

The third brother was Kakoran, whose fair is held in the monsoon month of Saavan at Manihar Shirki. This is an area where many families of Bhars still reside. They all have several tales to tell about their brave ancestors. A fourth brother,

Baidan's fair is scheduled for the Monday before the festival of Holi in Bahai. The local potters make baked clay idols of donkeys that are offered at his shrine. The fifth brother was called Rehmaal and his fair, well-known for its wrestling matches, is held in the monsoon month of Bhadon (Bhadrapad). Not much is known, however, about the remaining two brothers.

We planned a trip to Bhira Govindpur and Dalmau for the next day. Bhira was the village where Rana Veni Madhav Baksh Singh of Rae Bareilly had fought the British and Dalmau was likely to yield some more stories about another Muslim native rebel, Maulvi Ahmed Shah, who had sent a letter to Rana Veni Madhav during his stay here. I had seen this letter at Dr Rizvi's house in Lucknow. But Dalmau disappointed me. The locals were indifferent to the name of the patriotic Maulvi. When quizzed about local history, all of them would go back to ancient tales about the original inhabitants of the area, the Bhars and their battles against the Muslim invaders.

Pandit Gopinath, the head of the Dalmau panchayat, pointed out to us several old ruins of forts of Bhars on the banks of the Ganga. These were reminders of the multiple battles the Bhars had fought against Muslim invaders in the past. That perhaps had left a stamp somewhere in the mind of the local public, I wondered. Gopinath-ji told us that the Bhar warriors were attacked by Muslim invaders during the festival of Holi because it was well known that on that day the Bhars would not touch arms and would drink heavily. The enemy therefore took advantage of this and attacked the forts when the Bhars, the raja and all his soldiers were lying in a drunken stupor. Apparently, there were secret gates for flooding the fort with water in case of an emergency. When the Bhars found out that the Muslim army had entered the premises of the fort, they opened the floodgates and drowned their women in order to prevent them from meeting a fate worse than death at the hands of the enemy. Ever since, not only have the folks in Dalmau stopped celebrating Holi, but also observe it as a day of mourning followed by three days of abstinence from cooking fresh meals.

The panchayat head told us that Latifan, an old Muslim courtesan still lived in the village and may be able to tell us something about the elusive Maulvi Ahmed Shah. Latifan was almost ninety years old and hard of hearing. She knew nothing about the ghadar days, but when we kept prodding, she said, 'My abba used to say that once there were many cannons mounted along the big fort here, and also down below. Even the badshah had come here from Delhi. I do not know anything else but Liyakat's son Munnan has some books. You could go and meet him. Now, since you have come from so far away, let me sing for you at least. I will treat you to a lavani (a lascivious folk song from Maharashtra usually accompanied by dance). With some effort, Latifan tried to heave a few youthful notes into her throat and sang a lavani for us. The recital, however, ended up sounding more like a devotional bhajan than a hearty lavani.

Latifan told us that about fifty years ago there were several houses of courtesans and fabric dyers in the area, but they were no more. The slow wipeout of these two vocations spell out the dwindling fortunes of any village in India.

We then moved towards the forts described so graphically by the Hindi writer Nirala in his novel *Prabhavati*. Nirala's wife belonged to Dalamau and he had immortalized Kulli Bhat, a local character in one of his short stories. As I sighted the sparkling expanse of the river Ganga from the top of one of these forts, any regrets I may have had about my inability to get a good ghadar story at Dalamau disappeared. Earlier at the Pandavas' fort at Naimisharanya, I had been mesmerized by the sight of the Gomti river, but here I realized that the Ganga has a beauty and grandeur that no other river can match.

I spotted a little hut on top of a hill. We were told it belonged to a sadhu who had been staying here for a few years. All by himself he had cleaned up the entire area and after making it habitable, built a little hut for himself. We met the sadhu—a young man, in his mid-twenties. He seemed honest and looked at peace with himself. He offered us *batashas* (a sugar confection) and a pot of clean drinking water. We struck up a conversation.

'How long have you been living here?' I asked him.

'I am not in the habit of counting time on my fingertips,' he smiled, 'but I think I have spent around ten years here.'

'Did you come across any old coins or artefacts from ancient times?' I asked.

Baba-ji, we were told, had found three old locks, an old necklace made of Tulsi wood and a couple of elephant tusks when he began digging. When he cleaned up the dry choked up water tank here, he even found three large snakes.

'The tank is absolutely clean now and the water you just drank was fetched from there,' he said. The snakes were caught and later released in the forests as per the sadhu's orders. He'd thrown away the other things in the area where the ruins of the old fort began.

We stood there awhile, quietly taking in the beauty of the area. Then we climbed a short wall and arrived at an open veranda of twelve pillars (barahdaree). This was the only part of the old fort that had remained intact. Right below the Barahdaree, the Ganga ran in a loop of sorts. A little temple stood by the side of the river, next to a paved ghat. It looked empty and derelict now and the paved courtyard that led to it was no more. We were told that a pond still existed behind the temple–something that was once within the premises. The trees that flanked the river were thick and green and some more ruins dotted the open spaces. Only a cracked stone plaque marked the designated spot for a non-existent museum.

We now moved towards Bheera Govindpur, another Bhar village full of ancient ruins. Some students saw us entering the village and after we told them the purpose of our visit, they ran around collecting people. Soon we had an audience of about twenty-five to thirty people. A brahmin, Pandit Bhagwati Prasad Bhatt, told us that during the ghadar most of the villagers had abandoned their homes and run into forests, except a few who'd stayed back to protect their properties.

'The British came and ordered everyone to vacate the village,' he said. 'One elderly ancestor of ours was sitting on his roof and was spotted by the battalion parading the lanes. A British soldier shot him dead. Long after the villagers returned, they found his decomposed body lying in his courtyard on the day of the Dev Uthan Ekadashi (the eleventh day of the month of Kartik when gods are supposed to come out of their long hibernation).'

'My ancestors were the zamindars who owned this village,' said Kedara Singh. 'My father told us that when the government troops arrived along the Badaila pond from Lalgunj, our people met them bearing the usual gifts of food and chicken that they expected from the villagers. The British asked them if there were any militant rebels in the village. The villagers said that there were none. But little did they know that their village was destined to become a battleground. Rana Veni Madhav Baksh Singh's armies had arrived in the area via Shankargunj Maheru, and had halted near an old wall outside the village to keep a watch over the enemy.

'The Rana said that he loved this village and did not wish to cause a bloodbath, but his men disagreed. It being the holy day of Ekadashi, a day on which a Kshatriya must attack his enemy, a cannon was fired around noon and the two-day long battle began. It eventually ended with the Rana's defeat. The British attacked his army from the north and east and Rana's men fought until they had exhausted their ammunition. Then they ran away and took shelter in various homes within the village. After that, the British arrived here and cracked down on the villagers.'

A man called Gayadeen quipped that his grandfather's elder brother was killed in the Ekadashi battle and the door on their family house still bore the mark of an axe that was used by the British soldiers to break it open.

Another villager, Shiv Chandramani said that he had heard it from elders in the family that the goras had burnt down many houses in the village and treated women badly. A woman from the family of Raj Bahadur Singh, in whose house the Rana had apparently performed his ritual puja that morning, saw the goras come rushing in, feared the worst, jumped off the roof and died.

Shri Lakshmi Narayan Shukla said that Rana and his men were present in the village before the attack. But when the goras asked the villagers if they could locate where the enemy was, they pointed in the direction of Binhara, a village where the British troops were already present. When the British army was passing through the village, one of Rana's men said, 'There goes the enemy!' Rana said, 'Shhh... let them pass.' But his men would not listen. They fired and the British fired back. Soon, gunfire erupted from both sides. When his men ran out of ammunition, the Rana urged his men to retreat. But one man said that they would rather stay and fight till death.

Finally the Rana fled on horseback while his men kept firing stray bullets till they could and took shelter in an abandoned house, to which the British set fire, killing everybody inside. Even now one can see the marks of cannon firing upon some old trees in that area.

Much later, when Lakshmi Narayan Shukla was about nine or ten years old, a short man with a small white beard arrived in the village, dressed in the ochre robes of a sadhu. He was accompanied by two dogs. He hung around speaking to many villagers and asking about their well-being. He even tried to cajole them into coming with him, but no one obliged. Interestingly, many of those who saw him agreed that it may have been the Rana himself in disguise. Later, they had heard that back in Chahlari, the Rana's son had been paid some sort of compensation.

By now there was a slight drizzle in Bheera Govindpur and it was a moving experience to hear the group of young men sing folk songs commemorating the Rana. Folk singers Gayadeen, Sooraj Bakas Singh, Bhajaniya Satyanarayan, Krishna Narayan, Shiv Chandra Mani Shukla, Bholanath, Bajrang Singh and Sharada Prasad performed, accompanied by drums and cymbals, as the rain fell. We just listened.

Driving through the downpour over kaccha roads, our car got stuck in the mud and the driver had to go back to the village for help. He soon returned with about thirty young men from Bheera. They lifted our car as though it was a flower and replaced it on dry land. Several of them walked alongside the car to ensure it reached the pucca tarred road without any further mishap.

Those memories will remain with me as long as I live. Those warm and generous folk singers of Bheera, who even after a hundred years of the ghadar, pay their musical tribute to a rebel who rode out alone against the enemy, to save his land, his honour and his people.

Shankarpur

Early next morning we arrived at Shankarpur, the land of Rana Veni Madhav Baksh Singh, one of the most celebrated native heroes of the ghadar. It is said that just like Chhatrapati Shivaji, the goddess manifested herself in front of this warrior, and gifted him a sword with her own hands.

Somebody pointed out the temple of the goddess to whom the Rana offered his prayers. Located in the middle of a small grove of trees at the entrance to the village, the tiny temple has no idol of the goddess, since it is a peeth. There is just a small square in the centre of tiny room, and that's where a stone shaped in the form of a shield rests. This was the goddess's perch.

Two disfigured idols stood in alcoves on either side and the four walls had four figures, two male and two female, painted on them in a crude manner. There were two paintings—one, of a man wearing a turban believed to be Rana Veni Madhav Baksh Singh, while the other painting depicting a man with a drooping moustache, hung on the opposite wall is the Rana's father. The two paintings of women on the remaining walls were of the Rana's mother and wife. Outside there were a few crudely made idols of Lord Ganesha and of a man brandishing a sword. I was told that once upon a time, the temple was within the fort, near the gates to the male quarters. The Rana would come there regularly to worship the goddess.

A large and ancient banyan tree stood to the right of the temple and opposite that was a play centre for children, inaugurated by the chief minister Dr Sampurnanand. A small cluster of huts near the temple is called Fulwari ka Purva (the area of the garden). Obviously a garden stood here once. It is also said that the fort was once full of riches of various kinds and was protected by a thick forest that made it difficult for an enemy to pass through. A moat ran around the entire fort and it was further protected by gates that were unusually large and solid. The villagers told us that the man who could provide some authentic information was Thakur Gajadhar Singh, the head of the village panchayat of Shankarpur. They asked us to proceed to his house and in the meantime, they'd try and gather a few ballad singers from Fulwari who would meet us there.

The thakur's impressive dwelling stood at a distance of some two furlongs from the fort and was easily noticeable. His aged maternal uncle, young son and a few neighbours had been waiting for us there. Thakur sahib told us that although the area we were visiting was now known as Shankarpur, the original Shankarpur village was clustered only around the fort that we had just visited.

'Thakur Shiv Prasad Singh was the lord of Shankarpur,' he said. 'His brother was Ram Narayan Singh and Fateh Bahadur Singh was his son. Fateh Bahadur's part of the zamindari, called Fateh Singh Ka Purva, is located towards the north-east and is now known as Shankarpur. Ram Narayan had three sons: Rana Veni Madhav, Babu Narpat Singh and Babu Yuvraj Singh. You can still see the ruins of Ram Narayan's palatial house behind the local police station.

Fateh Bahadur died young while his father was still alive. So after him, Thakur Shiv Prasad Singh's elder nephew Veni Madhav, who was not yet an adult, inherited the throne. The second brother stayed on in Ram Narayan's house, today known as Babu Bangali ki Kothi, and the youngest, Yuvraj Singh, later moved to Bhawani Baksh Ka Purva, where his fortress still exists, known as Purana Thana.

Babu Bangali was a Brahmin from Bengal. His actual name was Dakshina Ranjan Mukherji. He had been rewarded with this house and twenty neighbouring villages for having displayed exemplary loyalty towards the British during the ghadar. His grandson, Kunwar Bhuwan Niranjan Mukherji later sold it to Ram Narayan's family and left the village.

Rana Veni Madhav had an uncle, Thakur Shiv Gopal Singh. When the Rana clashed with the British he implicated his entire clan including his sons, nephews and brothers. But after he ran away to Nepal, his family returned and they were given some land at Chahlari by the government for their upkeep. Veni Madhav's son Rana Raghuraj Singh died before he could make a formal will, and therefore his uncle Shiv Gopal's sons inherited the land. The local Raghuraj Singh Bazaar is named after him. The aged wives of Chandrabhal Singh, Shiv Dayal Singh and Surya Vikram Singh from this family are still alive. The Rana's mother belonged to Nain and when Khan Ali's forces invaded Nain, the Rana fought the enemy and was wounded in battle.

As a Nazim appointed by Nawab Wajid Ali Shah, Rana Veni Madhav went on to win a battle for his nawab and was graced with the title of 'Sirmaur Rana Bahadur Diler Jung' and the ownership of 239 villages. Later after the Nawab was deposed and exiled to Matiaburz, the Rana's lands were attached by the British. The livid Rana then went and joined the Begum of Awadh's forces. The British tried to win him back and one 'Biru Sahib', who the Rana was close to, was sent to act as a go-between. He told the Rana that if he sided with the British, they would give him half of the total area they win back. But the Rana refused saying it was his dharma to support his Begum and he would always stand by Prince Birjis Qadr.

The British then mounted an attack against him. They sent one set of troops from Pardespur and another from Gurubakasgunj. On the way they were also joined by troops from Semri. The Rana left Shankarpur and after crossing the Gadhi rivulet, landed at Narendrapur and soon arrived at Bheera. He did not wish for a bloody confrontation. He was a great devotee of the goddess Durga and sat for a long time at her temple within the fortress. The battle between the Rana and the British took place in Bheera Govindpur village.

A long time after the ghadar, the absconding Rana visited the village twice, dressed as a sadhu. I was too young to remember his first visit but when he came again, I must have been thirteen or fourteen years old. I remember him as a short man with a dusky face wearing ochre robes. He called himself Ravinath Ojha Vastradhari.

Let me give you an interesting story about that visit. There was a Parsan Maharaj who lived in the traders' area (Baisan Ki Umri) and had served in the Rana's army. He had lost his eyesight by the time the sadhu's visit took place. So he decided to test if the visitor was indeed the Rana. He told him, 'I cannot see. Tell me something about Bheera.' The sadhu replied, 'What will you do with that?' But Parsan Maharaj remained adamant. As soon as the mysterious visitor said, 'Ek kuchdi dahi' (a little claypot of yoghurt), Parsan Maharaj ran and hugged him, weeping and exclaimed, 'Ah, my raja!'

He explained to us how when the Rana was at the battle-front in Bheera village, he was famished but had no time to dismount his horse. He had then asked Parsan Maharaj to get him something to eat. The maharaj had somehow managed to procure a little claypot of yoghurt for him and the reference to the claypot was his raja's way of affectionately reminding him of the incident.

My father's name was Thakur Yadunath Singh and he had continued to attend Rana's court daily even after he went missing. During the Rana's second visit to the town as a sadhu, he told my father that after he had heard about Shivraj (Rana Shivraj Singh, from the nearby Khajur village) having incurred a big debt, he'd sent for Shivraj but he did not turn up. Had he come, Rana Veni Madhav would have told him about his secret treasure and he could have thus cleared his debts.'

Thakur Jagatpal Singh, the elderly maternal uncle of Thakur Gajadhar Singh, who was sitting close by and listening, now began to speak.

'I had also come here with the Rana. He held court daily near the temple. I attended one meeting where he asked me where I was from. When I said I belonged to Taraul village in Pratapgarh district, he began to speak of Babu Gulab Singh, the Rana of Taraul. He said they were very close friends and shot birds together. The memory brought tears to his eyes.'

Thakur Gajadhar said his father had asked the Rana about the source of funds to meet his daily needs during his long exile. He replied that the Begum had made arrangements that took care of his daily needs that came to some ten to twenty rupees per day. He had a retinue of two or three servants and an assistant conversant in English who could be described as the Rana's secretary.

'The Rana loved to read the Mahabharata. It had always been a favourite. He also loved to hunt and said that if the deer die of old age in a king's forests, he goes to hell.

'Then Lallan, a courtesan from Nawabgunj turned up. She had heard about the Rana's arrival at Bheera and wished to perform a dance for him. After her performance, she received a shawl and some money as reward from the raja. After this, Ali, the wrestler came to visit the raja. He and his brother Imami were two well-known wrestlers in the area. The Rana asked him where his brother Imami was. Upon learning of his death, he expressed his condolences. Ali expressed a desire to play drums in honour of the Rana, and received a reward too, after playing them. The Rana also sent for the family of his Brahmin guru Trivedi of Sarai and gave them a proper feast, followed by ritual gifts of cash. The Rana's face was still ruddy and only when he got up, the villagers noticed that his back was somewhat bent with age. He stayed in the village for about a fortnight.'

I could not contain myself here and asked the obvious question. How could the absconding raja's visit to Bheera village have gone undetected by the British, after all that dancing and beating of drums in public?

'The first time, the Rana visited the village in disguise,' thakur sahib said. 'The Bangali babu (Babu Dakshina Ranjan Mukherji who had bought the Rana's uncle's house) sent a man who asked the Rana to leave. The Rana refused pointing at the goddess's temple and said that she alone can ask him to leave, since she herself got him to migrate.

'The villagers wanted to lynch the impudent Bangali babu's messenger, but the Rana didn't allow them. He was later arrested from the village and sent to Lucknow, but no one there agreed to identify him as the wanted rana and was therefore released. During his next trip to the village he had had a few thorny shrubs chopped down for fire and the Bangali babu complained to the police yet again. The station house officer arrived and left after having a private conversation with the Rana. After a couple of days, the Rana departed as well.'

At this point, a man by the name of Vijay Bahadur Singh capped this Rana story with another one he had heard from Gajadhar Singh. According to his version, a certain Thakur Kali Baksh Singh of Siddhaur had also come to meet the Rana when he was staying in the village incognito. The thakur had confirmed that the sadhu was indeed Rana Veni Madhav Baksh after he saw a scar from an old wound that the Rana had sustained in a sword fight at the battle of Nain. Both of them hugged each other and wept.

I asked Thakur Gajadhar Singh if it was true that the Rana had once been arrested and jailed within the fort at Rae Bareilly, but had managed to escape with help from a notorious thief Hira Passi.

'Ah, yes,' said the thakur, 'during the nawabi rule, once the Rana quarrelled with the Nawab of Lucknow, and was confined within the fort at Rae Bareilly. Hira Passi alias Shivdeen was a famous thief and it was believed that he drove a stake into the walls of the fort each time the hourly gong struck. When he had secured the escape route for the Rana, he climbed up the walls and arrived at his cell. However when he offered his headgear to the Rana to use as a rope, it fell short. He then took off his dhoti and handed it to the rana, but that still didn't seem enough. The Rana said that it was still short of him, at which the Passi said, "I am sorry, but that is all I have!" The Rana somehow climbed down the steep walls safely and made good his escape upon the back of his royal steed Sabza, who had been conveniently tethered nearby to take his master back to safety. At Shankarpur, the fort warden had already been instructed to fire a cannon once the Rana had reached. This was also a signal to the soldiers at Rae Bareilly not to look for him. In exchange for his services, all the Passi asked for was that all earlier thefts lodged against him be expunged from the royal registers. This was duly done.'

Shri Dharmendra Bahadur was reminded of another story.

'Rana Veni Madhav was once riding towards Lodhwari. He heard a Passi woman asking her son to take the pigs out grazing. The boy refused, saying that he'd rather join the Rana's army and fight. The Rana overheard this conversation and called the boy. He told him only those with a mighty heart may enter the Rana's army. The boy replied, 'I have a mighty heart.' The Rana said, 'All right, let me test you.' Saying so, he punched the boy hard on his chest. The boy withstood it well. This pleased the Rana and he recruited the boy into his army immediately.'

Gajadhar Singh came up with another anecdote. 'There was a lonely, old woman whose ancestors had been working and were cared for by the Rana. Since she had no successors, she decided that she must return to the Rana whatever remained of the gold and money the family had received from him from time to time. Tired after a long walk, she was once resting by the roadside when the Rana came by, riding Sabza, his royal horse. The old woman did not recognize him and requested him to take her to the Rana explaining why she wanted to meet him. The Rana sat her on the horse and walked alongside her to his palace, holding the reins. Upon arrival, he gestured his servants to express no surprise. The old woman was accompanied inside and seated, while the noble Rana went in and changed into his royal robes before meeting her.'

Gajadhar Singh also talked of how the Rana made arrangements for his kin's safety:

'After the Rana went to call on Birjis Qadr and ate the *bida* (a rolled betel-leaf signifying lifelong loyalty and friendship), he went to meet his brother and his family at Khajur village, even though the relations between the two brothers were somewhat strained. He gave gifts to everyone there but when his younger brother Yuvraj Singh told the Rana that he should not take up arms against the mighty British, the stubborn Rana disagreed. Then his middle brother said, "All right. In that case, at least leave your sons here with us. He will be safe with the family." But the Rana declined the offer. He said, "For now, my sons must remain on my side. In case we lose," he told them smilingly, "I know you will still be there for them." Such was his trust in family ties!

'When the ghadar broke out, about 36,000 of the Rana's soldiers were joined by the native rebels. It is also worthwhile to note that Rana's son Raghu Raj Singh was married to the daughter of another great native rebel leader, Babu Kunwar Singh.'

Babu Gajadhar then began singing a popular Awadhi poem:

After bringing lustre to the people the Rana left this world.
The first battle was fought at Bheera, the next one at Simri,
The third clash that took place at Purwa made news
even in vilayat (England)
Even the laat (the governor general) was scared of the man.
The laat wrote to the Rana, why wander like a madman?
Why not meet me at Baksar?

The Rana smiled as he read.
Rana called all his family members and said, you have
joined the white men
But I shall remain with my God.
I shall do as I please.
The Rana beat back the enemies and escaped,
The whites were deeply embarrassed at heart.
The poet Bhagwat Das says with folded hands, may god
take care of him.
My heart, remember Ram
Oh my heart, pray to your god.

Parashurampur Thikhai

The village of Thikhai in Nain, Shri Shiv Dularey had told me, is the natal village of Rana Veni Madhav Baksh Singh's mother. We decided to call on Baijnath Baksh Singh, the grandson of Thakur Bhagwan Baksh Singh who ruled the Nain area during the ghadar years. Bhagwan Baksh Singh was not too high up on my list of venerable ones, since my sympathy for the sufferings of the ruling class is somewhat limited.

A few days ago, someone said that a memorial to Raja Lone Singh should be erected since the poor man had been indicted and sent to jail in the Andamans. The idea baffled me. Even if such a memorial was built, who would it inspire and why? Lone Singh had not joined the native rebel forces of his own volition but was just caught in the maelstrom of historic events. Personally, I would not place him on the same level as Rana Veni Madhav Baksh Singh. I believe Mohammad

Nazim Hussein of Gorakhpur deserved more of our veneration, because despite having helped several British soldiers escape the carnage by carrying them to safety, he remained loyal to the native cause. Bhagwan Singh had done nothing of the sort and his men at Nain had basically joined the native soldiers to be able to loot what they could.

Anyway, since we had come this far, I thought we might as well meet Baijnath-ji and see if he could come up with some interesting trivia. Baijnath Baksh Singh told us that his grandfather Bhagwan Baksh Singh had parted ways with the British in 1857.

'He was later punished for it when he lost twelve of his villages and was given back only one village in Unnao district for its upkeep. It is believed that Bhagwan Baksh Singh was visiting Vrindavan with Rana Veni Madhav at the time of the ghadar. The Rana escaped, but Bhagwan Baksh Singh was arrested. He was asked about how many family members he had and how much money he needed to meet his family expenses. The thakur refused to divulge the details because there was a rumour that the British would shoot all those they suspected of being rebel sympathizers. He told them that he lived alone with his horse and groom, and spent around two rupees per day. By way of a meagre compensation, he was given just one village, Manya, in Hadha taluka at Unnao.

'I belong to Bhagwan Baksh Singh's brother's family. Fearing British reprisals, we kept our relationship with him discreet until we heard about Bhagwan Singh being awarded compensation. Then we came to Rustampur and made the family connection public. Later, our family moved to Chandaniha where we had some relatives. Chandaniha was basically an area of the Bais folk. My family belongs to the Kanpuria branch.

'From Chandaniha, my ancestors came to Basadh where they invested some money to set up a money lending business. As the business grew, they were able to buy land in about twenty-one villages. That's all I know. And yes, we were told that the Nain folk were all-powerful in the area and the drums, whenever they were played in Tiloi, were only played for them and no one else.'

Harchandpur and Kathwara

Tales about titles and vanities of princelings, about the multiple advantages of employing an English-speaking secretary, and last but not the least, the tragic end of the Khan Bahadur of Kathwara, loyal servant to the Rana, whose estranged wife willed that she be buried next to the family pets, but not her husband

In an article on the native leaders of the ghadar published in the Hindi daily *Swatantra Bharat*, I had come across the name of Yadunath Singh of Harchandpur. Thakur Jaidev Singh, a respected elder of Harchandpur told us upon arrival, that there was no such principality and that he'd never heard of a ruler by that name. Nevertheless, we struck up a conversation with him about local participation of rulers of various principalities of Awadh in the events of 1857. The thakur said that he had spent a lifetime in the company of various nobles of the kingdom of Awadh and begun to recount the various hierarchies and glory of the various durbars that existed then. There were rulers like Raja Shri Rampal Singh of Kurri Sidhauli, who may have been ruling over a small territory, but whose governance was rock-solid. He would employ men who were proficient in English and having given them secretarial training, would find them suitable employment with some raja. He had thus managed to embed 'his men' in various durbars. They would happily oblige him and advise their rajas according to Raja Rampal's wishes. He was also very close to the British and while most rulers took their shoes off when they went in to meet the British bosses, Raja Rampal could walk in with his shoes on.

Jaidev Singh recounted to us an interesting story reflective of the vanities that prevailed among the local chieftains. A durbar was held to thank native rulers for their loyalty towards the British during the ghadar. All the rajas present were handed laudatory citations except the Rana of Khajuri village (perhaps because he was related to the rebel leader Veni Madhav). The rajas present felt one of their brothers was being insulted. One of them, the Raja of Mahmoodabad stood up waving his citation angrily and demanded to know if their royal status was now limited to a mere piece of paper. The result of this rather spectacular display of anger was that the Rana of Khajuri was also handed a citation.

The folks in Harchandpur, it seemed, were still stung by the memories of their rulers who had chosen to side with the British and not their own native brethren. One Pandit Shiv Sahay Tiwari recited to us a portion of a 'name and shame' poem composed by a local poet, Bachchu Singh. It ran thus:

> When the vast armies of the British descended,
> The cowards ran away into various lanes and bylanes and hid.
> The sly wretches Yagnapal, Hindpal, Lal Madho and Raghunath
> Plunged their daggers in the back of brave men like
> Shiv Ratna Singh.

Says the poet 'Bachchu', they cut off the nose of our brotherhood
Bravery, ah, she left the land with our beloved Rana
(Veni Madhav Baksh Singh).

Tiwari-ji explained that of the cowards named, Yagnapal was possibly the Raja of Rajamau, Hindpal of Kurri Sidhauli, Lal Madho of Amethi and Bachchulal, the poet belonged to Bachhravan.

Shri Bajrangbali Shukla told us that during the early days of the ghadar, Begum Hazrat Mahal had visited Kathwara where one of her trusted sardars lived, and asked for support for her side in the name of the young prince Birjis Qadr. Rana Veni Madhav and several others were deeply moved by her lecture and agreed to lend her their wholehearted support. This strengthened earlier stories about the Begum going around the Awadh personally to garner support for the native side. That tough fighters like the Rana were moved by her lecture shows that she must have a way with words. Perhaps, it was she who had composed the hard-hitting reply to Queen Victoria's declaration.

After hearing these tales we decided to visit Kathwara which lay on our route and met the village headman, Manglu Khan who told us that Rana Veni Madhav had left his principality to Khan Bahadur sahib when he escaped with the begum and others to Nepal.

The Khan Bahadur took good care of the principality while he was in charge. He was a great lover of animals and buried all his pets, namely various dogs, cats, parrots and mynahs in marked graves. He had set aside the earnings from one village called Kutiyamau to spend on his pets. The British captured the Khan sahib and took him away and the entire area, from

Anni Hilalgunj, Kutiyamau in south-west, and attached Sora to the east. Kathwara was fortified and one can still make out the ruins of a moat and walls. There is a Shiva temple near the village which was bombarded by the British armies. The walls of the temple still bear the marks.

Manglu Khan did not know if the begum had visited Kathwara. He said he came from a poor family and had been put to work as a daily wage labourer when still a boy. He was appointed as the village headman many years later. The Begum may have come and gone while he was working and so he had failed to notice her.

'She was the queen of the entire Awadh after all, and free to go wherever she pleased,' he added.

We visited the Shiva temple and saw the walls that were marred a century ago by heavy fire. We also saw the grave of the Khan Bahadur sahib. We were told that he and his wife had a fallout over something and spent the rest of their lives without ever looking at, or even speaking to one another.

Before the wife died she had willed that under no circumstances should her body be buried next to her husband's. She carried her anger to the grave and was buried away from the mausoleum where her husband was later cremated. Outside the mausoleum, one can still see the graves of the lonely man's beloved pets.

The tales that old graves hide!

8

SEMRI AND GADHI BAIHAR

*Searching for Lal Saheb and running headlong into small town poets
and bad poetry instead*

A letter of introduction to Lal Saheb of Semri from Pandit
Anjani Kumar of Rae Bareilly had already preceded us. Pandit-ji
was himself travelling with me to Semri and talked a blue streak.
A lawyer, occasional poet and newspaper correspondent, he
certainly was a man of many parts. After being jailed during
the Indian freedom struggle, he became a local Congress leader
upon his release. Despite doing well as a lawyer, he was unable
to put heart and soul into his practice. As he entered politics,
he had swiftly risen through the ranks as a popular Congress
leader in the Rae Bareilly region. He still fancied himself as
a creative writer of both fiction and poetry, who was yet to
showcase his full creative potential, but as a lawyer with a
flourishing practice and a popular leader, he could never find
enough time to devote to his writing.

By now he had turned into one of many ageing and
somewhat dissatisfied men I often come across in small-town
India. They write occasionally and get published locally, but

are not really into serious writing that demands more of their time and attention. Eventually, they recede behind delusions of being an unrecognized genius of their times and whenever they come across a serious writer, they make sure he/she knows how the literary world would have been so much richer had he not been so preoccupied.

A local poet Ramavatar Shukla 'Chatur', handed me three stanzas of the late Krishna Shankar Shukla 'Krishna's' unpublished ode to Rana Veni Madhav Baksh Singh:

> *In anger your sword, says Krishna, writhes*
> *And drops severed heads upon the earth, one after another.*
> *Like flies, it makes heads fly in battlefield*
> *And covers itself with the blood of white men.*
> *It covers the cannons with writhing dead bodies*
> *Guns count for nothing to the enraged sword*
> *Like a cobra it leaps at the enemy*
> *And bathes its wielder in blood from head to toe.*
> *Veni (the rana) of the Bais Kshatriyas alone was a man*
> *The rest were women in men's clothes*
> *Indrapal, Madhav Singh, Chandrapati, Raghunath*
> *All got together and deceived their own to the firangee.*
> *It was the Rana alone whose raised eyebrows sent tremors of fear*
> *Making the whites of the (East India) Company*
> *tremble in England.*
> *He grabbed the cannons from the shaken enemy*
> *Who cannot eat till the Rana stands in the battlefield.*

In another equally ornate poem Krishna blamed the dissipated rule of Nawab Wajid Ali Shah for allowing the British to grab power from the natives:

Says Krishna, the poet, when Nawab Wajid Ali ruled Awadh
Law and order of the Mughals was thrown into a blind well.
He hung around with transvestites, hermaphrodites and whores
And destroyed this great land bit by bit.
He cared neither for his life, nor his kingdom, nor the
laws of morality,
Uncaring of rules for prudent eating, drinking, or the holy Quran.
As he whiled away his days singing and dancing
The British entered through the Beli Garad and stole our flag.

So much for bad poetry written with the best intentions.

After our arrival at Semri we were told that Lal Saheb, whom we sought, had gone to Ikauni. Pandit-ji wanted to send another letter to him through a courier on a bicycle. But that would not have brought him back since he had left much earlier by bullock cart and it would take at least two hours for the cyclist to catch up with him and then another two hours to return with his reply. I suggested that we drive eight miles to Ikauni and catch up with Lal Saheb there.

At Ikauni we were received warmly by the local school teacher Thakur-ji and after an excellent lunch, we set out once again by the tarred road, accompanied by Lal Saheb. On the way we saw the Shiva temple built by an ancestor of the Rana, the Bais Maharaj of Satan. It is an old temple and has mediocre paintings of animals and birds and praying sadhus on its walls done in Mughal style. According to Lal Saheb, this is a holy spot for all Bais Kshatriyas built by Maharaj Satan, a well-known ruler. When he refused to lend his palanquin to Muslim invaders, he was skinned alive in Kakoran.

Under the Bais Raja Veni Madhav, the Bais army once marched up to the Nawab's to avenge the death of their ancestor. But after the Nawab declared him as a weak man unworthy of being killed even for revenge, they returned without shedding blood.

When I look at the landscape of India during those days, I realize that the history of India has seen the most amazing ups and downs. The Hindus have usually stood divided along caste and clan lines, bolstered constantly by feudal rivalries and internecine wars. There were few rare eras when a smart ruler brought people together.

Today we may praise the personal qualities of bravery and courage displayed by men such as Prithviraj Chauhan, but they failed to keep the invaders out of their land. What use are personal qualities such as courage and bravery in the absence of a larger sense of national unity and a national purpose?

The tale of Durga Baksh Singh, 'the persistent rebel', who lost his sons in the battle near the Loni river

Gadhi Baihar is actually part of the Unnao district, but borders old Awadh. It housed the descendants of two rebel leaders, Shiv Ratan and Jag Mohan Singh. Baihar, my companion Lal Saheb said, was a corroded form of the word Vihar or a Buddhist monastery. The ruins of several of these still remain. The house of the rebel leaders' present day descendants is also located on a high mound surrounded by old ruins. As we climbed up, Lal Saheb clarified that Shiv Ratan actually had no children. So the present day occupants were actually the descendants from his brother's family.

A long verandah with a straw roof ran along the front of the house where we saw someone lying on a string cot reading the popular religious magazine *Kalyan*. Seeing us arrive, he sat up. He was Venkateswar, one of the three great-grandsons of Jag Mohan Singh, and he taught at the intermediate college at Unnao. His younger brother Pratap Bahadur was serving in the Indian army as a subedar, and his elder brother Vindhyeshwari Singh looked after the family lands in the village. When we explained to him the purpose of our visit, Vindhyeshwari Singh was immediately sent for.

We learnt from him that Durga Baksh Singh, the father of Shiv Ratan Singh and Jag Mohan Singh had always been anti-British.

'He is described in a tract of the then commissioner of Awadh Mr Burrough (dated 1868), as a "persistent rebel". In 1857 he threw in his lot with the rebel leader Rana Veni Madhav Baksh Singh. He was too old and infirm by then, but his son Shiv Ratan participated in the battle and was killed along with his brother on the banks of the Loni on 13 May 1858. After that, our taluka of Patan Bihar was attached and the family fortress was destroyed by the British, who went on a looting spree and carried away all they could. This is also mentioned in Sir Hope Grant's account of the mutiny.'

A typed copy of all these facts was available and was sent for. According to Sir Hope Grant, he arrived at the city of Nagar (Bhagwant Nagar, as Vindhyeshwari-ji later clarified) on the morning of 12 May. He was told that the enemy had entrenched itself at Sirsi, five miles to the east of the city. It was a very hot summer noon, marked by hot cyclonic gusts of wind, as he and his men proceeded towards Sirsi. By five in the evening they arrived at the spot and found that the enemy had positioned itself near the Loni rivulet with about 1500 infantry, 1600 cavalrymen and two cannons. A dense forest lay behind them and the land surrounding them was uneven. Their cavalry was eyeing the British booty, which they did not know had been deposited at a safe spot, where 200 foot soldiers, two cannons and a posse of cavalrymen stood guarding it. The British artillery, comprising of the Sikh regiment and infantry, began shelling and firing their guns. They soon managed to force the enemy to retreat from the site. The firing killed the leader Amar Ratan Singh and his brother, both from a family of rich landlords, and grabbed their cannons. A British contingent was thereafter sent to drive away the rebel forces, while the rest camped in the area through the night. The enemy attacked once again under cover of darkness. The sudden attack at night caused some damage and a bullock cart driver was killed.

Thakur Vindhyeshwari Singh clarified that it is customary in the Awadh area for the parents to address their first born, not by his given name but by a pet name. The Amar Ratan Singh mentioned by Sir Hope Grant, was actually the pet name for Shiv Ratan Singh. His doting father used to address him by the former. After his sons were killed, the aged father Durga Baksh Singh was arrested and sent to jail for almost two months. When asked why he had not come up to receive the royal pardon proffered by Queen Victoria, Durga Baksh Singh had said that accepting it would have been an act of disloyalty towards the Nawab. He was then asked if he had instructed his men to kill the British men, women and children. He said that he considered it sinful to kill innocent people and had instructed his men to never harm innocent men, women and children.

Today in Jamipur village, a junior high school named after the martyred Shiv Baksh Singh stands as a memorial to Durga Baksh Singh's much loved first-born.

'Oh where are you Beni Madho! Beni Madho!'
Or, how Rana Veni Madhav Baksh Singh escaped the British siege
with his women, his soldiers, his treasure and his cannons

Lal Saheb, the erstwhile talukedar of Semri had participated actively in Mahatma Gandhi's Civil Disobedience movement and founded a school in his village named for his hero Jawaharlal Nehru. The school is now a college. At Semri, Lal Saheb gifted me an old hand-drawn portrait of Rana Veni Madhav Baksh Singh. He said it had been given to him by one of the villagers whose grandfather had fought alongside the Rana. The sketch showed an impressive face with an unwavering gaze and a beard parted in the middle, Rajput style. Something about the face told you that this was no ordinary man. I looked intently at his face, and when Lal Saheb said he had been waiting for a good man he could leave the Rana's portrait with, I told him that even if he had called me an evil man, I would still have grabbed the proffered gift.

Raja Veni Madhav, like the other major rebel leaders Tatya Tope, Maulvi Ahmedullah Shah and Babu Kunwar Singh, was a great guerilla fighter and leader of men. When the British laid siege around Shankarpur, they did not expect a native leader to give them the slip along with his women, his treasure and an entire army and complete weaponry. In his book *My Diary in India*, Sir William Russell has given a graphic account of that memorable escape on the night of 16 Novenmber 1858. He describes how the British had surrounded the Shankar Garh fort, with the chief of the British forces Lord Clyde himself setting up camp towards the south-eastern side. In addition, General Hope Grant, a seasoned army man himself, was stationed towards the north-west. A Hindi writer, Shravan Kumar Shrivastav quoted a song to me that he said had been composed by a witty English soldier while the British lay in wait for the Rana: 'Oh, where are you Beni Madho! Beni Madho! Beni Madho!'

The Rana bided his time quietly till two in the morning, and then made good his escape from the western side. He and his retinue passed close to General Hope Grant's post like a band of shadows. Next morning when the British woke up they were astounded to find that the Rana and all his men had escaped under cover of darkness. Even the royal cannons were gone.

'Oh, where are you Beni Madho!' they must have screamed.

Lal Saheb then took us to meet seventy-three-year-old Thakur Ran Daman Singh, an enthusiastic and energetic man who spent the last two years preparing a history of the Bais Kshatriyas. The book, he says, is progressing slowly because he has limited means. But he went on and on about his grandson who had just cleared his final school year exam in the first division with distinction in Sanskrit. I felt a little embarrassed to stall his joyful recital of his grandson's brilliance, but Lal Saheb finally took him by the shoulders, turned him around to face us, and told him firmly that he must first answer my queries about Rana Veni Madhav and the ghadar before going on any further about his own family.

'Ah the ghadar!' the thakur exclaimed in Awadhi. 'It is not as though it costs me fifty-six rupees, sir! Certainly I will tell you all I know.'

The thakur began speaking. He was going so fast that I could barely keep pace with him. He told us that when the British displaced the Nawab Wajid Ali Shah from the throne of Awadh, a loyal Veni Madhav Baksh Singh asked all fellow landlords not to pay their taxes to the British. All agreed, except the Raja of Tiloi. Veni Madhav then went and captured him.

'When the Rana arrived at Semri there were 3,000 men in the army. 1,600 were foot soldiers and 1,500 formed the cavalry. The white army (gora paltan) entered the town at noon. At the Semri ruler's home there were no male members present, just his aged widow. She did not know the Rana but looked upon him as a young clansman. Like a matriarch she insisted, "You must not leave without first eating a few morsels of our food," adding mischievously, "unless of course, you consider yourself too high and mighty to share our humble repast. If you do, we shall go out and chop the tails off all your horses."

'The polite man that Rana was, he smilingly said, "Yes, grandmother!" and came and sat on a wooden seat like any ordinary man and finished his meal.

'Traditionally, when a senior nobleman in Awadh visits another who is ranked below him in the power hierarchy, he is supposed to receive a ritual gift of money (nazrana) from his hosts before sitting down for a meal. But Rana Veni Madhav chose to respect age before hierarchy, and waived off all considerations of seniority as he ate meekly without letting on who he was. That's not all. When the shelling began and the cannon balls came flying towards the fort, two of Rana's men, a trader from Maharanigunj called Barkhandi, and Har Prasad Singh were ordered by him to carry the old lady to safety to the nearby the Barha village.

'Even as she was being carried away, the spunky old lady screamed at the British: "You just wait! Shiv Ratan Singh of Baihar will soon be in Simri and will roast you all with his fire!"

'In Semri, the legume crops had been harvested and hard little stumps were left embedded in the fields. The water in the wells too was brackish. The British first made an allegation that the old lady had had the fields planted with hidden arrows and poisoned the local wells. Then one British man said that a lone old widow and her young son could not have managed this. There were two cannons in Semri named Nakti and Baldev Ban, the British carried them away.'

Rao Rambaksh Singh of Dondiya Khera village emerged here as a strange anomaly. Thakur Ran Daman Singh seemed to be somewhat miffed with the Rao, who he said had fought no battle but created plenty of trouble for Rana Veni Madhav Baksh Singh. The Rana had told Rao that he should go and fight. There was enough food stored in the fort to last three years at least. But Rao collected all his treasures and ran to Kashi to hide because he had burnt alive some British officials hiding in the Shiva temple after his men had capsized their boat. Rao now feared for his life, because if the truth was leaked out, the British would punish him severely. Eventually when he was caught and killed, no one came forward to identify him. Finally, Chandan Lal Khatri of Mauravan village and Durvijay Singh of Murar Mau identified his body.

Lal Saheb also remembered hearing that the late Rao sahib was a sadist who liked to see young boys drown in the river. He would sit on the river bank pretending to meditate and when young boys dived into the water, he'd drag them deep into the river and enjoy the spectacle of their panic as they struggled to stay afloat. I recalled Surendra Nath Sen quoting two survivors, in his book *1857*, on events that followed the capsizing of British boats in Rao Ram Baksh's area. The seven British men whose boats were stuck in the sands, ran through a hail of bullets and took shelter in a nearby Shiva temple. It is somewhat surprising though, that Sen does not go on to describe the subsequent burning of the temple by the villagers. He only states that the British took shelter in a temple when they could not outrun their tormentors. There was no food inside the temple. However there was a stinking pool whose waters they drank to quench their thirst and fled towards the river soon after. Had the temple been set on fire, I am sure that as a great supporter of the British cause like Mr Sen—he refers to the natives as 'the enemy'—would not have spared us this gruesome detail. The fact remains that the idea of attacking the British escaping in the fire boat was someone else's, and Rao Ram Baksh Singh became a party to it. According to Pandit Devi Dutt Shukla's book *Awadh Ke Ghadar ka Itihas* (A History of the Ghadar in Awadh), the temple was set on fire by the irate public. He does not either confirm or deny Rao Ram Baksh Singh being present at the spot.

Interestingly, later when we visited Rao Ram Baksh Singh's village of Dondiya Kheda, his family members showered glowing colours of praise on him and said that he was a 'much misunderstood martyr'. So, just like Raja Man Singh of Ayodhya and Lone Singh of Mitauli, his actual role in the ghadar remains somewhat dubious.

Of egos and eccentricities of rural princes; a great debate on who ranks higher, a Rana or a Rao? Count their ploughs to find out

While discussing the actions of the complex ruler Rao Ram Baksh, our talk veered towards other tales of eccentric minor rulers and their enormous egos. Thakur Ran Daman Singh said that once the Thakur of Gaura told him that the actual yardstick for measuring eminence among rural princes was the number of ploughs each owned. Measured thus, a man bearing the title of Rao from the Bais community actually ranked higher than one with the title of a Rana. Rao Ram Baksh must therefore be considered higher in status than Rana Veni Madhav. He quoted a couplet to support his theory:

> He who owns ten ploughs is a Rao,
> He with eight ploughs is called a Rana,
> The owner of four ploughs is merely a well-to-do farmer.

Ran Daman Singh challenged this as flawed and recited what he considered the correct lines:

> A Rao owns ten ploughs, a Rana owns twenty
> A well-to-do farmer has but four.
> One who has two ploughs is an ordinary farmer
> He that owns just one plough, would be better off wielding a spade.

It is believed that the Bais Thakurs were originally related to the ancient line of Shalivahan King Sri Harsha. In Awadh, their history begins from the year 1250 onwards. It is said that two brothers, Abhay Chand and Nirbhay Chand had come to bathe at Buxar on the banks of the river Ganga. At that time there was a tussle going on between the Muslim subedar (provincial representative) of the Ghulam rulers of Delhi, and the local Hindu King of Argal, who belonged to the Gautam clan. While the two brothers were getting ready for the holy dip, they heard the queen crying out for help from any Kshatriyas in the vicinity, to defend her against a sudden attack by Muslim infidels. It turned out that she and her young daughter, who had also come for a dip in the holy river, were surrounded by enemy troops and on the verge of being kidnapped. The two courageous brothers managed to chase away the attackers, but

Nirbhay Chand died fighting. Abhay Chand then escorted the queen and the princess back to Argal. The grateful king married his daughter to the brave lad and gave him twenty-two (bais) villages as dowry. Hence the name Bais Thakur.

Even as the Bais family prospered, they were constantly at war with Muslim invaders and simultaneous internecine quarrels began to surface within the clan, resulting in kicking sprees between brothers. Rao Ram Baksh belonged to the village of Daundiya Kheda, the original seat of Bais Thakurs. The most prominent Bais leaders were lords of Shankarpur and Khajur village. Rana Veni Madhav's association had brought renewed vigour and prosperity to the state of Shankarpur. There are three main branches of the Bais Thakurs: Murar Mau, Daundiya Kheda and Purwa. There were several clashes between the three branches, mostly due to envy. However, once the ghadar broke out, all Bais clans came together to fight the common enemy.

As I have said before, throughout Indian history, periods of great prosperity and peaceful coexistence are invariably followed by spells of discord and constant infighting that eventually lead to subjugation by a powerful outsider. The ghadar was somewhat different simply because despite being a period of great unrest, it managed to forge a rare Hindu-Muslim unity that outlived the ghadar. And in 1919, it was this same bond that Gandhi further strengthened and utilized to create a massive nationalist movement against the dreaded Rowlatt Act of the British government. The rest, as they say, is history.

Hardoi and Unnao

Visiting Hardoi and Unnao was next on my agenda. However, by now I was beginning to realize that the sort of research I had undertaken was extremely demanding and could only be sustained if the researcher was either not burdened by family duties, or else had a very affluent and indulgent father who could bankroll the effort. Since I belonged to neither category, I was occasionally forced to take shortcuts against my wishes. In Hardoi I wished to learn more about three major local leaders: Thakur Gulab Singh of Berua, Raja Narpat Singh of Ruiya and Chaudhary Hashmat Ali of Sandila. I had read about Chaudhary Hashmat Ali in the book *Savan Hat-e-Salateen-e-Awadh*. It was believed that he had been asked by Begum Hazrat Mahal to help her, and after receiving her letter had arrived in Lucknow with an army of 4,000 men. But my travel itinerary that included Hardoi and Unnao districts had to be revised suddenly at this point and I had to leave for Lucknow to take care of urgent some family matters. By the time I had sorted things at home, the monsoons had arrived and travelling to those villages became very difficult.

So, the following details that I have about the Raja of Ruiya and Gulab Singh of Berua are largely based on articles published in two Hindi dailies: *Navjivan* (article by Buddhi Sagar Verma) and *Swatantra Bharat* (article by Bachnesh Tripathi).

Raja Narpat Singh of Ruiya
A principality carved with help from local Muslim rulers of Bilgram

The Ruiya village lies at a distance of some ten miles from the principality of Bilgram in Hardoi district. It is said that Rana Pratap Bhanu, an ancestor of the clan ruling Ruiya, had arrived and settled here, after being driven out of his original village in the Udaipur district of Rajasthan. After arriving in Awadh, he struck up a friendship with the Syeds, who ruled the Bilgram state and received the Ruiya village from them as a gesture of friendship.

Raja Narpat Singh was fourth in line from Rana Pratap Bhanu and inherited the throne from his cousin Sumer Singh. A brave man, Narpat Singh respected those who practised martial arts. It is said that any one desirous of joining his army was expected to eat and keep down at least a seer (1.4 kilos) of food at a time. As per ancient tradition, his men came from sturdy agricultural families and visited him at Ruiya twice a year for training and instructions. It is this casual attitude towards training armies that, in my opinion, led to the native armies' defeat all over Awadh. When these informally trained farmer soldiers were pitted in battles against the well-trained British soldiers, their defeat was almost certain. The soldiers who reported for duty only when the enemy stood knocking at the door and who were prone to acting like indisciplined barbarians during battle, were no match for the well-armed and orderly British army.

When Narpat Singh joined the anti-British front being forged in Awadh, it was at the behest of a fellow thakur, Sati Prasad of Shivrajpur with whom he attacked a British loyalist landlord of Gunj Muradabad. The begum had sent him a letter inviting him to Lucknow but he had declined the offer citing troublesome circumstances. He would, he assured her, stay at Ruiya and hold the enemy back. After the British failed to have

Narpat Singh join them, Colonel Hope mounted an attack on the fortress of Ruiya from the eastern side. Raja Narpat Singh marshalled his troops to defend his territories, but fear of the British weighed heavy on them, despite being extremely well-fed. Of these, two men from the village of Rosgunj chose to run away rather than risk their lives in battle. Of them, Sardu was a Brahmin, while the other, Laltu, was a Kurmi. Sardu's aged father was preparing a drink of bhang for himself when Laltu landed at his doorstep. 'Oye Laltua,' asked Sardu's father, 'how come you are home?'

Taken aback by his ferocity, Laltu replied, 'Kaka, the firangees are about to attack the raja's fortress and his future is insecure. Who wants to jump into that particular fire with eyes open? Many other soldiers have also gone home, so even I decided to leave. Your son too will be following me shortly.'

The old man, appalled at what he'd just heard, stormed inside and brought out his rifle, waved it him and thundered, 'Saala, you have spent a lifetime eating the raja's namak and have already been paid in bullock cartloads of grain for the whole year. And now, when the raja needs you, you have chosen to leave him alone? Go back! Or I will shoot.' The scared kurmi boy ran back, they say, dragging his brahmin mate with him.

So as Colonel Hope's armies surrounded the raja's fortress and began shelling, the natives lined the inner courtyard with wet gunny bags, and as soon as a cannon ball fell through water to diffuse it, their soldiers shot at the enemy. Arrangements had also been made—in case the enemy managed to storm in—to kill the women to save them from possible torture and rape. A basement room had been sprinkled with gun powder which was covered with a beautiful carpet. A charcoal burner was kept ready and women were told to congregate in the room as soon as the enemy entered the fortress and light the fuse for a final blow-up. It was said that a seven-year-old girl had predicted victory for the rebels. She reportedly told Narpat Singh, 'Bapu, do not be afraid. You are going to win.'

Her words came true. Colonel Hope was killed in a freak accident when a bullet hit him. The battle lasted just a day. Soon after their leader died, the British army brought out a white flag and retreated. They suffered heavy losses.

But this did not conclude the battle. A little later the British sent another set of troops via the river Ghaghra. They were carrying tall step-ladders to help them scale the high walls of Narpat Singh's fortress, which was protected on all sides by thick groves of very tall bamboos and a deep moat. Intense shelling began once again and this time the battle lasted for three days. The end of this onslaught is somewhat dubious. According to Mr Sen's account, Narpat Singh tricked the British and escaped, whereas according to Buddhi Sagar, on sensing imminent defeat, Narpat Singh and his men threw open the gates and were killed in battle.

Gulab Singh of Berua
A caretaker ruler and a Nana Saheb acolyte who followed him
to Nepal after losing to the British

Gulab Singh originally hailed from Bhind, now in the state of Madhya Pradesh. He belonged to the clan of Bhadauria Rajputs and migrated to Berua principality in Sandila where he rose to be the diwan (vizier) to Raja Chandrika Baksh Singh of Berua. Since the raja was then a mere seven-year-old minor, as diwan, Gulab Singh became the real power behind the throne. When he decided to make common cause with the anti-British native rebels, his brother Gopal Singh warned him of the dire consequences it would have. But obstinate as he was, Gulab Singh did not change his mind. His dejected brother killed himself by slashing his throat.

Gulab Singh idolized Nana Saheb and fought bravely in several battles against the British forces at Lucknow, Kanpur, Rahimabad, Malihabad, Sandila, Jamu, Malhera, Berua and finally on the banks of the river Betwa. It is said that after the fall of Lucknow, when he had been declared an absconder by the British, Nana Saheb Peshwa had visited Berua with Gulab Singh. When Nana went into exile in Nepal, Gulab followed him there and a little later, succumbed to malaria.

Rao Ram Baksh Singh of Dondiya Kheda
A fearless hero, or a cruel sadist?

Dondiya Kheda was one of the main seats of the Tilkachandi Bais Kshatriyas and its ruler Rao Ram Baksh Singh was a leading light of his community. It was he who was chased and killed by the British at Varanasi for having allegedly set their boat on fire and killing some British officials by setting fire to their shelter. In a letter to me, Pratap Singh Chauhan, a lecturer in the Yuv Dutt College of Lakhimpur wrote:

'Rao Ram Baksh Singh was a proud, fearless and religiously inclined man. During the 1857 mutiny, he led the Unnao front and was the last to put his sword back in the scabbard. He used to worship his sword and it is said that his sword would rise and float to him on its own. On being invited to his village, our ancestors were presented with agricultural land in four villages: Bhaya Kheda, Pahadpur, Kapupur and Bijai Kheda. The lands are still with our family. It is true that he drowned a British boat and set fire to a village temple where some British men had taken shelter. Some may call his actions heartless, but as the British themselves say, all is fair in love and war.

I am still somewhat unclear about the exact sequence of events that took place at Daundiya Kheda village during the ghadar. What I'm sure about, is that thirteen British men had for some reason left their boat in which they were travelling down the Ganga at Najafgarh, and arrived at Buxar by land. As soon as Yadunath Singh of Daundiya Kheda saw them land, he chased them and tried to stop them. He was however shot dead, thanks to a bullet fired by one member of the British group, as they ran along the riverside to save their lives. When Yadunath's men saw their master fall, they got busy trying to revive him and stem the flow of blood. Meanwhile, news spread all over Baiswada that some British men had shot Yadunath-ji dead.

A crowd of young men led by Rao Ram Baksh Singh then began to look for the killers, who had by that time entered a temple in the middle of a garden. Both the temple and the garden belonged to Rao sahib. The British had thrown out the temple idols in the garden outside and locked themselves in.

When the crowd reached the spot and noticed the holy idols lying out in the garden and the temple doors locked, their suspicions were aroused. Since the temple had been desecrated by the enemy who was hiding inside, the enraged crowd decided to set the building on fire. A certain Major Delafauz (sic) survived and escaped to Gahrauli village with two other men. The rest of them perished in the temple fire.

Rao Ram Baksh escaped to Benaras after the fall of Baiswara and Awadh and lived in hiding till Chandi. He carried a price on his head and lured by the reward on offer, one of his own servants had him arrested. The British tried to force him to beg for pardon, but after he refused, he was hung on 8 June 1861 in Buxar.

Like Raja Lone Singh of Mitauli, the life and death of this enigmatic leader who had fought against the British in the battle of Semri, remains shrouded in mystery.

9

LUCKNOW, 1857

Lucknow, the capital of Awadh (Lt Major McLeod Enis, R.E.V.C., *Lucknow And Awadh And The Mutiny*, pub. 1857), stood on two sides of the river Gomti, and covered a total area of five and a half miles in length and two and a half miles in width. A deep semi circular canal embraced its three sides, segregating the relatively congested western and south-eastern parts of the city from the green and picturesque north-eastern area, home to a rich and powerful aristocracy. The upscale part of Lucknow housed many vast palaces, private gardens, bungalows, elite graveyards and mausoleums. It was connected to the less privileged 'other' Lucknow by an old stone bridge called Patthar Ka Pul and further downstream by Lohiya Ka Pul (an iron bridge), built later by British engineers. Both these bridges led to Mandiav Chhavni, the cantonment area which housed the British garrison. The road leading to the nearby industrial town of Kanpur ran along the British Residency to the south. It crossed the canal near the Char Bagh gardens. Both the Machhi Bhawan (also known as the Nawab's palace, called the former because of the Awadh insignia of two swimming fish or machhi, that marked its gates) and the British Residency (also referred to locally as Beli Garad due to the presence of a large guard house, the first among the cluster of British designed buildings in the area) lay close to the river. The native palace Machhi Bhawan stood close to the old stone bridge and the Residency to the new (iron) one.

During the mutiny of 1857, the major roads and bridges of the capital city proved to be of great importance in navigating the area for both the natives and the British. And so after the ghadar was over, maintaining them in good shape became one of the biggest priorities of the government of Awadh.

Unfortunately, the administrators who took good care of the roads and bridges, totally neglected the beautiful native heritage buildings in the city. Badly scarred as they were by the shelling and arson that followed the fall of Lucknow, these historic buildings were slowly reduced to rubble. A few such heaps of rubble are still visible around Lucknow. The old roads however, are serviceable and in constant use. It is hard to believe today how grand and beautiful old Lucknow was. The deposed Nawab Wajid Ali Shah, while being taken away under armed escort, bade this city a tearful farewell in verse:

I cast a last sad glance at the familiar walls and doorways
Be happy my fellow countrymen,
We set out on a long journey.

Nawab Wajid Ali Shah's beloved fellow citizens were not a happy lot after the Lucknow gazetteer (dated 11 February 1856) announced that the principality of Awadh and its capital were being placed directly under British rule. This news rendered the highly respected members of the old aristocracy, the mighty band of bureaucrats that had served under the Nawab, a vast web of lawyers, clerks and revenue officials of the state of Awadh totally redundant almost overnight. With the old nobility thus made obsolete, dozens of businesses patronized by them also came to a halt and a horde of shopkeepers and traders in fine goods too found themselves reduced to abject poverty.

The sudden and total disbanding of the Nawab's personal armies after his deposition also badly affected the law and order machinery of the state. With the old order gone, street ruffians and gangs of common criminals lost no time in escalating their activities and terrorizing the citizens, who were deeply apprehensive of the new system of British jurisprudence suddenly foisted upon them by the East India Company. These new laws overtook the customary legal systems and personal laws pertaining to property transfer and marriage, and people found the changes to the justice system to be unacceptable. The British Resident Colonel Sleeman, who had seen the erstwhile administrative systems at close quarters during the reign of Nawab Sadat Ali Khan, also testifies to the dissatisfaction with the new laws among the common citizens of Awadh. According to him, most people preferred to live within the jurisdiction of the Nawab's Awadh because they found the new legal system imposed by the British both opaque and time consuming. They disliked not only the complicated procedures but also the arrogance and rapacity of the new legal fraternity patronized by the British rulers. They were deeply resentful of the rampant corruption in the new, many layered courts of law where the cases were decided after prolonged deliberations and decisions were arrived at, not on the merit of the cases, but by the nature of bribe, offered by the litigants.

The stories recounted to me by villagers and citizens of Lucknow made it amply clear that the East India Company Raj, following the exile of Wajid Ali Shah, brought with it a sudden proliferation of new taxes that burdened the people. It also created inflationary pressures that shot up the prices of all commodities. Opium, the favoured drug of the nobility in Awadh, now became a very scarce and expensive commodity.

Several other insensitive measures, namely the conversion of Kadam Rasool, a pilgrimage spot of Muslims, into an army godown for storing gunpowder also angered and alienated the masses. They began to feel that whatever their flaws, the nawabs had at least been sensitive and caring. They had also displayed a far greater respect for native traditions of Hindus and Muslims from both Shia and Sunni communities. These 'red-faced invaders from vilayat', people said, rode roughshod over popular sentiments and were thoroughly corrupt to boot. As a result of all these factors, the irate citizens refused to rent out their properties to the officials of the East India Company.

Meanwhile, the Company, instead of trying to gauge the reasons for their reluctance, decided to wield the legal whip and managed to acquire any local properties they fancied, after Chief Commissioner Henry Lawrence gave his permission to the British for occupying any local buildings deemed fit for housing the Company's officers and men, by force, if necessary. Soon the much-loved palace Chhatar Manzil was taken over by the British and turned into a residential area for the Company's European officials. Another adjacent palace Khurshid Manzil, became their kitchen and dining area. Chaupad Astbal, the royal stable, was turned into an army camp and all the houses of royal attendants that were in good shape and located nearby, were forcibly vacated and occupied by British army officials.

Tara Kothi, which was once built as an astronomy research centre, became a courthouse. Other historic homes like the Asafi Daulat Khana and Sheesh Mahal were also summarily vacated under government orders and made available to Company officials. To further drive home the point, the British army's presence was visibly increased all around Lucknow. From Moosa Bagh to Mandiyav camp, Mudkipur and the Chakkarwali Kothi in Sikandarbagh—all the grand heritage properties were turned into army barracks to house large units of the Company's army.

The traditionally well-bred, polite and peace-loving citizens of Lucknow felt acutely terrorized by these enormous changes and were deeply resentful of the crude tactics used by the British to disrupt native lives for their own comfort. With each rapacious assault by the sahibs upon Lucknow's rulers and their native culture, the atmosphere in the city grew more and more tense. The visiting British Archbishop Hebbar, who came to Awadh during Ghaziuddin Hyder's regime, could clearly sense the hostility and before his departure from the city, warned the British officials not to venture out under any circumstances, unless riding an elephant or accompanied by armed guards. There had been several reports of how unescorted Brits riding their horses had been attacked and murdered by unknown men.

Maulvi Ahmedullah Shah

When a society is forced into silence, it turns paranoid. What follows is the growth of superstition and religious fanaticism. An example is the rise of Muslim leader Maulvi Ahmedullah Shah, a resident of the Ghasiyari Mandi area in Lucknow upto February 1857. Old citizens of Lucknow still refer to him as

'Danka Shah Maulvi'. Syed Kamaluddin Hyder writes that he was also well known among the Awadh nobility as 'Nakkara Shah'. Shaida Begum, one of the begums of the exiled nawab, explained why these names came to be attached to the Maulvi. She wrote from Lucknow in a letter to the Nawab (whom she addresses as Jan-e-Alam), that after his departure (to Calcutta), the Ghas Mandi area had become a central point for the maulanas of Lucknow. Among them, a Sufi called Ahmedullah Shah had thousands of followers and went out in a palanquin, preceded and followed by drummers playing drums (Nakkaras or Dankas).

'...I have heard it said that the followers of Danka Shah would chew burning coals in public and the Maulvi would tell the congregation that these young men who were chewing them were going to spout fire very soon and go straight to heaven. His followers also spread many tales about the Maulvi's closed door sessions, wherein he was supposed to confer with Allah. When that happened, they said, the dark room would suddenly begin to glow with a celestial light (noor), and up in the skies, lightening would crackle and clouds would roar. The disciples said that while all this would happen, they would stand outside the room with their ear next to the door, listening to the holy dialogue taking place within and then they would tell people what they had reportedly heard.'

In February 1857, the Maulvi went to Faizabad and a little later, according to Sunder Lal Shukla's account (Bharat Mein Angrezi Raj), the Maratha noble and rebel leader Peshwa Nana Saheb of Bithur visited Lucknow on 18 April 1857. Nana was extended a very lavish welcome by both the Muslim clerics and ordinary citizens. Apparently, the Chowk area's prosperous jewellers' community had covered some gates with gold ornaments to welcome the esteemed royal guest from Bithur.

Even though Nana's visit to Lucknow was aimed at gauging the level of dissatisfaction against the Company rule among the nobility of Awadh and strategizing its overthrow with like-minded people, being an astute man, he called upon major functionaries of the Company to make sweet talk with them.

The very day Nana Saheb was being welcomed in Lucknow, Chief Commissioner Sir Henry Lawrence, who was out for a ride in his horse carriage, was publicly humiliated when an irate citizen sprayed mud on him. This incident should have alerted the Resident and his men, but it was allowed to pass. But the Company's troubles had only just begun. Some contempt was festering even within the British army.

Mirza Mustafa Ali Shah, the native commander of the Company's armies at the time, was the elder son of the late Nawab Sadat Khan. He had been denied the throne by his father who felt he was unworthy of it. Everyone in Lucknow knew how, after his younger brother Wajid Ali Shah had inherited the throne, a miffed Mirza Mustafa had sworn never to wear headgear unless it was a crown. This statement upset the public who had remained loyal to the deposed Nawab. This too had been duly reported to the Company's higher officials by their spies as a possible source of future flare-ups.

At the beginning of April, when Henry Lawrence was humiliated in public, another ugly incident occurred at a local hospital. A visiting doctor Colonel Walter Wells along with a group of white doctors was inspecting the stores. He had reportedly picked up a bottle (of carminative mixture), and taken a few swigs of the liquid. It could be that he was feeling unwell and wanted quick relief for an upset stomach. But what he did not realize was that the natives observed strict laws of pollution regarding the ingestion of all kinds of liquid or solid stuff. To them, by touching the bottle to his lips, the doctor had polluted its contents. Although, according to reports, Colonel Wells had duly recapped the bottle and replaced it, it set in motion an angry buzz among Hindu soldiers. The fury refused to die down and the men suspected that the colonel, who was a Christian, may have deliberately flouted the Hindu laws of pollution that strictly forbade anyone eating or drinking straight out of a container. The long and short of it was that the native sepoys in the 48th battalion of the British army—most of whom belonged to the upper castes—thereafter refused to accept medicines from the store.

When Colonel Palmer, the official in charge of the hospital heard of this, he immediately sent for all native officials and had the supposedly polluted bottle of medicine smashed in front of their eyes. He also made sure to give Colonel Wells an earful in front of them. But the sepoys' anger refused to die out. One night, the doctor's bungalow was set on fire. It was obvious that this was the handiwork of the disgruntled men of the 48th battalion. But again, things were brushed under the carpet and nobody was penalized. A few days later, some ugly rumours about bags of wheat flour—meant for the sepoys' meals—being contaminated with finely ground animal bones wafted in, raising temperatures further in April 1857, a month of simmering discontent in Lucknow.

On 2 May, the Seventh Irregular Battalion of Awadh at Moosa Bagh, a camp that was already resentful of their British masters for several reasons, was provided with cartridges for their new Enfield rifles. It was widely believed that these cartridges that had to be opened using one's teeth, were laced with highly forbidden fat from cows and pigs. Despite much counselling by officials, the sepoys refused to touch these cartridges. They were then threatened with strict legal action which further heightened tensions between British officials and their native sepoys, who continued to remain adamant about not using the new cartridges. As pressure began to mount, one of the sepoys finally lost his temper and ran out of the camp yelling, 'Please save us from forcible conversion to the firangees' religion!' Although the sepoy was arrested immediately, the news of this dramatic revolt created a sensation in the city.

Thirty other sepoys who were displaying similar signs of gross insubordination, were asked to stay back and their entire battalion was ordered to disperse. But by now, things had gone out of control and the 1000-strong battalion, comprising both Hindus and Muslims refused to either disperse or allow their brethren to be apprehended. They said that as Indians, they would not allow thirty of their fellow natives to be taken away and killed. During this tense confrontation, a few natives went up to the British officials and said, 'Huzoor, give us a chance to calm down the defiant boys by tomorrow.' As a face-saving measure, this proposal was accepted, but both sides retired angry and began to plan retaliation. The soldiers knew that the ultimate punishment for such open insubordination would be death. Hence, to ward it off, they captured all the weaponry they could lay their hands on and sent a letter to their 'elder brothers' of the 48th regiment at the nearby Madiyav camp. The letter urged them to support their brothers and defend their faith which was being endangered by 'the white infidels'. The aforesaid regiment had already defied its officers a few days earlier and the letter writers felt they would be sympathetic to the native cause. Unfortunately for them, their messenger entrusted with the vital letter, did not deliver

it to the sepoys and handed it to the Commissioner Henry
Lawrence instead.

*Henry Lawrence arrives at Madiyav camp firing all guns and gory
retaliations begin; Sir Henry tries to incite Hindus against Muslims
by quoting past humiliations, fails; a vital letter gets delivered at the
wrong address, exposing plans for revolt*

Sensing an imminent rebellion at the already restless barracks
at Madiyav Camp, Henry Lawrence arrived there with 1500
soldiers the very next morning, shelling, as he came. The
rebellious soldiers surrendered immediately and were then
ordered to line up. As soon as the jawans of the Seventh
Irregular Battalion saw the cannons mounted at the maidan,
they realized what was going happen to the rebels. Petrified
of the impending reprisals, they broke into a run, many
abandoning their rifles in their panic. Of the thousand-strong
battalion, only 120 stayed on. They were made to surrender
their arms, and a few were ordered to disband. Forty men were
then sentenced to life imprisonment and thirty were charged
with sedition and summarily sentenced to death by hanging.

The hangings that took place in the heart of Lucknow were
rather beastly in nature, primarily intended at driving maximum
fear in to the hearts of all those who planned to revolt against
the sahibs. Those condemned were hung one by one from
scaffolds placed in front of Machhi Bhawan and the corpses
were left to rot there till sundown, by which time vultures and
dogs had defiled them completely. Whatever remained was
taken down and interred at the gates, instead of being handed
back to the families. More hangings followed the next morning,
and this series of daily killings stunned the city so badly that the

traumatized citizens could not bring themselves to talk about these deaths.

Henry Lawrence remained impervious to the deafening silence that descended on the city. After he felt sure that he had established an English stronghold, he began the process applying salt to the natives' wounds. He richly rewarded the soldier from the 13th battalion who had exposed a seditious plot by three men against the Company's officials. He subsequently announced a scheme for rewarding all jawans who, in the future, would similarly help the government uncover such seditious plots. A durbar was held on 12 May to which all British and native officials were invited. In a break from tradition, the native officials were offered chairs to seat themselves, and Lawrence made an impassioned speech in an accented Hindustani. He minced no words in underlining various atrocities committed in the past by Muslim invaders against native Hindus. He also chose to remind his audience (a majority of whom were Hindus), of how Aurangzeb and Hyder Ali had destroyed thousands of Hindu temples and smashed idols within homes and forcibly converted thousands to Islam. Till the Company took things in hand, Sir Henry said, no Hindu could build a temple for Lord Shiva in a Nawab-ruled Lucknow. He then went on to remind the Muslims that the Sikh ruler Ranjit Singh had discriminated against them in Punjab, and how, during his regime, no azaan calls could be made in the mosques at Lahore. He reiterated how the Company's government, like an indulgent and fair-minded parent, had treated Hindus and Muslims alike.

After this speech, several men from the 48th and 13th regiments—Subedar Sevak Tiwari, Havaldar Hira Lal Dubey, soldier Ramnath Dubey and soldier Husein Baksh—were awarded titles and bags of cash as reward for their loyalty. And while a few native officials came forward to record their appreciation of the Company bahadur's leadership, the soldiers stood silent and sullen.

I have often wondered how some soldiers of the 13th and 48th regiments could have chosen to hand the sensitive and confidential letters meant for their brethren to the same British officials that they had openly defied. Did they want to stab their comrades in the back in the hope of milking a few petty favours from the British? Or did they just expect to ignite more disaffection and catalyze a major retaliation that they could sense brewing all over? Had they failed to foresee the swift and severe reprisals that the British would mount against the rebellious jawans at the Madiyav camp?

Whatever be the truth, as I met and spoke to more people, I was convinced that the soldiers' initial defiance of the British was a precursor of the non-violent (Gandhian) Civil Disobedience movement. Gandhi adapted the very same tactics, but made them more broad-based and sophisticated before using them successfully to challenge the well-entrenched colonial rule in India. The violent turn of events in 1857, such as the burning of the doctor's bungalow, was largely a result of the insensitive and oppressive countermeasures used by officials like Sir Henry Lawrence to quell disaffection. The brutal public hangings further ensured that the fires of the ghadar that had been ignited, would continue burning even though no one knew exactly when matters would come to a head.

After the public hangings, a series of alarming incidents took place in Lucknow at regular intervals. At odd hours, people would hurl burning rags inside the bungalows of British officials, or a collage of incendiary posters and pamphlets would suddenly appear on the city's walls, urging the citizens to revolt and reminding them that it was the religious duty of both native Hindus and Muslims to kill the firangees defiling their land and religion. This tense atmosphere made even Sir Henry Lawrence, the chief commissioner and commander of the Company's armies in Awadh, wake up and realize how, after the the sullen restlessness in Lucknow, its army cantonments could erupt suddenly. By that time, the neighbouring regions of Meerut, Delhi and several north-western districts of the United Provinces had openly revolted against Company rule and declared independence.

A pugnacious Sir Henry set about putting the house in order without losing time. First, he regrouped his forces and put the precious garrison under the charge of trusted British officials. After that, within just five days, he had Machhi Bhawan—the most important building that housed his officers and a large part of his forces—repaired and readied for military activity. Several trees were cut down to make room for mounting cannons at strategic locations, and large quantities of grains were purchased and stored in government buildings. By demolishing several neighbouring properties, the Residency area was spruced up and geared to withstand a prolonged siege or a sudden, armed onslaught by the natives. So obsessed was Sir Henry with safety and security of his officials and their families, that apparently when local nobles or prominent merchants came visiting and politely asked if they could be of any service, he would unhesitatingly ask them to provide him with as much foodgrain, ghee and other edible items as they could.

*Malihabad gets its own back with a practical joke as Sir Henry and
Gibbons sahib solicit help from the native elite*

In Awadh, fear and absurdity are close relatives. Irate citizens
of the neighbouring town of Malihabad, fed up with the fuss
created by Sir Henry's men, decided to play a practical joke
on the obtuse and pompous commissioner. Word was sent to
him that Malihabad was on the verge of a bloody revolt. As was
expected, Sir Henry immediately rushed his troops under the
leadership of Captain Weston to Malihabad. As soon as the
army entered the town, the men realized that they had been
conned. The town was rocking with silent laughter while the
citizens calmly went about their daily chores without any worries.
The army marched back, feeling rather foolish, and all of Awadh
showered praise on Malihabad for this well-executed hoax.

Sometime towards the end of May 1857, when it was
almost time for the Muslim festival of Eid, Sir Henry and
his deputy Martin Gibbons invited all the eminent citizens
and moneylenders of Awadh to a party. Nobles and elites
from all over Lucknow, namely Nawab Ahmed Wali Khan,
Munavvaraula, Mirza Hussein Khan (uncle-in-law to the
deposed Nawab Wajid Ali Shah), former minister Muhammed
Ibrahim Sharaf-ud-Daula, former diwan Balkrishna, Nawab
Mumtaj-ud-Daula and many others turned up and asked the
British powers that be, for protection in case of an outbreak
of violence. The commissioner said that he would deploy his
own men to guard them.

The 71st Light Company sets off the fuse

Eid on 22 May passed off peacefully, but the mood continued to
remain tense. Late evening, on 30 May, as soon as the cannon

was fired, signifying the disbanding of troops for the night, the native soldiers of the 71st Light Company refused to disband. Instead, they began shooting randomly and a group of forty-odd rebel soldiers began to march menacingly towards the officers' mess. As soon as they entered one gate, some cavalrymen from the same regiment entered through another gate and met them. This demonstrated that they were following a well-laid-out plan to subject their officers to a two-pronged attack. The rebel soldiers first set about destroying the army mess, but fortunately for the officers, they had been alerted in time and had escaped.

Anticipating more trouble, Sir Henry had already put his men on alert and asked his own soldiers to take charge of the garrison. But as the soldiers began firing, oblivious to their officers' efforts to calm them down, it was obvious that things were about to take an ugly turn. Sir Henry ordered that the cannons be fired, and this forced the sparsely-armed natives to flee towards the Mudkipur army camp. This proved to be very dangerous because once they arrived there, they ended up inciting the already restive men present there. The next morning, when a troop of British soldiers of the 7th battalion arrived from Machhi Bhawan to defend the Mudkipur camp, a rebel subedar emerged, holding up his sword threateningly, and raised anti-British slogans, calling out to his native brethren to join him against the firangees. Stirred by this, several men of the Seventh Battalion broke ranks and joined him. About a thousand rebels now faced Sir Henry's troops and fought them bravely, although they were soon crushed by the superior fire-power of the British. Sir Henry's men gave them a good chase, motivated by the commissioner's announced reward of a hundred rupees per captured rebel soldier. Hundreds of rebels were thus caught and butchered.

The clashes at Mudkipur camp deeply affected the city of Lucknow and the citizens joined the soldiers as open rioting began on the streets. Eventually, ruffians and bands of robbers also joined in. Syed Kamluddin Hyder, formerly a member of the Nawab's durbar and later a retired pensioner of the Company's bureaucracy, in his historical *Sawavhaat-e-Salaatin-e-Awadh* describes it thus:

'The ruffians along with the rebel soldiers and mounted cavalrymen created mayhem all over the city. In the mohallas of Mansur Nagar, Saadat Gunj and Mashak Gunj, they grouped the people under the banner of the Prophet (Nishan-e-Mohammadi). Hundreds first left towards the army camps saying that they wished to join the rebels' army, but they retraced their footsteps after they heard about the natives being defeated by the firangee troops. Agha Mirza, a well-known personality who had hidden himself with a blanket, was busy urging people to revolt despite being advised by other god-fearing men to desist from such foolhardy schemes. The sole reason for his disaffection was revenge, because his pet dog had been killed by a firangee sahib. He and his cohorts finally managed to enter the sahib's house, kill him and loot everything possible. Well-known goons such as the fabric dyer Chhotey Khan of Do Gavaan and Evaz Ali also joined in this melee.'

As news of the rioting spread, a large crowd from Aishbagh area left for the army camps. Barring 200 armed rebel soldiers, the rest of the rioters were carrying whatever they could hastily lay their hands on, be it a small knife, a spear, an ancestral matchlock gun, or even ordinary bamboo sticks. Syed Kamaluddin Hyder describes them as a mob of lumpens (*badmashon ki bheed*) and there is no hard evidence to prove otherwise. However, I must point out here that his point of view was somewhat biased in favor of the British. His work, under the guise of being a history book of the nawabs, chooses repeatedly to describe the British as Sahib-e-Alishan (The Grand Sahibs). Like many of Wajid Ali Shah's begums and several of his nobles (whose descendants I've interviewed), Kamaluddin has witnessed the violence and bloodshed that marked the ghadar, but described it as mere riots.

Coming back to the aggressive natives surging towards the British army camps, they left via Gau Ghat, passed through the ramparts of the Imam Bara and crossed the Gomti river to arrive at the Madiyav camp. Since hardly anything remained there by then, they turned back and en route halted at Huseinabad. Hunger drove them to loot green grocers' shops, attack armed guards and snatch their weapons.

For two days, rioters created scary scenes of lawlessness and vandalism in Huseinabad, before being attacked by the British forces and butchered mercilessly. Horrific reprisals by the British followed, and an entirely new phenomenon of public hangings was introduced to instill fear of government's law and order machinery. Laxmani Tila, Akbari Darwaza and scores of ancient trees were chosen as sites for these activities.

Despite such barbaric and public reprisals, the native leaders did not desist from inciting the soldiers in the British army. On 2 June, Carnegie sahib arrived in Mansur Nagar with his army and began apprehending and punishing the rebels. But on 11 June, the infantry and cavalry divisions of the military police went on a rampage. After setting fire to the British officials' bungalows, they left, and were soon chased by the Company's men. Survivors of this onslaught joined Nana Saheb's troops of rebel soldiers, led by Begum Hazrat Mahal.

All the British could hear now was bad news, and their much-celebrated post and telegraph services were in a state of disarray. The only saving grace was that their network of native spies, liberally bribed by them, was still up and running and providing them with various kinds of valuable information.

As the natives begin to gain and the British, panic, spies
fan out all over

The rebels too had their own network of spies and agents. Munshi Rasool Baksh of Kakori was an Awadh native who had joined the rebel forces with his son Hafiz. He continued to incite the native soldiers in the British army through messengers. Two of these emissaries were caught trying to exhort Subedar Karam Khan of the Nadari Paltan near the Huseinabad tank under a mulberry tree. When the subedar noticed a British spy nearby, he looked frightened and reported the matter to his superiors. The next day, when the munshi's men came to meet the subedar again, he asked them to take him to their house for an intimate chat. The three left, tailed by the British spy. The men took the subedar to Raja Hulas Rai's house at Raja Tikaitrai Bazaar. The munshi and a couple of his friends, including an old man called Mir Khalil Ahmed, were sitting there and chatting among themselves. In a house nearby, a wedding party of Sankata Prasad Khatri's family from Kashi was camped. After the British spy reported the subversive activities being carried out at Raja Hulas Rai's house, British troops soon landed up at the spot, and arrested everyone and sentenced them to death on charges of sedition. Curious onlookers from the wedding party next door were taken captive but released later after it was established that their presence near the raja's house was a mere coincidence.

The Company's men had also learnt that some native officials from among their ranks were secretly in talks with erstwhile native rulers of Awadh to provide shelter and support to the rebel troops. As soon as their suspicions were confirmed, they swooped down on the traitors and captured them. These included Nawab Saadat Ali Khan's son Nawab Muhammad Hasan Khan Ruknuddaula and the former nawab's elder brother Mirza Mustafa Ali Khan. Two princes from Delhi, Mirza Hyder Shikoh and Mirza Humayun Shikoh, who had been residing in Lucknow for a long time, were also apprehended. All of them were imprisoned in Machhi Bhawan. The young royal scion of Tulsipur who had been imprisoned at the Beli Garad was also transferred to Machhi Bhawan since it was considered a safer venue. All the precious possessions of the British army, including their armoury, were also relocated to the Machhi Bhawan. The British tried to keep things under control physically, but over a period, the consistency of violent outbreaks soon proved that brute force was not enough to quell a revolt that was too widespread and had very deep roots.

After 30 May, while Lucknow remained under Company rule, the British, preoccupied as they were to save their own, were not bothered about maintaining law and order in a city that was increasingly becoming lawless and unsafe. At the same time, a hundred mutinies began erupting elsewhere in Awadh: Sitapur, Muhammadi, Aurangabad, Sekraura, Gonda, Bahraich, Mallapur, Faizabad, Sultanpur, Salone, Begum Gunj and Dariyapur—places where British men, women and children found themselves surrounded by hostile crowds threatening violence.

On 25 June, the British had some reason to feel good, when an insider by the name of Ali Raza Khan helped them locate and dig out a vast royal treasure that lay buried at Kaiserbagh. Khan was a trusted noble and official in the court of the deposed ruler Wajid Ali Shah who turned traitor after the British exiled the nawab. He bargained for the lucrative post of a deputy collector, and in exchange provided a secret map for the carefully hidden treasure to the finance commissioner Gubbins. He rushed to the spot with Major Banks and his men, and together they carried away the rich booty—twenty-two boxes of priceless crown jewels, a gem-encrusted throne and many precious objects imported from Europe by the nawabs.

Meanwhile, the fires of the ghadar had spread till the Himalayan foothills in the north. Around Awadh, the rich and powerful states of Azamgarh, Gorakhpur, Shahjehanpur, and Kanpur had become centres for rebels to regroup and replenish their arms and ammunition. By 28 June, the rebel armies of Awadh had also found shelter at Nawabgunj in Barabanki. This was the day a British boat was destroyed when it got stuck on the riverbank near Daundiya Kheda in Unnao district. The native ruler Rao Ram Baksh Singh's soldiers killed several British officials while they were fleeing from the boat.

The Battle of Chinhat after the early victory for the native side, the lamentable rise of the tilangas and the growing disenchantment of ordinary citizens with revolutionary forces

On 29 June, the native army under the leadership of Barkat Ahmed, came close to Lucknow and camped at Chinhat to prepare for a final assault on the capital. They were joined by the fierce Afridi fighters from Malihabad. As soon as he heard of this development, Sir Henry ordered his troops to leave and take on the rebels outside the town for a decisive battle. The native armies fought bravely, assisted by the troops of Subedar Ghamandi Singh and Subedar Shahabuddin, and won the round. As the British armies fled, the rebels managed to capture four of their cannons and a large cache of gunpowder and cannonballs. The news of the natives forcing back the soldiers of the Company, spread like wild fire, and motivated the military police jawaans at the Imambara and Daulat Khana to go on a rampage, attacking the British officers and looting all their possessions.

In no time, the natives began to chase away the British. The defeated army ran up to the iron bridge, where they were given cover by cannons fired from the Residency. When they reached the stone bridge, the cannons at the Machhi Bhawan were fired on the native armies, who retaliated with equal firepower and managed to capture the town eventually. Now victorious, they could be seen celebrating all over, from Kothi Farhat Baksh, Chhatar Manzil, Badshah Bagh, Shad Manzil and Khursheed Manzil, to Mubarik Kothi, Kothi Rasadkhana, Hazratgunj, Dilkusha, Muhammad Bagh and Asafi Imambara. The begums residing in the royal pavilions at Kothi Farhat Baksh and Chhatar Manzil were a little alarmed by the sudden influx of soldiers, but were reassured by their leaders who promised that they'd be gone by the next morning.

Alarmed at the fall of Chinhat, the British officials and their families living at the Residency were keen to escape. The rebels camped all around the area began to bombard its walls before dark, causing further panic. The people of the city were going wild with joy. On the morning of 1 July 1857, word came that the men guarding the government stores at Kotwali Imambara and Musafir Khana had absconded, and precious government properties including the armoury were available for loot. The mobs rushed there in no time and began looting and destroying everything in sight. According to *Savaanah-e-Haat-e-Awadh*, a goon from the Roomi Darwaza area called out to his colleagues from other areas and told them that it was foolish to destroy cannons. Instead, it would be beneficial in the long term, if they mounted them at Machhi Bhawan. This idea appealed to all and the cannons were relocated—two of them to the roof of the drummers' quarters (Nakkar Khana). Wooden seats from shops were used to barricade the area and fend off British gunfire from Machhi Bhawan. The success of this arrangement inspired some people to pile up a large amount of cotton next to the Bhawan's gates and set fire to it.

Sir Henry now realized that the British would be safer at the Residency and so it'd be a good idea to shift the women, children and treasuries there from Machhi Bhawan by midnight. He tried to relay this message to Col Palmer at the Bhawan by paying an emissary a thousand rupees, but the man was killed en route by rioters. Repeated attempts were made thereafter to get the message across, ordering Col Palmer to leave immediately with families of the officials and simultaneously, to set fire to the gunpowder stored in Machhi Bhawan. Given the curfew on the streets, Sir Henry was not sure if any of those messages would reach the colonel, but luckily, one of them did, and Col Palmer managed to escape with his charge after setting the gunpowder stocks on fire.

The natives were totally surprised as the building suddenly erupted into flames and dark fumes enveloped the entire area. According to Syed Kamaluddin, by the time the rioters could wrap their heads around what was happening, the British forces had made a clean escape from the disturbed area. There were some casualties along the way—some British officials, lost in the city's lanes—and some native gunners who ran off, but more or less they were able to dodge the shelling by rebel forces camped on the Hasan Bagh side of the city. The fleeing group was given protective cover by several cannons that were leading them and it finally managed to enter the Beli Garad area (The Residency) through a secret passage in one of the princes' homes.

The gruesome events of murder, looting and arson that followed the victory at Chinhat somewhat stigmatized the triumph of the Indian rebels. As the British fled Machhi Bhawan, the rebels came to the erroneous conclusion that they had chased the firangees out of India forever and began celebrating by indulging in lawlessness. In a stark contrast to this, Sir Henry demonstrated a deep and humane concern for his fellow Britons till his last breath. Even after he was fatally wounded by the shelling of the Residency on 2 July, he continued guiding his forces and planning for their safety. It was reported that he asked his doctor how long he could expect to survive, considering that he was seriously wounded. Upon being told that he did not have much time, he urged his men to pull up their socks and ensured that they felt protected and cared for. One must bow to such bravery and grace.

The Indian soldiers increasingly began to display a lamentable arrogance and dishonesty after their short-lived victory at Chinhat. Groups of them would land at homes of noblemen and demand that they be allowed to look for enemies that may be hiding. Once inside, they would ransack the house and leave with whatever they could lay their hands on. They robbed the homes of many eminent citizens like Muhsin-ud-Daula, Sharaf-ud-Daula, Amin-ud-Daula and Hakim Mir Ali. One of my grandfather's rich friends, the well-known jeweller Babu Jay Narayan Tandon who lived in the Sone Wali Kothi, was also robbed. His descendants showed me an old gate at the back of their ancestral house. It was broken down by rioting hooligans after the battle of Chhatar Manzil. On close inspection, I noticed that it was still intact, thanks to some haphazardly nailed planks. I was told that the rebels had stood rioting in their backyard until the house-owners distracted them by throwing gold coins at them. Clearly, this was a revolution gone astray, turning upon itself to finally self-destruct.

Begum Hazrat Mahal

Fate now introduced a new leader, Begum Hazrat Mahal into the mutiny. At a time when male leaders seemed to be losing out to the East India Company, this young and charismatic woman took over the reins quietly. She remained the centre of authority in Awadh through all the volatile months that finally ended in defeat for the native armies, and a harsh and determined British backlash against all native supporters of the ghadar. The lives of the two women leaders of the ghadar—the Rani Lakshmibai of Jhansi, and Begum Hazrat Mahal of Awadh, largely sum up the state and situation of Indian women in the feudal society of that era.

The rani's motherless childhood was spent in company of a father who was not too well-off, but who more than made up for it by giving his only child Manu, alias Chhabili, a solid education, and by inculcating in her a love for martial arts. This bright and precocious young girl was also deeply loved by the generals of the Maratha Peshwa's army, among whom she had grown up while they were students at her father, Moro Pant Tambe's school at Bithur. They had helped their guru's motherless daughter learn to fight in combat and train like a man. Tambe was a brahmin priest at the Yagna Shala of Srimant Peshwa Nana Saheb of Bithur, where he also ran a

training school for the sons of aristocrats. Chhabili rose to be
a queen when she was married to the eccentric ruler of Jhansi,
Baba Gangadhar Rao. The tomboyish and ebullient child-
bride, once faced with the harsh feudal mores, empowered
an ageing and ill-tempered husband to keep her in purdah
under a strict and constant vigil. A nineteenth-century Marathi
book, *Maaja Pravas* by Vishnu Bhatt Godshe, gives an incisive
eyewitness account of the ghadar as it panned out in the
north. According to his descriptions of the Jhansi royal family,
Chhabili was at least fortunate because she was her husband's
sole wife, and therefore did not have to face hostility from
other wives. Also after Gangadhar Rao's early death within the
next few years, she regained her freedom and mobility, and
as dowager queen she could revert to her regimen of vigorous
physical exercises and frequent interaction with learned men.
This kept her physically fit and mentally agile. I am sure, had
she not died in battle at the young age of twenty-two, she'd
have lived a long life and remained an exemplary, although
somewhat eccentric ruler till the very end. Rani Lakshmibai
belonged to the tradition of royal wives like Sita, the consort of
Lord Rama, who accepted traditional social mores with grace,
but contested them when they became unjust, oppressive and
deprived her of her natural dignity.

Begum Hazrat Mahal's life reveals another side of the
oppressive social values prevalent among feudals in India.
Unlike Chhabili, she grew up as a trained courtesan, happy
to please men, sing and dance for them ever since she was a
child. It is said that she was introduced into the harem of Wajid
Ali Shah, the second son of Nawab Amjad Ali Shah, by two
notorious madams (kutnis) of Lucknow, known as Amman
and Amaman. They had trained her in the art of pleasing male

clients. She was accepted in the harem and renamed as Mahak Paree (the fragrant fairy).

Sajjad Ali Mirza Kaukab Qadr, great-grandson of Begum Hazrat Mahal had confirmed to me that his great-grandmother was born to an unknown and poor family in Faizabad, and that her parents had sold her to Amman and Amaman in exchange for some money. He said that there were no other details available within their family about his great-grandmother's childhood and parentage. He denied Najmul Ghani's statement about her real name being Umrao Jaan, a well-known Urdu poetess and courtesan. He further added that she was very young when she was inducted into the Nawab's harem as Mahak Paree. She got pregnant and gave birth to the Nawab's fourth son (named Mirza Ramzan Ali Khan, also known as Prince Birjis Qadr), but even after he elevated her to the status of a begum, in his letters to her from Calcutta, he continued to refer to her as a commoner (Jan-e-Khanagi).

What happens to the soul of a proud woman who is sold by her own parents for purposes of sexual slavery, when she is a mere infant? Perhaps it was the anger rooted in repeated abuse that turned her into an aggressive woman who not only guarded her infant son's right to the throne of Awadh, but also openly challenged the might of the East India Company. Sir William Russell has also spoken of her spirited defiance and her capacity for leading from the front, despite being young and inexperienced. Every British writer who has written about the ghadar has expressed similar admiration for the Begum, describing her as an extremely intelligent and clever strategist with a rare capacity for organizing and leading men.

I would like to refer here to another story about the deposed Nawab and his harem as quoted by a British author in *The*

Private Life of an Oriental Queen. According to it, the Nawab had lusted after one of his mother's female attendants and wanted to bring her into his own palace. The mother was opposed to it, but instead of a frank expression of her disapproval, she played on the superstitious Nawab's fears. She told her son that she was against sending this girl into his harem because she bore the inauspicious tattoo of a snake on her back. It was believed that a woman with such a tattoo could cause her lover to die an untimely death. Wajid Ali Shah, whose weak heart was already giving him trouble, was predictably scared. After he came back to his quarters, he asked his harem's hermaphrodite guard Khwajasara Bashir-ud-Daula, to strip all his women immediately and expel any who had similar tattoos on their bodies. This created mayhem within the harem and the clever Khwajasara apparently became a very rich man overnight. To retain his credibility, however, he singled out eight begums who he announced, were found to bear the unlucky sign of the snake. These were Nishat Mahal, Khursheed Mahal, Shaida Begum, Badi Begum, Chhoti Begum and last but not the least, the nautch girl turned begum, Hazrat Mahal. The Nawab quickly declared talaaq (divorce) for all of them and showed them the door. At this point, some sympathizers who knew the Nawab's great attachment for some of the expelled begums, advised him to send for a Hindu tantrik (black magician) who would perform some secret rituals and render the marked begums safe for cohabitation. The talaaq orders were withdrawn but only two of the eight exiled begums chose to return to the harem. Begum Hazrat Mahal was one of them. If this story is true, the unfair expulsion must have further traumatized her and could well be the reason behind her determination to hang on to her privileges as a royal wife and mother of a boy who would be the next Nawab.

After Nawab Wajid Ali Shah's impeachment by the British, no one had given a serious thought to Prince Birjis Qadr succeeding him as heir. And had another senior begum or prince laid claim to the throne, there is no way attention would have been paid to a junior begum such as Hazrat Mahal who was just a commoner. In reality, after winning the battle of Chinhat, when the native generals sat down to mull over a good successor for the throne of Awadh, they found it to be a daunting task. In 1857, the court of Awadh was full of tired and lazy royals who loved to have a good time but would be reluctant to fight for their rights. Pandit Devi Prasad Shukla notes in his *Awadh Ke Ghadar Ka Itihas* (The History of the Ghadar in Awadh):

'There were no royals available in Lucknow who were fit to carry on the nawabi rule in Awadh. When rebellion broke out in the city, it did because little mutinies were erupting all over. Had the people of Awadh really wished to rise in revolt against the British rule, they would have defied the orders to depose Nawab Wajid Ali Shah instead of welcoming the Company's administration. The landlords that had been defiant of the Nawab's revenue laws not only began to pay their taxes on time but also upon being reprimanded by the Company's officials, returned lands acquired illegally, to their lawful owners. When the mutiny broke out in Lucknow in April, Awadh had been fifteen months under British rule and the people, by and large seemed content with the new law and order system enforced by the police. The commissionaries at Khairabad and Bahraich had been organized under new laws (Mulki Bandobast) and the tax limits had been defined and tweaked to reasonable rates. It took just a few incidents of lawlessness to undo all that.'

After scoring a victory over the British army, the generals Barkat Ahmed, Umrao Singh, Jaipal Singh, Raghunath Singh, Shahbuddin and Ghamandi Singh formed a war council and began to discuss the question of succession to the throne of Awadh. As a representative of the civilians, the very noble Raja Jaya Lal Singh was sent for. He complained to the generals that the public was fed up with the reign of terror unleashed by some infamous hoodlums (popularly referred to as tilangey). The public expected the generals to rid the city of this menace. The generals then asked Ali Raza Kotwal and Meer Nadir Husein to take charge and restore law and order as soon as possible. Since both of them had been in the service of the Company, the generals considered it prudent to post Muhammad Qasim Khan to supervise them. They also asked Maulvi Ahmedullah Shah to have his own police pickets removed, something which caused some bad blood.

The first name chosen as the prospective Nawab was that of Mirza Dar Ur Sitvat. He refused, as he was scared of reprisals, should the British manage to reassert their authority. The next name was that of Mirza Naushervan Qadr, but he too turned down the offer. Finally, two nobles: Nawab Mahmood Khan and Sheikh Ahmed Hussein advised the generals to anoint the infant son of Wajid Ali Shah, Mirza Birjis Qadr as a symbol of nawabi authority, provided that the other begums agreed to this arrangement. If they did, the nobles and people of Awadh would accept him as the new Nawab.

Just as a pebble hurled into the stagnant, unmoving waters of a pond will part the scum on the surface and reveal unseen depths, the common peasants' and soldiers' defiance of the alien rule of the East India Company had some unforeseen consequences. For one, it provided a rare window for the downtrodden to come up; for another, the deaths of men threw open the gates of veiled pavilions where queens and begums lived in total isolation from the outside world. This was how women like Lakshmibai and Hazrat Mahal were able to emerge from their gilded cages to become leaders of the masses almost overnight.

According to various stories emanating from the harem, the women there lived a life of great splendour, but underneath all that lay deep insecurities and many unspoken grievances. The ageing and debauched nawabs prided themselves on having a full harem, but were hardly in a position to satisfy the normal sexual needs of all their wives, especially those that were brought in very young. The favoured ones threw their weight around while the less fortunate ones lived in fear and frustration. Both Rani Lakshmibai and Begum Hazrat Mahal came from ordinary families and represented the mindset of commoners thrown suddenly into royal harems with all their intrigues and bewildering restrictions. As girls, both had suffered discrimination and injustice and were denied the many freedoms their male counterparts never had to fight for. But both were also highly intelligent, energetic, and were happy to get a chance to break out of their restrictive lives and participate in a struggle for freedom for all fellow Indians.

Anyway, to return to the coronation of Prince Birjis Qadr, the begums gathered when they were invited by Raja Nusrat Jung and Mehmood Khan to give their opinion on the matter. They said they feared for their exiled husband's life, should the generals choose to defy the Company yet again by putting the deposed Nawab's infant son on the throne of Awadh.

'Suppose the British decide to avenge our action by killing the Nawab imprisoned in Calcutta's Matia Burz? What happens then?' they asked. Disgusted by the impasse, Raja Nusrat Jung left. But a persistent Mehmood Khan got a willing Begum Hazrat Mahal to send out letters inviting all the nobles to

attend her son's formal coronation on 7 July. The generals
got the Begum to agree to four conditions in exchange for
her elevation as the dowager queen. The first condition was
that the exact designation for the new Nawab was to be left to
the Mughal Emperor Bahadur Shah Zafar of Delhi. It was he,
they felt, who should decide whether Prince Birjis Qadr, upon
coming of age, would be addressed as an independent Nawab
of Awadh or continue as a Nawab wazir like his predecessors.
The second condition, was that the salary of soldiers in the
Nawab's army would be doubled, and the backlog of pending
wages would also be paid by the new government of Birjis Qadr.
The third condition made the generals the final authority in
the appointment of all army officials and also the diwan (prime
minister), and the fourth condition mandated that the council
of generals must be consulted by the Nawab prior to taking any
major decision. After she had agreed to all these conditions,
Begum Hazrat Mahal was appointed the sole guardian of the
young Nawab and was authorized to run the state on his behalf.

On the designated day, General Barkat Ahmed duly crowned
the young prince and a twenty-one gun salute was fired in his
honour, as the generals unsheathed their swords to salute the
new Nawab of Awadh and celebrations followed in the city. The
Begum appointed a few trusted men to her council of ministers.
These included men such as Sharaf-ud-Daula, Raja Balkrishna,
Raja Jaipal Sigh, Mammoo Khan and Hisam-ud-Daula. A
declaration was made, whereby thirteen new battalions for the
army were sought to be created. Another declaration ordered
all the major talukedars, landlords and princes of Awadh to
gather in Lucknow with their personal armies. According to
Syed Kamaluddin, those that turned up included Raja Devi
Baksh Singh of Gonda (with 3,000 men), Anandi and Khushaal,

the landlords from Gosain Gunj (with 4,000 men), Raja
Sudershan Singh of Semrauta, Chandapur (10,000 men) and
Ram Baksh, a well-known landlord of Chandapur (with three
cannons and 2,000 men), Raja Lal Madho Singh of Amethi
(with four cannons and 5,000 men, plus 200 cavalrymen), Rana
Veni Madhav Baksh Singh of Baiswara (with five cannons and
5,000 men), Rana Raghunath Singh of Khajur Gaon (with four
cannons and 2,000 men) , Chaudhary Hashmat Ali of Sandila
(with 4,000 men) and Mir Mansab Ali of Rasoolabad with a
thousand men.

However, it was not as though these men arrived as soon
as they were summoned by the Begum. During my travels
through Awadh, I have learnt of several conferences held by
the Begum personally, in various parts of Awadh. At each of
them, she personally pleaded with the princes and landlords to
help her mount a joint attack against the enemy. Many of the
local rulers, won over by her personal intercession, had signed
various documents confirming their allegiance to the native
government of Prince Birjis Qadr (Sarkar-e-Birjisi). It was, of
course, very unusual for a Begum to abandon purdah and tour
ceaselessly and there were those who fussed about this. When
she was fleeing after the defeat of her armies, Raja Mardan
Singh, the landlord of Bharawan is said to have told her that
he would have given her shelter but for the fact that she was a
busybody and would continue to hop around like a frog. But
I think that is the usual attitude exhibited by people towards
a defeated leader. Had the same Begum emerged victorious, I
am sure Mardan Singh would have been heard loudly praising
the great Begum Hazrat Mahal's (Janab Aliya Begum Hazrat
Mahal's) whirlwind touring capabilities for having saved the
day for Awadh!

The Begum may have perhaps remained aloof from the ghadar, but once her infant son was declared the heir apparent to the throne of Awadh, she became passionately involved with the native cause and remained totally committed to restoring native rule in Awadh. By and large, I have heard the common folk of Awadh refer to her with affection and reverence. The fact that shrewd and forthright men like Rana Veni Madhav, Raja Devi Baksh Singh and Muhammad Nazim Hussein also respected her and fought on her behalf, is additional proof of the Begum's dignity, intelligence and personal integrity.

During my travels, I came across several families and individuals who had the letters that the Begum had sent to local rulers urging their support. I was also told that the rajas of Ruiya, Katiyari and Rajpur had extended a warm welcome to the Begum's emissary and accepted her plea for help. The rajas of Charda and Chahlari were leading her men when the royal native army attacked the British at Beli Garad (the Residency). The rajas of Kalakankar (Hanumant Singh) and Taraul (Babu Gulab Singh) had likewise arrived in Lucknow with their personal armies and helped fight the British forces within the city. There were also some minor rulers like Makhan Singh of Bangarmau, Mir Ghulam Jaffer of Usmanpur, Mir Alam Ali of Sandi Baavan and Bhikham Khan of Salone, all of whom had pledged their support to the Begum when her letters reached them, but didn't participate when the battles were actually fought.

According to *Awadh ke Ghadar ka Itihas*, the total number of soldiers in the employ of various rajas, talukedars and landlords of Awadh who gathered in Lucknow at the behest of the begum, was around 1,50,500. In contrast, the total number of the Company's own soldiers and those of their British supporters was negligible, and yet the natives were defeated. Why? The answer according to Devi Dutt Shukla lies in the typical Indian attitude—aversion to following regular training schedules, lack of strict discipline within the cadres, susceptibility to factional infighting during crucial moments. We have had brave leaders who were let down by their army's indiscipline and internal squabbling among the generals, ever since the ancient days when the brave King Puru lost out to Alexander, despite having a million-strong army. The battle that took place at Beli Garad reflects the same age-old weaknesses within the Begum's forces and our inability to learn from failures made in the past.

Internal squabbles, mutual suspicions and envy had marred relations between the ambitious native generals and other begums from the harem ever since the new chain of command was formed under the Sarkar-e-Birjisi. Among the military commanders, General Barkat Ahmed had become a target for belittling ever since the native side won the battle of Chinhat under his command. Mammu Khan, who had managed to get very close to the begum and had her ear, liked to play the boss. And Maulvi Ahmedullah Shah, considered even more popular and respectable than General Barkat Ahmed, let go of no opportunity to show his clout. These leaders were certainly upright and proud men, ready to die for their country, but at the same time they were all quite unmindful of the need for training their men scientifically and forming a proper joint strategy before going to battle. They raised stirring slogans, but their minds were frequently led astray by petty gossip and old misgivings.

Even before the actual battle at Beli Garad, the native side had been regularly mounting small acts of subversion against the British colony there through men from the Passi tribes who were adept at planting landmines and guerilla tactics. This had weakened the British defence considerably. When the Begum and her generals heard that Major Havelock had been asked to come with his men from Kanpur to defend the endangered British holed up at the Residency, they decided to move quickly and seize control of the area on 10 August before help arrived. But there was utter chaos when General Barkat Ahmed and his forces arrived at the Beli Garad. They found that the infamous ruffians, the tilangas, had moved in, and after surrounding the building, were raising the religious slogans of, 'Bum Bum Mahadev!' Soon, the Muslim leader Maulvi sahib arrived with his men, and summarily ordered the royal armies not to move till he told them to. Since he commanded a lot of respect among the common folk, ordinary soldiers and gunners obeyed him and froze in their tracks. The tilangas in the meantime had reached the walls and tried to bring them down using dynamite, but being rather inept, they messed it up because the fuse they lit refused to ignite. They were left with no option but to dig underneath the walls and enter the premises. Then they headed towards the British treasury building and the church, raising slogans and flourishing firearms. Even before they could accomplish anything, word was sent to the Begum and her trusted advisor Mammu Khan at the palace that the native side was close to victory. Naturally they were very pleased. The next day however, they were equally shocked to learn that the squabbling native side had actually lost 220 men and 150 rebels had been severely wounded.

Meanwhile, the royal harem had also become a hotbed of intrigue. One day, a group of begums called on Begum Hazrat Mahal and gave her a dressing down. They told her that her troops killing the British did not augur well for the life of their beloved husband, the Nawab who was languishing alone in a prison at Matia Burz in Calcutta. They told Hazrat Mahal that Jaan-e-Alam was at the mercy of his British captors, and they could use him as revenge if she continued to subject them to further humiliation in Awadh. They demanded that she immediately abandon all her military plans and call for truce. An angry Begum Hazrat Mahal alleged that they were all saying this because they were jealous that her son Birjis Qadr had been selected as the regent. A loud squabble broke out among the royal women. Since nothing remained secret in the feudal court for long, it was a given that news about these ugly squabbles and allegations would find its way into public domain.

Money worries of the Begum and her generals, and Mammu Khan, the malevolent and corrupt companion

When news of this fracas reached the powerful generals, they apparently remarked that it seemed as if the other begums had sympathies for the enemy, and for the sake of safety, they should immediately be thrown out of the palace.

Meanwhile, financial concerns had been mounting ever since the coronation of Prince Birjis Qadr in July 1857. The tilangas were looting citizens and the public was getting restless. One day, the Begum sent the prince out on horseback to try and talk to the tilangas and to get them to behave themselves. It is said that they gave their prince a thirty-three-gun salute and heard him out patiently. Once he was done speaking, they told him that they were hungry, and would stop looting if they were given a firm assurance that their daily needs would be met by the government. The Begum, by now, was fast running out of the 24,000 rupees which was all the cash she had. Her treasurer, Muftah-ud-Daula was asked to produce more cash, but he said the royal treasuries had none. All he had were royal ornaments and vessels made of gold and silver. The generals asked him for the keys, so that the bullion could be sold or melted and turned into coins. According to Syed Kamaluddin, the house of a rich noble Nawab Mashuq Mahal was raided for cash after Mammu Khan lured his men into giving him information about a secret cache by promising them a seven per cent commission on the total amount they recovered. The secret treasure was dug out and yielded five lakh rupees in cash. Only part of it is said to have reached the government, the rest found its way into Mammu Khan's personal lockers. Syed Kamaluddin also claimed that by this time, Mammu Khan had also been secretly running a protectionist racket from the palaces. He would give cover to the dreaded tilangas for loot and pillage, and extract a certain amount as his commission in exchange. Protected by him, the tilangas became so daring, that they began to loot homes of various eminent aristocrats like Nawab Mumtaj-ud-Daula and Nawab Afsar Bahu. The begums kept complaining to him, but Mammu Khan turned a deaf ear to their consistent appeals.

Mammu was an important figure in this intrigue-ridden period in Lucknow. The British writers documenting this era have alluded to an illicit relationship between him and Begum Hazrat Mahal. Sheikh Tasadduk Hussein, an eminent historian of Awadh has also hinted at it, but most members of old families in Lucknow deny the possibility. According to them, the Begum was without fault and was being unjustly maligned by various quarters by the spread of all kinds of false tales, as punishment for leading the fight against the British and their native supporters. Raja Raza Hussein, a descendant of the famous Raja Nabi Baksh of Bhatwamau got very excited when I asked him about the Begum's relationship with Mammu Khan. He felt that it was sheer misfortune for the royals that most of the records those years were unavailable. As a result, people with mischief in their hearts had passed along all kinds of vicious lies. His own grandfather, Nabi Baksh Khan and his two brothers, Tajammul Hussein Khan and Kazim Hussein Khan, had participated in the ghadar against the British. He had overheard family elders stating that a lot of ugly tales had been deliberately spread about Mammu Khan by jealous courtiers because he was close to the Begum sahiba.

But I still have my doubts about Mammu Khan being a noble man. The reason why he was important to the Begum may have been because he was a trustworthy link between her and the all-male world of her generals. Another reason may have been that Mammu Khan was able to generate the necessary funds for keeping the fight against the enemy going. After the ghadar, the British lodged cases against both Raja Jay Lal and Mammu Khan, and those papers are still available. They reveal Mammu Khan to be a somewhat shady man who was neither well-educated nor propelled by a sound common sense or a grand vision of any sort.

But for the stories of the brave young Hazrat Mahal's tenacity of purpose in the face of the most adverse circumstances, one could perhaps write off the entire rebel attack on the Residency as an embarrassing farce. The native side, with its funds almost gone, intense internal rivalries between the army generals, and the endemic problems between Shias and Sunnis, were saddled with lax administrative machinery that was weighed down by the atmosphere of fear generated by political uncertainties.

It was going through the motions of a war towards the end, only to sustain its honour. One must give credit to the begum though, for not hiding behind old and trusted nobles like Mammu Khan, Maulvi Sahib, the various army commanders and district officials. Sir William Russell notes in his well-known diary that Begum Hazrat Mahal had incited all of Awadh to protect the interests of her infant son and all the leaders swore allegiance to the young prince. She boldly sought and won the unwavering loyalty of both Muslim and Hindu rulers when she set out on a whirlwind tour of the entire principality of Awadh. She addressed dozens of public rallies and made personal pleas for help to all major princes. It was because of this that Hindu Kshatriya rulers like Rana Veni Madhav, the head of the Baiswar community, Hardutt Singh, the leader of the highly respected Raikwars, Raja Devi Baksh Singh of Gonda and the Rajas of Gaur Kanpuria and Janawar, all stood by her through the struggle. Several of them accompanied her all the way to Nepal even after the native forces were defeated, and several of them died in exile.

Given the volatile times and the regressive social mores all young women were subjected to, the forging of a unified front by the begum was no mean feat. I do not believe that the arrogant feudal males supported Begum Hazrat Mahal merely because they pitied a lonely young mother fighting for her son's rights. Somewhere within them, they must also have felt a strong urge to protect their turf, their self-respect and the interests of their people that were being increasingly threatened by the expansive designs of the British. The Begum was young and from a questionable background. Any slip on her part, any act that could be construed as silly, would have invited sharp reactions and adverse comments immediately. The fact that this did not happen, further proves that just like Rani Lakshmibai, the Begum too was too committed to the greater cause, to spend her time in audacious displays of feminine guile.

As Wajid Ali Shah's young wife, Hazrat Mahal may not have had the courage to step out in public, but being the regent's mother Begum alia gave her the right and the authority to come out of the harem and solicit help for her son despite the fact that she could not have been more than twenty-six or twenty-seven years old. Having shed the purdah, Begum Hazrat Mahal also tried to create special female battalions that, according to Surendra Nath Sen, fought so fiercely—almost like wild cats—that the fact that they were women could be established only after they were killed. One of these women is said to have climbed up a peepul tree and shot many British soldiers from her perch until she was shot dead. Another old woman beggar who was often seen gathering rags under the iron bridge was found dead, killed while making an abortive attempt to blow up some underground tunnel.

All through the months of July, August and half of September 1857, the Begum managed to keep up the morale of her forces and also round up vital resources for a prolonged battle. Then in mid-September word arrived that two British commanders, Havelock and Outram were seen coming towards Lucknow with additional forces. To incite the panicky citizens against the enemy, pamphlets were distributed by the royal sympathizers. They said that in case the British won, they would forcibly convert all the citizens to Christianity, and that they'd already done unspeakable things to natives in cities like Meerut, Delhi and Kanpur. The tilangas now dug themselves in to defend the city. But they remained resentful of the Birjisi government for not being paid for their efforts.

It was pouring when the British troops arrived, but the native forces, infected by the tilangas' rancour, appeared listless. Mammu Khan and General Hisam-ud-Daula rode among them in a horse-drawn buggy and made efforts to cheer them up, but they were forced to run back when the enraged tilangas let loose a volley of foul words at them. The aristocracy was more proactive. Raja Raza Hussein of Bhatwamau had told me that when British forces entered the city, his grandfather and his two granduncles had just sat down for a meal. His grandmother rushed in, and said that she had heard that the city was under siege and asked them leave their meal and go defend the city first. 'What are you waiting for? Do you want the firangees to pull you out by your hair?' she screamed.

The three brothers stood up and left immediately. Unlike the tilangas, they had refused monetary help offered to them by the government of Birjis Qadr. Raja Man Singh of Ayodhya also joined them with 9,000 men and together, they all fought bravely in the name of the Begum. As the Alam Bagh park filled up with men, the Begum made a personal appearance to encourage her forces. Later, one of the other begums, Sarfaraz Begum wrote petulantly to another co-wife in Calcutta:

'Oh sister! Who would have thought earlier that this young woman (Hazrat Mahal) riding an elephant to cheer her forces in battle, would turn out to be such a bag of tricks (*aafat ki parkaala*)?'

But whatever gossip may say, this spunky young woman who, without any training, funds or even backing from her own family, led a whole army of feudal lords and their semi-trained men against a vast colonial power, has earned my respect, thanks to her courage and sheer tenacity of purpose.

Some untold tales of Hindu-Muslim camaraderie, individual
bravery and selfless service

I heard several other tales of individual bravery and easy camaraderie between the Hindus and Muslims who fought against the British during the ghadar. At the battle near the dome of Ghulam Hussein Khan's palace, the noble Nabi Baksh and two of his brothers, who had been sent by their mother before they could sit down to a meal, were severely wounded. Nabi Baksh died fighting along with his Hindu friend, Thakur Amar Singh. When the bodies of her three sons were brought into the house, one dead and two severely injured, the mother reportedly exclaimed, 'I thank Allah for protecting the honour of our family. Those that I fed with my breasts have died fighting for their motherland. I shall make no motherly claims on these martyrs.'

Another poet friend, Chandra Prakash, told me how his mother's grandfather and two of his cousins Madhav Singh and Kalika Singh, personal bodyguards to Prince Birjis Qadr, carried the Begum and her son out of Lucknow to safety. They had to force their way through slippery mounds of bodies and firing from all sides, he said. When they arrived safely in Nepal with their charges, the Begum burst into tears and told the loyal brothers:

'We now face a life of terrible uncertainties. You may go back now and may god be with you.'

Chandra Prakash also said that the brothers always remained loyal to their patroness and thereafter took care to attend every major function dressed in the uniforms provided by their erstwhile employer.

The Begum and the rebel leaders, when they escaped to Nepal, were accompanied by a fairly large group of their loyal soldiers. Many of them were carrying the much-reviled British Enfield rifles and the cartridges allegedly laced with cow fat and lard. How could they, I wondered.

A historian friend of mine, Dr Satyanarayan Dubey of Agra College said that the Hindu dharmshastras state that embattled men are to follow the Apad Dharma (dharma in a state of emergency). This, he told me, was the special religious provision that had helped his Brahmin ancestors and also the upper-caste Hindu soldiers in the British forces (who were in a majority) sustain themselves during prolonged battles. They continued to observe the usual food taboos and carried home-cooked meals in saddlebags, but when they needed to shoot the enemy, they would open the suspect cartridges as required, by using their teeth. Obviously both the Enfield-carrying Begum's guards and the rebellious ancestors of my friend believed that saving their side was their prime duty and resorted automatically to the by-laws provided conveniently under the doctrine of Apad Dharma.

Ali Naqui Khan a.k.a Nakki Nawab

Perhaps in the course of time, historians will confirm the real route through which Begum Hazrat Mahal and her son had escaped to Nepal. From the various tales we heard, it seems possible that when Lucknow fell, the last battle was fought under the leadership of Maulvi Ahmedullah Shah. The begums may have fled the besieged city of Lucknow two days earlier, but Hazrat Mahal was not one of them. The story about the badshah giving away his kingdoms to the British at the behest of his father-in-law Ali Naqui Khan is proof of this. Ali Naqui was the father of Khas Mahal (the chief begum, not Hazrat Mahal). One of Wajid Ali Shah's long autobiographical poems *Husn-e-Akhtar* describes at some length what actually transpired between him and the British.

> *Stop the reasoning, my tongue, and begin to speak*
> *Of the sad tale of this Wajid Ali, the son of Amjad Ali.*
> *It was the tenth year of his rule when the terse letter came*
> *Friend! Give up this kingdom now, were the governor general's orders!*
> *The six crores who live in Awadh, theirs was the badshahi, theirs the power*
> *But their Shah-e-Awadh was being declared an unwanted presence,*
> *Thus end ten years of my rule.*
> *That man, one Lord Dalhousie by name, writes to us in his letter,*
> *The people are deeply displeased with you and you have a bad name*
> *We cannot have that, so you must be a king only in name*
> *who shall be sent*
> *A sum of one lakh rupees every month, without fail.*
> *The letter of the governor general when handed me by resident general*
> *Made hell break loose within the palace, the day turned into night,*
> *But the British battalion of soldiers rode in, enormous like a sea wave.*
> *Ali Naqui Khan, my vizier, alone was privy to my grief.*
> *So this was the way things were destined to end, thought I, why be sad?*
> *Put your stamp on the agreement, I say, the kingdom is lost for no reason!*
> *I, the Nawab warily signed the papers divesting me of the kingdom.*

Such unquestioning acceptance of his supreme humiliation shows Wajid Ali Shah as a man whose calm, I fear, springs not from a reasonable and philosophical attitude, but an extreme cowardice. From what one gathers during one's readings about the last ruler of Awadh, Wajid Ali Shah was a simple, generous and easy-going man. As a young nawab, he had even shown some interest in sprucing up his armies and administrative machinery, but he was unable to summon any courage and challenge the gradual tightening of the British Resident's grasp over his kingdom. Finally, things reached a point where he had delegated all the administrative decision making to the British and receded into living a life of song, dance and womanizing within his palace. Divested of state administration and the strict discipline and sense of duty it imposes, the Nawab's life was soon enveloped in every kind of perversion. His chief begum (the daughter of his vizier Ali Naqui Khan) was a sophisticated and well-brought-up lady of noble lineage. But it was his youngest begum, Hazrat Mahal, who was a late entrant to his harem as a dancing girl and was soon enacting the role of a young fairy in his favourite musicals, who was to become his best-loved wife, as she bore him a son, Birjis Qadr. In contrast to the chief queen, Hazrat Mahal came from an unknown and impoverished background. She had been sold while she was very young, to the debauched and ageing Nawab's harem by Amman and Amaman, two notorious procuresses of Lucknow, who had bought her from her parents in exchange for hard cash. The role of this young khawasan-turned-queen—who refused to accept her infant son being denied the throne and turned into the commander-in-chief of the rebel armies to fulfil her ambitions for her son—deserves careful and closer scrutiny.

What a pity that we Indians have no formal written record of that historical uprising dating back to 1857. None of the available Urdu books like *Kaiser-ul-Tawarikh* or *Savanhat-e-Salateen-e-Awadh* or *Tareekh-e-Awadh* present the ghadar as experienced by the ordinary Indian of the time. I have heard the elders say that the people feared British reprisals and so even families that had had a history of participation in the uprising, were reluctant to write anything down. The ghadar tales have all come down to us through word-of-mouth, and have undergone many changes over the years. We were told that many people burnt the papers they had in their possession, and that many others were washed away in a particularly heavy monsoon of 1915.

Arrival of the Begum at Nepal Border, protected by her band
of loyal men carrying the hated Enfield rifles and the polluting
cartridges and then suddenly, an amazing about turn

On her way to Nepal, Begum Hazrat Mahal passed through Achava Garhi in Tulsipur and thereafter to the Baradari of Asaf-ud-Daula located close to the border of Nepal. But even before she arrived there, on 27 February 1859, Captain Niranjan Manjhi came to the Baradari, carrying a letter from the ruler of Nepal addressed to Hazrat Mahal. The letter said that she should not expect immediate help from him. Under the circumstances it would be more prudent for her to first apologize to the British and restore broken ties with them.

Mammu Khan wrote back to the Rana saying that they neither wanted his help, nor were they willing to make friends with the firangees. The Rana replied saying, in that case, the British would attack them from India and he, from his kingdom. He also severed their food supplies at the same time, thus underscoring the threat. Begum Hazrat Mahal now acted with caution and prudence. She went to meet the Rana in her palanquin, unaccompanied by her men, carrying a cache of priceless crown jewels. Those she presented to Rana Jang Bahadur along with a written statement from her on behalf of her son, stating that he had been forced to lay claim to the throne of Awadh by the rebel leaders and that mother and son remained loyal to the British.

The Begum was then granted entry along with her son and courtiers and began to live in a small cottage in Kathmandu as a state guest. The British sent word to her that if she returned to Lucknow, she would be given a handsome pension and her privileges and palaces would also be restored to her and her son. But the cautious Begum turned down these offers and chose instead, to stay in Nepal, living on a small monthly pension of 500 rupees per month from the Rana of Nepal. My younger brother later made a copy of the faded photograph of an ageing Hazrat Mahal that I had. In it she looks pensive and her face bears a resigned air. This was the mother that in 1869 got her son Birjis Qadr married to Mukhtar-un-Nissa, the daughter of another royal, Shahzada Mirza Daud Beg of Delhi, who was also living in political exile in Nepal. The princess, after her marriage, was renamed Mahtab Ara Begum, and her grandson, Mirza Kaukab Qadr of Lucknow had told me that after the wedding, the young couple paid a secret visit to Calcutta to visit Birjis Qadr's father—very ill at that time—to get his blessings.

In 1874, this amazing woman who left an indelible imprint upon the history of the ghadar, breathed her last and was buried quietly within the premises of a mosque in Kathmandu.

Prince Birjis Qadr, his murder by his own and the sad fate
of the last Nawab's children

Prince Birjis Qadr went on to sire eight children: Agha Jani, Hashmat Ara, Shitwat Ara, Badr-e-Qadr, Jamal Ara, Khurshid

Qadr, Husn Ara and Meher Qadr. His father, Nawab Wajid
Ali Shah died in Calcutta in 1887. With his passing away, a
colourful chapter in the history of Awadh came to a close. He
was a man with an artistic bent of mind who loved music and
theatre. He wrote several musicals and acted in them with
young dancers from his harem. He did not involve himself
much with politicking, and if the British had not been so
keen to amalgamate his kingdom, may even have grown into
a compassionate ruler and a great patron of the performing
arts. Like Baba Gangadhar, the king of Jhansi, he became an
eccentric and an aesthete when he found that the wily British
had restricted his activities and controlled the revenues of
Awadh completely. He abhorred violence of any sort and was
at heart, a completely guileless and transparent man till the end.

After his family grew in numbers in Nepal, Prince Birjis
Qadr badly wanted to return to his land. He was fed up with his
strained circumstances and increasing alienation in the country.
So in 1893, he decided to go on a pilgrimage to Mecca and sent
a request to the British government in Calcutta through his
wife Mahtab Ara Begum for permission to travel through India
en route to the holy city. After he learnt that the government
of Queen Victoria was willing to let bygones be bygones and
consider his request favourably, he arrived with three of his
children: eighteen-year-old Princess Jamal Ara, fourteen-year-old
son Khursheed Qadr and twelve-year-old daughter Husn Ara.
His wife was then expecting their fourth child.

The Nawab and his family were housed in the government
guest house at Sadar Street in Calcutta. He then began working
on the issue of his succession with the government. At this
point, he was invited by his cousin Sir Mirza Jehan Qadr, to
move in with his family in Matiya Burz, which he finally did.
It was a foolish move. On 13 August 1893, Nawab Birjis Qadr

was invited to a family dinner that he attended with his son Khurshid Qadr and his eldest daughter Jamal Ara Begum. Soon after partaking of the meal, they all died, possibly poisoned. The wife Begum Mahtab Ara and the younger daughter Husn Ara, who had not attended the feast, survived. The hosts did send them a platter, but being pregnant, the Begum refused to eat the heavily spiced meal and so did her daughter. They were the only survivors.

On 27 September 1893, a few months after the sudden demise of Birjis Qadr, a son was born to Begum Mahtab Ara. He was named Mirza Meher Qadr and he continued the royal line of Awadh. Husn Ara Begum died in 1949. Meher Qadr is alive, but paralyzed. He has three sons: Anjum Qadr Roshan Ali Mirza, Kaukab Qadr Sajjad Ali Mirza and Naiyer Qadr Wasif Ali Mirza. All that is left of Begum Hazrat Mahal is a copy of the holy Quran Sharief that she read for long hours as she aged in exile, some royal seals and few other tidbits.

The aftermath of the ghadar when hell broke loose and the fearful people of Awadh learnt to swallow their words, or simply lost their mind like the old man that lived near the Kali temple

'Chop the heads of these insubordinate rebels! Kick them, shoot them and rob them of whatever cash they have!'

These commands were issued by British officials frequently all over Awadh after the thrashing of the rebel armies and their return to power in Awadh. Many rebel leaders including the Begum of Awadh had managed to escape to Nepal, leaving the city and the villages to the mercy of the firangees raring to avenge the deaths of their men and women at the hands of the natives.

According to Pandit Devi Dutt Shukla, as horrific reports of mass slaughter began to pour in from each corner of the state, there was great panic among the citizens of Lucknow. Many people packed up whatever they could carry with them and went into hiding with their families. Thereafter, thieves and robbers had a field day, looting their unprotected homes. The only safe place in the capital was the Saadatgunj Naal Darwaza in the Chowk area, where the moneylenders always had protection of armed guards. Those who were fortunate enough to have found some shelter there, escaped being beaten up and robbed by bands of firangees, Sikhs and Nepalese soldiers of the British army, all of whom poured into the city and began an orgy of pillage, loot and rape. The unprotected citizens went through hell.

My grandmother, who belonged to Allahabad also corroborated this with similar stories from her own town. When we were children, there was an old woman who lived next to our house. She used to tell us that the victorious firangee troops would enter the town on horseback and from several directions, firing their guns in the air. While the city was under siege and rebels were being smoked out, curfew permits used to be issued to allow ordinary people to move within the city. These were issued from three points—Lala Chaturamal Seth's Haveli in Sondhi Tola, Rai Bishabhar Kakaji's Haveli that faced the smaller temple of goddess Kali, and Shah-ji's Kothi in Mirza Mandi. The late Sri Gaurinath-ji, a retired honorary magistrate who was a friend of my grandfather's, used to recount a heartbreaking story about an old man who lived near the Kali temple. As the rampaging firangees stormed into his house, his wife and daughter killed themselves by jumping into the well within their family compound. No sooner had the son shot his young wife (so she would not face humiliation), than the soldiers arrived. The father and son were tied to a pole and the soldiers shot them both. The son died on the spot, but somehow the badly wounded father survived. His body did heal later, but he never quite recovered from the emotional trauma of the incident. He would emerge exactly at seven every morning from his house, or whatever was left of it after the soldiers had ransacked it, after smoking his daily chillum of tobacco. Then he would set off to buy a new chillum for one paisa. He never used the same chillum twice. The distance to the tobacco shop was not much, but it took the feeble old man several hours to get there and return. He was constantly accosted by his neighbours as he moved. The elders would greet him politely, with affection, and he would mumble something in return. But the children in the lane were merciless. They would provoke him by asking him, why had he not visited Chowk for so long? Didn't he want to go there that day? At the very mention of the word 'Chowk', the old man would chase his interlocutors, waving his stick and cursing the firangees with the choicest words of abuse. After he died, each room—even the terrace within his house—was apparently found littered with clay chillums and hookahs.

The avenging firangees did not spare anyone. Rumour had it that they had even defiled several hundred veiled women from local families who had taken shelter in the dargah of Hazrat Abbas, the famous Sufi saint. Later, one of the officials interceded on their behalf and all of them were given a rupee and sent home in covered palanquins. Hundreds of washer men had also been hiding at the dargah. They and their bags of laundry were stripped. Even the properties of the dargah, including a solid gold alam, a mace weighing almost thirty kilos was stolen. Later, the local goldsmiths bought it piecemeal from the firangees, many of whom made a lot of money by selling their loot. It was said that they used it to buy properties and pay off family debts in England.

Of the loyalists of Begum Hazrat Mahal, the lot of Sharaf-ud-Daula Ibrahim Khan was rather sad. He suffered with her while the battles were fought and had even given her shelter, briefly. But he refused to flee with her and her men to Nepal, saying that he had switched sides, and was now loyal to the British. He was quickly declared a turncoat by the tilangas, who had a sharp memory, and killed as a punishment for his duplicity. Mammu Khan, said to be very close to Hazrat Mahal, also met a tragic end. He was betrayed and taken back to Awadh in captivity from Nepal. A long trial followed. He presented a bunch of letters from the British trying to establish that he was instrumental in saving many British officials captured by natives during the battle at Kaiserbagh, and stated that he deserved to be released on compassionate grounds. His reasoning fell on deaf ears and he was finally sentenced to death by hanging. He went on to appeal and managed to get the sentence reduced to life imprisonment at the Andamans, where he opened a shop and later, breathed his last. Raja Jay Lal Nusrat Jung—known popularly as Raja Jaya Lal—who had been given a position of authority in the government of Birjis Qadr, was also tried and sentenced to death. He was hanged on charges of killing a British official of the East India Company on 1 October 1858, at the same spot where he had killed the official a year earlier, on 24 September in 1857. Legend has it that the raja remained proud and unafraid till the end, and at the gallows, he smilingly put the noose around his neck with his own hands.

The questions yet to be answered

I am sure there are many other stories, which, if they were to surface, could provide answers to several questions the hitherto recorded history raises. For one, why did the begum, so brave and defiant otherwise, buckle down in Nepal and give the Rana a written note saying that she and her son were forced to lead the revolt against the British? Having once sent a defiant reply to Queen Victoria's appeal from Lucknow, how could she change her stance so completely after reaching Nepal? Was it because her maternal instincts to protect her son had weakened her resolve? Or had she received some secret message from her husband about not endangering his life, since he was still being held captive by the British at Matia Burz? Was there a plot to regroup the rebels and mount an attack on Calcutta from Nepal to free the Nawab? Or was it because the Rana was facing an increasingly rebellious army of his own and did not wish to increase his trouble since he already had a defiant Begum's presence in Kathmandu at that point?

Another question that bothers me is this: could a perceived threat to their religious beliefs have been the sole reason for Hindus and Muslims in the army rising simultaneously in revolt against the British?

After all, as they fled, the Begum's men were also carrying the controversial Enfield rifles and their questionable cartridges, which they also used to attack the British during the ghadar in Lucknow, quoting Apad Dharma as an excuse.

If there is one silver lining to this cloud of otherwise unrelieved gloom, it is that the uprising of 1857 for once forced the Indians to emerge out of their age-old distinctions of caste and creed and accept their traditional strengths and weaknesses.

The frank self-analysis this generated among Indians, helped sensitize them to the void that exists, for creating strong communal bonds and shared cultural values across religion and caste. This alone is the cement, they realized, that can hold this colourful, diverse, quarrelsome but warm and humane nation together, despite all odds, and hopefully, will go on to create a unique republic someday.

I bow my head to this noble vision.

EPILOGUE

Some excerpts from, Begamat-e-Awadh Ke Khatut *(Letters from the Begums of Awadh), compiled by Intezam Ullah Shahabi*

Here are a few excerpts from letters written by Nawab Wajid Ali Shah and his wives that reveal the history of Lucknow during the tumultuous ghadar years.

To bring them the latest news about the world outside the palace, the large network of trusted servants and maids the palace employed, doubled up as a veritable news agency for the begums who lived seclusive lives within the walls of the royal harem. Thanks to this, some of the dates and sequence of events may appear flawed. But laced with poetry, they still remain a precious source of information about another, largely unreported history of Lucknow during the ghadar as it unfurled. They allow us a rare peek into the mind of the exiled Nawab Wajid Ali Shah and his begums, their bittersweet relations with each other, their romantic yearnings and deceptions, and the envy that existed between the various wives.

A letter from Begum Khas Mahal to Shaida Begum, dated 29th day
of Ramadan, Hijri year 1271

My melodious bird, you are the voice of a flower garden, my loving nightingale, my bringer of good tidings about blossoms in the garden, may your laudable aims prosper and bloom.

In these rotten times bearing neither blossoms nor fruit
Like little green shoots are we, trampled upon as soon as we emerge.

Dear sister Shaida Begum,

As long as I live, I will never forget the dark day when Sultan-e-Alam was ordered by General Outram to leave the kingdom handed down to him by his father and forefathers. We departed from Lucknow as a nightingale from its garden, as Joseph from Egypt, and as fragrance from a fresh blossom. What memories we carry!

The wordless grief of our darling husband Jan-e-Alam and his staff, who stood helplessly watching their king leave, with a dignified silence mopping up their pearly tears in handkerchiefs.... The women who brought up the rear of the long, sad procession that followed Jan-e-Alam into exile, were crying so hard that they developed hiccups.

'During the ten years of my rule, if anything I said or did caused you unhappiness, please forgive me for that. As I am taken away from your midst forcibly, I am truly repentant. God knows if we will ever meet again in this life.'

You would remember, my sister, how these last words of our beloved Jan-e-Alam reduced us all to tears.

You'd also recall how when the loyal Hazrat Munavvar-ud-Daula Ahmed Ali Khan said (to Wajid Ali Shah), 'Sir, please do not push away one who has always been a servant at your feet.' Jan-e-Alam remained silent. The queen mother, the queen, Malka Kishwar Ara Begum and (the Nawab's younger) brother (Mirza) General Sikandar Hashmat Sarmahoo and that piece of his liver, the light of his father's eyes, the Prince Regent Wali Ahad Bahadur Sarmahu left the palaces in sorrowful silence followed by us.

We wept all the way, and by the time we arrived at Kanpur, we were nearly spent. We halted at the bungalow of Palvan sahib for the remaining eight days of the month of Rajab. On the first day of the month of Shaban, we left and arrived at Benaras. The raja, true to his nature, welcomed us as his own. He and his family took good care of us, especially the queens who waited on our Begum sahiba hand and foot throughout our stay. Even a relatively unimportant personage like me was well looked after.

I spent most of my time trying to cheer up Jan-e-Alam by talking to him about this and that, but he remained morose. Ah, how it hurt to see him thus! At Benaras, we climbed into a fireboat and left for Calcutta by river. We were all exhausted by the time we arrived at Calcutta on the 27th day of Ramadan.

That's all I can describe in brief, about our journey. Please write back how you all fared after our departure.

A letter from Jan-e-Jan Begum to Sarfaraz Begum, dated 16th day of Shavval, Hijri year 1272

> *The city holds no charm for the heart*
> *The barren lands are unknown*
> *Oh my madness, on what rocks*
> *Should I bang this head of mine?*

Our fates have led us into days that are darker than the darkest night. Our hearts feel as though pierced by your wet eyelids. Our own eyes remain bloodshot.

So now we write to you about how we fare.

A 110 men were recruited to travel to England with Janab-e-Aliya, the dowager queen (Janab-e-Aliya Taj Ara Begum). Maulvi Muhammad Masih-ud-Din was appointed her legal counsel, with Mir Muhammad Rafi as his assistant. Haji Al Harmain, Sheikh Muhammad Ali Wayaz and General Wazaris-ud-Daula were to mentor the Prince Regent Mirza Wali Ahad, who was given 10,000 rupees for incidental expenses. For the grand Queen of England, the following gifts were carried—a gold necklace weighing three seer, another necklace studded with rubies (yakut), a hair-comb studded with diamonds and emeralds (zamurrad), several chips of diamonds (almas), many rings, and a beautifully handcrafted dress that cost 32,000 rupees to create. A necklace made of gold coins was also sent for her eldest daughter-in-law, along with a formal letter of agreement (Mukhtarnama) done in brocade and embroidered with gold threads and gemstones.

As they left, they carried five rukkas. On the 14th day in the month of Shavval of the Hijri year 1272, the delegation led by the queen mother departed for England by boat at midnight. She was given a tearful send-off by her dear ones amidst a cacophony of words of counsel and religious slogans. The ship left the port at dawn. As it passed close to the Matia Burz kothi, Jan-e-Alam came out in the balcony and the prince regent and his mentor, the general, saluted the badshah from the ship who returned the gesture by wishing them khuda hafiz. We all came inside feeling miserable. I couldn't eat for the next two days despite Jan-e-Alam urging me to. Thus, I have penned down for you whatever has been happening here.

Before we stepped out for a walk in the gardens,
The spring, alas, had departed!

Wajid Ali Shah's letter for Munna Jan, dated 22nd day of Rajab,
Hijri year 1273

'We languish here in Calcutta, surrounded by utter loneliness.'

My dearest, my life, the best sandal-balm for my aches, my hope amidst hopelessness, the abode of romance, the spring in my garden, my Munna Jan...

May you be well and remain close to your Akhtar (the badshah's pen name) in exile. Your letter that I received, courtesy Janab Kanzar-ud-Daula Bahadur, which gave us all the news about our beloved and distanced city, is more precious to me than my life. You described the grief and restlessness of our people. God knows I am even sadder and more shaken than they are. I left my home so they could be safe. What will happen in the future, one must leave to fate.

Nawab Farkhanda Mahal's letter to Jan-e-Alam, Wajid Ali Shah,
the Hijri year of 1273

'If only you'd show us your glorious face
This restless and eager heart would find peace!'

O sun to my garden, the radiance lighting up things from afar, things here are getting more and more strange with each passing day. But a few incidents brought us some cheer. On the eighth of the month, all of a sudden, their soldiers revolted against the British commanders over a matter of some new cartridges that had been distributed recently. Soon, it turned into a major confrontation, and the rebel soldiers who gathered thereafter at Moosabagh, were ready to kill all Christians. One horrific tragedy followed another, despite many sober people urging restraint. Sometime in the evening, these dimwits had finally forced hundreds of Europeans out of the building, and a fearsome massacre took place thereafter. At the time of writing this, some 1500 men have gathered at Aishbagh, and according to information received, they're angry and unruly. According to hearsay, the Ulema are also about to raise the flag of the Prophet in revolt. Let's see where it all ends.

Things seem to be just going out of control and for the Christians, going to Moosabagh is akin to risking their lives. I write these ugly things to inform and warn you, because my dear Jan-e-Alam, we do not know if your men are free any longer to bring you newspapers, or whether they have already been ordered by their supervisors to keep them out of sight. Please write and tell us exactly what is happening at your end. What can we do sitting here, except report to you the sad stories the local newspapers carry each day? This request is also being endorsed by your beloved Nawab Sarfaraz Begum.

Jan-e-Alam's letter to Shaida Begum Sahiba

The thought of death clutches at me
There is no release from this restlessness.

O my blessing of The One above, the sun at its gentlest, the pearl
upon the crown, our only sword
May you be happy always.

We hear from here and there
The times have just gone berserk.

We learnt that groups of rioters have gathered in Awadh and are defying the British government. Please tell those idiots to calm down. Why are they rioting now, after we left the city without raising a fuss? For a few days after arriving here, we were very ill. After we got better, our people celebrated the recovery by organizing a music and dance festival that lasted through the night. They are now busy fulfilling various religious vows they had made during my illness, to help me recover. Meanwhile in the early hours, a great hue and cry arose. I was fast asleep and woke up with a jolt and found that we were surrounded by British troops that had crept up upon us like locusts while we were resting. When asked why there was a commotion outside, I learnt that our man, Ali Naqui Khan had been arrested.

I needed to freshen up first, so I entered the toilet. As I emerged after my bath, the secretary to the governor forced his way into my chambers and asked me to accompany him. I demanded to know why, and to at least let us all know what the fuss was all about. He said that his government harboured certain suspicions. I replied saying that it was ridiculous to harbour suspicions about someone like me who had always avoided conflict of any sort. It was to only avoid unnecessary bloodshed in god's own country that I had quietly let go of my kingdom of Awadh and agreed to be exiled. What trouble could we be expected to create here in Calcutta?

He replied saying that he was aware of some folks from our erstwhile kingdom who wished to create disaffection. I told him that in that case, as the de facto rulers, they were free to take steps to tackle the deemed troublemakers. What was the need for me to accompany them? Wouldn't cordoning my residence and keeping watch through soldiers be sufficient, I asked him.

He said he had told me whatever he had been ordered to say. So I told him that I and my royal retinue were willing to leave with him. But the secretary said only eight of our men would be permitted to accompany me. Finally, uncles Mujahid-ud-Daula, Zihanat-ud-Daula, the secretary sahib and I got into one buggy and arrived at the fort where we have been put under house arrest. With me are Zulfikar-ud-Daula, Fateh-ud-Daula, the treasurer Kazim Ali, the rider escort (sawar) Bakar, Ali Hyder Khan Kool, the chaprasi Sardar Jamaluddin, my hookah carrier Sheikh Aman Ali, my masseur Amir Beg Khawas, the sweeper Wali Muhammad, the gunner Muhammad Sheikh Khan, the palanquin bearers Karim Baksh Sakka and Haji Kadar Baksh, and Imami, who cleaned our carriages. All of them forced their way into the fort where I was confined. Rahat Sultan, the water-carrier, the maid Husseini, who served us betel leaves, and Muhammadi Khanam Mughlani also arrived accompanied by my doctor Tabib-ud-Daula, who had come along with the others to have a look at the place. He flew into a panic and said, 'May Khuda relieve us from fresh troubles as soon as possible!' They tried to remind him of his loyalty to someone who had taken care of him for twenty years, but he just ran away!

I send you this letter by hand with the brother of Rahat
Sultan, the water-carrier.

The face of the one who has taken ill in your absence,
Is become such, that anyone who unveils it, covers it immediately!

Shaida Begum's letter for Jan-e-Alam, dated 26th day of Jamad Ur
Akhir, Hijri year 1273

O compassionate lover of your subjects, may Allah's shadow
be upon you. I just received your eagerly awaited letter of the
17th. As soon as I got it, I touched it to my eyes and my heart
leapt up! A seer read it out to us. The grief of separation and the
sorrow of hearing your words read out aloud brought a flood of
tears to our eyes. The master of the universe has played a strange
trick upon us, with you lying there and us pining for you here.
May Allah waive away these problems soon, and show us your
lovely face and soothe our hearts. Once the cause of the pain
is gone, our hearts will find peace once again.

Rakiya Bano has a bad cold.

Shaida Begum's letter for Janab Jan-e-Alam

The sorrows of these days of separation
Have lent strange colours to the heart,
How the heart is behaving now
Cannot be put into words

Why should one live thus, waiting for you, writhing in
constant pain?
But die one cannot, even if one wants to, living a life
turned to dust.

Life is a long tale of woe. There is no one to share one's sorrows with either. We are fed up with life and do not wish to continue thus. The heart aches and the sighs are deep and icy. The chest is heavy with sorrow, the skin dry, and fear has us in its grip all the time. I have come to hate the world.

If only when in love, one had two hearts
One to keep, and the other, to lose to love.

Darling Jan-e-Alam, ever since you departed from Lucknow, we have forgotten to dream. Weeping is the only way to spend time. Our days and nights are spent mourning your absence, but there are some of my fellow wives who look happy and prance about joyfully. Ever since you've gone, poison is being spread against the firangees, and all kinds of strange things are being heard. The heart is always aflutter with fear, not knowing what other calamities fate may have in store for us. The maulvis have gathered in the Ghas Mandi area, they say. We hear that a Sufi saint, Ahmedullah Shah has come to Lucknow from Agra. He is said to be a prince of Chinateen and is believed to have thousands of followers. He goes out in a palanquin preceded by drummers that keep up a steady beat. The most fearsome gossip is doing the rounds. Sultan-e-Alam, to cheer us, please write to us about yourself, and pacify our fluttering heart.

Jan-e-Alam's letter to Shaida Begum, dated 10th day of Rajab, Hijri year 1273

Life of my life, the empress of beauty, Nawab Shaida Begum Sahiba,

On the 9th day of Rajab, Anjam-ud-Daula Bahadur handed two of your letters to us. I felt better immediately and my heart began beating with new zeal. But my dearest, we are no longer what we once were. I write to you about myself to let you know what has been happening to us here.

Love and romance are all but gone. And sorrow nibbles our insides day and night. We are under house arrest at Fort Williams. The governor wrote to me, saying that we shall treat you on par with our own officials, but my life has become a burden to me now. After eight days we were shifted to a bungalow within the fort's premises. Now I have a staff of only twenty-three. Even a bird may not visit us here within the fort. The gates have been closed shut, and we feel suffocated. Mujahidu-ud-Daula Mirza Zainul Abedin, Diyanat Daula, Muttdin-ul-Mulk Muhammad Motimid Ali Khan–all our trusted generals who used to be with us all the time, circling us like devoted moths, ready to sacrifice their lives for us, are now no more. Of the remaining few, Mohtamim-ud-Daula and Zulfikar-ud-Daula Syed Muhammad Sajjad Ali Khan were initially involved in all our joys and sorrows but have slowly drifted away, tired of the problems and the tedium of a jail. First, Diyanat-ud-Daula asked the council for permission to go on a pilgrimage and as soon as he got it, he left the fort. Then Mohtamim Daula began to act like a violent and abusive lunatic and got himself thrown out. Muhammad Sher Khan, the gunner, chopped off Bakar Ali's nose and was arrested and sent to jail. Karim Baksh Sikka went down with tuberculosis. And after facing all this, I am fully fed up with my life.

Wajid Ali Shah's letter to some nameless begum

The sky had never made us laugh so hard
That it should now force us to weep in recompense.

I received your loving missive from the hands of Muhammad Jaan, the drummer (chobdar). We are still holed up in Calcutta. The pain of leaving my people, the shock of losing my throne and our beloved city and its gardens, then seeing off my mother and brother and the prince regent to London on the 14th day of Shavval, have bewildered and saddened me and left me feeling so utterly lonely. I am now left with only Begum Nawab Khas Mahal and four other begums to keep me company. Ali Naqui Khan and Nawab Munavvar-ud-Daula have just joined us. Be courageous and trust Khuda, who watches over everyone's welfare. He will certainly find a way of rescuing us all. My blessings to Rakia Bano.

The Unlucky 'Akhtar'

Shaida Begum's letter to Jan-e-Alam, 10th day of Ramzan,
Hijri year 1273

O Shah of Shahs, the bouquet of beauty and charisma,
    We were always infatuated by you. And may Prophet Ali's benign gaze always protect you. The pain you're going through is

killing us slowly. We continue to shed tears and heave sorrowful sighs. A mighty fear, a deep passion is ripping our hearts and roasting our insides all the time. We are left with no dreams in our eyes, or patience within the heart!

The fire of separation has devastated us so much so
That we are but a mote of dust in the eyes of the world now.

So strange have we become that sometimes we are deeply depressed, and then we begin to laugh. Sometimes we are so frightened that we begin tearing at our dress.

Who should we tell about this restless heart?
Who could be witness to this our tearful gaze?

Jan-e-Alam,

Ever since we heard you have been taken prisoner at the fort, we have been so worried that we're no longer able to sleep or dream, and that's a pity because we could have at least seen you in our dreams.

The world will never maintain its ways for long
This we have learnt from our experience.

Meanwhile at our end, there is a new development every day. Hazrat Mahal, that darling of yours, has joined the rebel forces and become their leader. She is under the spell of Nawab Muhammad Ali and showing muscle. Let's see where all this leads ultimately! Those who feel their power is on the upswing, rejoice.

Letter from Farkhanda Mahal to Jan-e-Alam, dated 10th day of
Ramzan, Hijri year 1273

Earlier blood oozed out of eyes through dark tears
Today pieces of the heart roll out with our sighs.

O my mirror image, one who's ever caring one of his people, one that knows the seas of longing...

We received your affectionate letter carrying the message of your love and learnt of Begum Khas Mahal leaving. Your efforts at holding her hand and trying to reason with her seem to have gone in vain. She was not so disloyal, and loved you deeply. Why then has she turned away and left you for no reason? There must be some provocation from somewhere that urged her to return. When you wrote 'Shame on the folks of Hindustan!' you were referring to the kind of people and cities emerging in the once glorious Hind! Let us tell you that good, god-fearing people still exist in the city of Lucknow and among the clergy. It is true, there are indeed some bad eggs and fools, but as a wise man once said, no woman is just a woman, nor a man just a man–after all, even Khuda has made all five fingers of different length. At this point, I conclude my letter with a quote from another wise man, Sheikh Saadi:

'An intelligent man will spot even a gnat, but there are some that will not notice a cow standing at the door.'

Sarfaraz Begum's letter to Begum Jan-e-Jan

I am Majnu's heart separated from his beloved Laila
I wander lonely in dark forests, unseen by eyes.

My balm for the suffering, may you always be happy and content. After Sultan-e-Alam's departure, Lucknow has gone from bad to worse. Each day, new troubles arise. It is as though the folks here have gone mad. Day and night, all kinds of stories do the rounds, scaring us out of our wits. God knows what else is going to fall over our heads from the skies in the days to come! The tilangas are creating havoc within the city. It was only after Maulvi Ahmedullah Shah arrived here from Faizabad and created police posts that the looting was halted somewhat. Many supporters of the rebels are with him. On the other hand are the supporters of Jan-e-Alam who wish that the throne of Awadh should not lie vacant for too long. Mirzadar-us-Sitwat's name was proposed as successor to the exiled Nawab, but after three nights, he refused saying that if even Nawab Shuja-ud-Daula could not get the better of the firangees, how could he? Raja Jawahar Singh and Nawab Dershan Singh then arrived at the consultation chambers of Nawab Khas Mahal Begum and proposed the name of her son Mirza Nausherwan-e-Qadr for the throne. But Shamsherullah, the daroga turned it down saying that though the young man was perfectly suited for incumbency, he could not be put on the throne without permission from the badshah (Wajid Ali Shah) and Khas Mahal Begum (who was in Calcutta with the Nawab). Mehmood Khan (Mammu Khan) and Sheikh Ahmed Husein then proposed the name of the young prince Mirza Birjis Qadr to the two generals, Raja Man Singh and Raja Jawahar Singh. They said the name was acceptable to the council of army generals but it should also be acceptable to the begums in the palace. Mehmood Khan then called Pir Wajid Ali and the begums, some of whom felt that to put another person on the throne while Jan-e-Alam was still alive, did not augur well. To this, Sarfaraz Begum countered by saying that after all, the person proposed was the legitimate son of the badshah, and by filling the vacant throne, he was actually paving the path for his father to return at a later date and resume his powers. Hazrat Mahal joined her palms together and said, 'He is your son as well. So please decide as you see fit.' Nawab Khurd Mahal then raised another objection by saying that if the begums were to sign for the accession of Prince Mirza Birjis Qadr to the throne of Awadh, the British may construe it as an insult, and consider killing Jan-e-Alam who lay within their clutches. Raja Man Singh and Jawahar Singh then left without any decision coming forth. But Mammu Khan's feet were itching for action on-ground. He made Begum Hazrat Mahal send letters to the army generals immediately. It was the 12th day of Zeekat of the Hijri year 1273 and it was pouring outside.

The raja arrived, followed by all the top officials of the army and sat down in the meeting room. Mirza Birjis Qadr rode in with great aplomb, all dressed for the occasion in an ornate buggy with Mirza Ramzan Ali Khan accompanying him, and the whole procession entered the formal sitting chambers Jannat Araamgaah and sat down. Someone whispered, exclaiming that the prince was too young. Another capped it by saying that he had been leading a protected life and may go astray if given all the powers (of a Nawab). At long last, Sahabuddin and Syed Barkat Ahmed, the leader of the 15th battalion got up and placed the crown on the head of Mirza Birjis Qadr. Everyone burst into applause and congratulations began doing the rounds. The officials unsheathed their swords and saluted the new Nawab and at Faizabad topkhana, the chief gunner Jehangir Baksh gave a twenty-one gun salute to the new Nawab.

It was a very hot day when Mirza Birjis Qadr stepped inside the palace. Ghamandi Singh, a district official (subedar) kept his customary negative chatter on. The name of Nawab Hissam-ud-Daula was proposed as the new prime minister, but he was unwilling. Shahanshah Mahal asked Muftah-ud-Daula, but he also refused. Then Nawab Sharaf-ud-Daula Muhammed Ibrahim was sent for. At this point, Mammu Khan lost his temper. Finally, a compromise was reached and peace re-established. Eleven gold coins were put upon the Janab-e-Aaliya (Birjis Qadr)'s palms as Nazr-e-Akeedat. Then Nawab Hism-ud-Daula got up and collected them and gave them to the queen mother (Hazrat Mahal). He was praised for this by Nawab Syed Barkat Ahmed Qasim Jaan.

The next day, the new Nawab made various appointments to his court. The title of 'diwan' was given to Maharaja Balkrishna, followed by police chief Mirza Ali Raza Beg and Meer Yavar Husein Muhtamim Aravind. The title of 'general' was conferred upon Hisam-ud-Din Bahadur. After this, all of them presented Mirza Birjis Qadr, his mother Hazrat Mahal and the chief of protocol (Shahanshah Mahal) with suitable gifts. Mammu Khan, officiating as the daroga for Diwan-e-Khas, left with Ali Mohammad Khan Bahadur. The post of chief law officer (Munshi Kachahri Khas) was given to Amir Hyder, while that of the chief police officer, in charge of the palace (Daroga Dyodhiyat), was handed over to Meer Wajid Ali, and the chief information officer (Akhbar-e-Mulki)'s job was given to Muhammad Hasan Khan, son-in-law to Nawab Sharaf-ud-Daula. General Hisam-ud-Daula was asked to take charge of the 13th battalion and start recruiting new men. He began the battle against the British and wasted no time in attacking the Beli Garad (the Residency) where the British had collected. The forces of Maulvi Ahmedullah Shah had pushed their way right up to the outer walls of Beli Garad, but had to pull back as he received no support. He returned badly wounded.

I have left the palace and am staying with friends within the city. Please do whatever it takes to have this letter sent to Jan-e-Alam. He is at present under house arrest in the Fort (William). His letter reached me with great difficulty.

Yasmin Mahal's letter to Jan-e-Alam

How should I write, oh statue of heartlessness
No day went by without me shedding tears for you.

Jan-e-Alam, it has been a whole year since you began rewarding all your favoured ones with your missives, but this unfortunate one did not receive as much as a scrap of paper from you to please her. Day and night, I am consumed by the fires of worry for you, and even as I die, you appear to remain indifferent to me.

My body is as though filled with fire
And my fluttering heart is a ball of mercury.

It is now just me and my broken heart and sighs that escape the chest ceaselessly. I go see Prince Birjis Qadr to console myself and feel soothed by the sight of this young boy who is as fair as his father. May god bless Hazrat Mahal's womb. The prince loves me and even I adore him. You must have heard that yesterday he celebrated his eleventh birthday and is now sitting on the throne. All the folks here dote on him. During the festivities for his birthday, a courtesan read out a poem praising him. I still remember a couplet:

Birjis Qadr puts the sun to shame.
A priceless jewel is our Birjis Qadr.

May god save the darling boy from the evil eye, and he that casts it, may his face be blackened! It is as though autumn is over and spring is here once again and the nightingales are singing happily in the gardens. But we, dear Jan-e-Alam, remain inconsolable. Please bless us with news about yourself whenever convenient, so we may emerge out of this bleak state of grief.

We, the living dead, try to soothe the ailing heart and enjoy the kiss of death. But then, we begin to die for you over and over again.

Jan-e-Alam's letter in the name of his fifth wife, Sarfaraz Mahal

Who is there that does not feel sorry for me?
But see how strong is my resolve I will not utter an uff!

What shall I write about? My heart is more and more restless. Some 500 of our people had accompanied me (from Lucknow to Calcutta). Of the women, the prince regent's mother, Malka-e-Khas Mahal, the mother of my general, Janab Tajunnisa Begum and our third begum, Mehbooba Khas are sick. I hope god helps them get well soon! The fourth, Kaiser Begum was neither willing nor unwilling (to relocate), but had, it seems, accompanied me for the sake of friendship. She asked me for some money and as soon as I handed her eleven thousand rupees, she left Calcutta. Once, my fifth wife, Jafri Begum: flirtatious, mercurial, playful, combative, quick to take offence, sharp-tongued and never lacking a colourful turn of phrase, sent me rolled betel leaves frequently at Fort William. But that is in the past. I have been pining for her for several months, but there's been no word from her. This was a woman who would not leave my side even for a minute. Without her, my heart withered like a blossom denied of water.

Our only two companions are fear and loneliness. We languish behind a very tight security cover comprising of twelve of our loyal men. Each of them is dejected and hopeless. Even when the waterman (bhishti) and the sweeper (khakru) arrive, they are accompanied by a firangee supervisor. They do not dare to open their mouths in his presence. The house we are in is comfortable enough but I have no use for such grandeur. Even fresh air, it seems, will not make itself available to the prisoners. The doors are always locked and the sultry heat bothers us greatly. When the doors are thrown open, intense heat rushes in and makes us even more uncomfortable. We have sent several letters of complaint to the governor general, but they remain unanswered. Be grateful to god that you are free. You sleep your own sleep and no one bothers you. Shaida Begum had sent a letter. We do not know if she did receive our reply though.

> *I am a nightingale deprived of both spring and autumn*
> *I belong neither to the skies nor to the cage.*
> *They have clipped his wings and tricked 'Akhtar' into imprisonment*
> *Is such treatment meted out to the hunted anywhere?*

Sarfaraz Begum's letter to Akhtar Mahal

My queen Alam Rafiq-e-Sultan-e-Alam,
I am sending you news about the sad state of Lucknow for Jan-e-Alam's information. The state of affairs here is so bad that I find it hard to put it down. This does not augur well. Recently, news came in that there was to be an army attack on the Beli Garad the next day. Apparently the native army was planning to slaughter all the sahibs and level their Residency after reducing it to rubble. When they heard this, women within the harem got together and sat worrying. Some said that when they kill the sahibs there, their mentors in Calcutta might take revenge on our Jan-e-Alam whom they have held captive there. Another said that even you and I will not survive. These firangees are like the wild grasses: the more you trim them, the faster they grow. Finally, all the begums like Nawab Fakhr-e-Mahal, Nawab Suleiman Mahal, Nawab Shikva Mahal, Nawab Farkhanda Mahal, Yasmin Mahal, Mehboob Mahal and many others went up to Hazrat Mahal and said, 'We wish you well and we congratulate you now that your son is the new badshah of Awadh. But we feel orphaned. We hear that the army is planning to attack, and we wish you to speak up for justice and tell them that if they do this, our Jan-e-Alam's life will be endangered. We'd rather that you burnt such an idea in the kitchen fire.'

The queen told the visiting begums coldly that she was convinced they did not wish well for her and were envious of the pre-eminence she now acquired as Birjis Qadr's mother. Thereafter, she picked up her son and went inside her room.

This incident somehow got leaked out to the army officials. Some of them came to Hazrat Mahal and told her that they felt the begums (opposing the attack against the firangees) had got mixed up with the enemy and therefore must be asked to leave the royal palace. The begum, however, counselled patience.

The next day, the native armies rode into town, pillaging and looting. Birjis Qadr rode on horseback and congratulated the tilangas for their bravery and appealed to them against harming the citizens and generating ill will. Their leaders stood with their palms folded, and assured him that they would not loot the city again. Thereafter a messenger was sent to Delhi to get Bahadur Shah Zafar's formal acceptance of Birjis Qadr's crowning. I never realized that Begum Hazrat Mahal would turn out to be such a bag of tricks! She rode an elephant and herself led the tilangas to battle against the British. She lost her shame and she was not at all contrite.

So there was this major meet at Alambagh at which Hazrat Mahal also met Maulvi Ahmedullah Shah. The native side faced the battleground bravely, but fate was not in their favour. On 22 December 1857, 40,000 soldiers of the British army were led into a battle against the Begum's men by General Outram and General Havelock. Rain was pouring down when the British began shelling aggressively. The tilangas were driven back and Mammu Khan and Ashraf-ud-Daula moved to Charbagh and set up post there. Raja Man Singh fought on bravely against the enemy with his 9,000 men and created mayhem. In the evening, the Begum had rich words of praise for Raja Man Singh. She rewarded him for his exemplary bravery by honouring him with the title of Farzand, and presenting him with a special stole, a shawl and a kerchief. But alas, despite Ahmed Raza fighting bravely, and a stalwart like Nana (Peshwa Bajirao's adopted son) coming to help her from Kanpur, just as a close relative General Bakht Khan Ruhela and the Mughal prince Feroz Shah came from Delhi, nothing could ward off their ultimate defeat. The British really knocked out the tilangas.

As shells began exploding at palaces in Kaiser Bagh, the begums ran out in panic. May even one's enemies not be forced to see such a day! Without slippers on their feet or a scarf over their heads, the dazed begums ran here and there, tripping and falling over their elaborate harem pants and trailing scarves. Around their slender waists, many had tied up boxes used for stacking betel leaves, which they had filled with their precious jewels. The respected mother (Janab-e-Aliya Hazrat Mahal) came out looking bewildered and surrounded by a circle of servants and her officials, made her way out of the palace through the gate that opens towards Ghasiyari Mandi. She was walking dressed in white, and an attendant next to her carried the Prince Birjis Qadr rolled up in a white protective sheet. Whoever saw this sad regal procession pass through the lanes, could not help beating their breasts and weeping loudly. This was the time of revolution!

The Begum somehow made her way through numerous lanes, went past the grave of Pir Jalil, and finally arrived at the house of Jawahar Ali Khan at Pul Maulvi Gunj. From there she left in a palanquin to Sharf-ud-Daula's. She spent the night at Shah-ji's. General Outram sent her word requesting her to stay in her own house comfortably and assured her that his forces would throw out the rebels and protect her. But Hazrat Mahal faced her dark hours with fortitude. On the 29th day of Rajab, she got into her palanquin with her son and left Lucknow with Mammu Khan riding on a horse by her side. They left through the entry point at Alam Bagh. On the way, Raja Mardan Singh, a landlord, was deferential and Maulvi Amanuddin alias Maulvi Mohammad Nazim of Biswan crossed a distance of three kos to greet and welcome her. He brought her to Mirza Banda Ali Beg's Imambara, with drummers and flag-bearers leading the procession. On the way, 2,000 rupees were distributed among the indigent on behalf of the begum and cannons were fired as she entered the city. Soon after, consultations were held and it was decided that they should go to Bareilly. So this procession left. My young maid Yasmeen, who had accompanied the entourage till now, returned thereafter. She is the one who gave me all these details that I am passing on to you for Jan-e-Alam's information. I hear the firangees are going to face the Maulvi Ahmedullah Shah now. Let's see what happens then. I am leaving for my niece's house in Khairabad. I am sending this letter through a man from Yuta-ud-daula's who is running off to Calcutta. Let's see if this letter gets to its destination or not.

Shaida Begum's letter for Jan-e-Alam, while travelling in the Hijri year 1274

May god make no-one witness the terrible incidents and problems that began to surface a year after your departure. Hazrat Mahal showed exemplary bravery and replied in kind to the enemy. She turned out to be a determined fighter who brought luster to her Sultan-e-Alam's name. One whose wife faces men with such daring must be a rare man himself. Nawab Sarfaraz Mahal has already sent you all details which one cannot contradict. Dear Jan–e-Alam, these firangees have shelled our Hazratbagh mercilessly. When shells began flying, I too fled from the palaces with all the other women. Most of our stuff got left behind and whatever little we could carry out, was stolen from us in the ensuing melee as we fled the burning palaces. Now things are such that if we cannot raise a loan somehow, we would have to go hungry. Let's see what else kismet has in store for us! In god's name, please send for us somehow or else we will make an effort to reach you on our own. How long can we bear these shocks?

Dear Jan-e-Alam, I am also taking care of my aged parents who have neither a pension nor a stipend available to them.

Hoor Begum's letter to Jan-e-Alam, dated the second of Zikad, Hijri year 1273

We are in bad shape—almost dead and exhausted. After I left the palaces with the princess, I faced a lot of problems on the way to Saadatgunj. After a lot of searching, we managed to locate an empty house and stayed there for two days. On the third day I felt threatened and left. Since then, I have been spending my days wandering from here to there and have lost all will to survive. On the road most of the time, I eat when I can manage a meal, or else I just go hungry. When I finally arrived at my natal home in Maali Khan Ki Saray, our daughter, princess Rahim Ara Begum fell sick, causing me further worry. How can I describe my great sorrow when she finally passed away during the month of Ramzan? As god is my witness, I have become part of the living dead since she passed away. Even now, each time I remember her face, my chest feels it will burst with grief. Aye Jan-e-Alam! God bears witness to my sorry state. I have nothing left, neither food to eat, nor a house to live in. Hour after hour, I carry my burden of grief, and no one cares. In these days of utter misery, everyone has turned away from us.

*Nawab Fakhra Mahal's letter to Jan-e-Alam, Ramzan,
Hijri year 1274*

Each house lies deserted. The natives are on a rampage. The
firangees are beaten back. But let's see what the next two or
three days bring...

Letter from Jan-e-Alam to Nawab Nishat Mahal Sahiba

The indifference of the firangees beats all assumptions. Real
news about us is infinitely worse than the details that may have
reached the members of the family.

Mehrunnisa Khanam's letter to Jan-e-Alam

Khuda's wrath visited the city of Lucknow and we all suffered,
and how! The shelling emptied out all dwellings, and everyone
looked dazed. We controlled ourselves with some effort and
left our homes and set out for the great unknown. I arrived at
Kanpur in a daze. Total strangers took pity on me and graciously
allowed me enough room to sit down. As I recounted my tale, I
noticed that everyone was moved to tears. When they realized
that I was one of the lesser co-wives of the ruler of Awadh, they
showed me great deference and love.

DRAMATIS PERSONAE

The Cast and Geographic Backdrop in
Ghadar Ke Phool

The clans, nobles, native generals and British officials

Awadh

This was the largest and wealthiest of the sovereign entities of
the British empire in 1857. In the first half of the eighteenth
century, the Mughal emperor appointed a Persian noble, Syed
Saadat Khan of Khorasan, as the nazim (governor) of this
province. As measured during Akbar's reign, the (Akbari Ilaka)
area measured 24,000 sq. miles and ranged from the Himalayan
region in the north to Allahabad in the south, and Gorakhpur
in the east to Kannauj in the west. It then had five districts:
Lucknow, Faizabad, Khiri, Bahraich and Gorakhpur. In 1857,
the number of districts had grown almost threefold and part
of the eastern region (Tulsipur Dang) was by then a part of the
territory of Nepal.

Most of the population (around one million at the time of the ghadar) lived off the land cultivated under the zamindari system by tenant farmers and landless labourers. The province had about 70,000 villages and only eighteen towns.

In 1858, the area was expanded, reorganized and named 'The United States of Agra and Awadh'. In 1902, it was renamed The United Provinces. Since Independence, it is called Uttar Pradesh.

Titles of the Royalty in Awadh

The original title given to the rulers of Awadh (by the Delhi rulers whose vassals they were), was that of vizier (minister). Until 1817, the rulers in theory at least, were not monarchs but nazim (governor). Nawab was a title given to Muhammad Ali Shah by the emperor at Delhi, and although it was equivalent of a viceroy, it had no claim to sovereignty. After the decline of Delhi's authority, the British recognized the last Mughal only as an emperor of Delhi. They also let it be known that they considered the Nawab Vizier of Awadh as the King of Awadh, entitled to a twenty-one gun salute. The Nawab thereafter assumed the title of Badshah (king). However, letters reveal that at Birjis Qadr's coronation, Delhi's nod, although sought, was not received, and the emperor continued to address him as 'prince' in his letters.

Nawab Wajid Ali Shah

Tenth in line of the original nazim of Awadh, Sadat Ali Khan, he was born on 30 July 1822, and bypassed his elder brother to be crowned as Abdul Mansur Nasiruddin, Badshah-e-Adil,

Kaiser-e-Zaman, Angasha Sultan-e-Alam, Muhammad Wajid Ali Shah, the fifth king and the tenth and the last nawab of Awadh in 1847. He was dethroned on orders from Governor General Lord Canning in 1856, on charges of misgovernance, and exiled to Garden Reach bungalow in the Matia Burz area in Calcutta. Although he left without protest, he did petition against the charges levelled at him through a case filed in London, citing his loyalty to the Queen. The case got nowhere and he finally accepted a small pension and died in 1887, having fathered twenty-five sons and forty-five daughters.

Wajid Ali Shah's father, Amjad Ali Shah, was an austere and deeply religious man. Although he placed his son and heir under the apprenticeship of learned and pious men, the young Wajid was naturally inclined towards the arts—music in particular—and preferred the company of courtesans, poets and dancers. By the time he ascended the throne of Awadh, he was an accomplished but somewhat frivolous dilettante. According to Abdul Halim Sharar's *Guzishta Lucknow*, initially, the badshah showed an interest in raising an army and therefore created several new battalions. But his interest remained focused primarily on giving them poetic names like Banka (the crooked one), Tirchha (the tilted one) and Ghanghor (the thunderous one); or framing poetic terminologies for military commands in Persian such as: 'Raast Rau' (straight ahead!), 'Pas Bayan' (turn around!) 'Dastar Chap Bagurad' (turn to your left!). A small female army (Janaani Fauj) was also raised where beauty was an essential criterion for acceptance.

Wajid Ali Shah was deeply interested in folk theatre and music. He loved the traditional rahas (musicals) of Hindus with fun-loving gods like Krishna and his consorts frolicking upon the stage. He composed several musicals (like *Kissa Kanhaiya aur Radha Ka*) and also acted in them, donning the roles of Hindu gods Krishna and Indra. He revived Kathak dancing and several other crafts, including the culinary ones. Even during his exile, he introduced the eastern city of Calcutta to the fine art of Lucknavi dining and classical dance and music.

Nawab Begum Hazrat Mahal

Born in 1820 in Faizabad, died in 1879 in Nepal. Her maiden name was Muhammadi Khanum. Her parents of whom not much is known are said to have sold her as an infant to two procuresses. She was introduced in Wajid Ali Shah's harem, first as a khawasan and was soon promoted to the rank of a pari (fairy), thence to a begum as the Nawab's concubine, and finally after the birth of her son Birjis Qadr, was made a junior wife and awarded the title of Hazrat Mahal.

Birjis Qadr

Son of Wajid Ali Shah and Begum Hazrat Mahal, born in 1845 in the Nagina Wali Baradari at Kaiserbagh, the rebel forces crowned him as the Nawab in 1858 with the title of Sikandarjah, Iqbal Shah Muhammad Naiyyaruddin Khallallullah Mulak Hu. It remains debatable whether the badshah at Delhi recognized his rising to the Masnad as badshah of Awadh. Even after he requested this recognition, the emperor continued to address the twelve-year-old as Mirza Birjis Qadr Bahadur.

He received the royal pardon at the time of Queen Victoria's jubilee in 1862 and came to Calcutta with his wife (related by birth to the Mughal emperor Bahadur Shah Zafar) and children.

By now, his father had died and the elder brother Qamar Qadr was receiving the largest pension among the late Nawab's sons. Birjis Qadr represented his case as the erstwhile crowned Nawab and asked for two-thirds of his late father's pension. This caused much heartburn within the large family. He was invited by one of his numerous family members for dinner and was poisoned. He was thus killed allegedly by his own family members in 1893, and he died along with his daughter, leaving behind a pregnant wife and son.

The Queen Mother

Janab-i-Aliya Malika Kishwar, wife of the late Nawab Sadat Ali Khan and mother of Nawab Wajid Ali Shah boarded the ship S.S. Bengal to London in 1856 as the leader of a diplomatic delegation seeking to reverse the annexation of Awadh. She had a large entourage of over 140 people that included, among others, the heir-apparent Muhammad Hamid Ali Mirza Bahadur, her younger son, General Mirza Sikandar Hashmat Bahadur, nine daughters, twenty-one female servants, seven eunuchs, her personal interpreter, the Englishman Captain Rose Brandon, the plenipotentiary to Nawab Wajid Ali Shah, Maulvi Muhammad Museehuddin Khan Bahadur, and numerous aides and courtiers.

When she arrived in London, an interview was arranged with Queen Victoria who received the dowager queen and the two princes with courtesy. However, in the summer of 1857, when the revolt broke out in India, Begum Hazrat Mahal joined the rebel groups. This disturbed the equations. A petition presented in August 1857 was turned down by the House of Lords. The royal house presented a memorial promising continued loyalty to the Queen. Justice was not granted due to 'the deplorable incidents' in India, and the mission failed. Back at Matia Burz, a cabal of ministers led by vizier Nawab Naqui Ali Khan (a.k.a. Nakki Nawab), managed to convince the Nawab that if he withdrew the case he had filed for the restoration of his kingdom in London courts, and accepted the pension proffered instead, he would be able to live comfortably. The British accepted his receipt of this pension with alacrity, and the case, filed in the courts of London, stood annulled. The shock was too much for the dowager queen who left England and died in Paris on the way to Mecca, followed soon by her doting son Mirza Sikandar Hashmat. Both were interred near a mosque in Paris in the Muslim graveyard.

The Prince Regent

Mirza Muhammad Hamid Ali Mirza Bahadur (1836-1874), son and proclaimed heir to the throne of Awadh. He accompanied his grandmother, the dowager queen to London as a member of the last diplomatic delegation from Awadh in 1856. After his father—contrary to the expectation of the delegates—suddenly chose to accept a truncated and paltry pension from the British in exchange for his kingdom, they left for Mecca. On the way, after the heartbroken dowager queen and her son died one after another and were interred there. The heir apparent, faced with uncertainties in India, finally chose to settle down in Paris.

Nawab Ali Naqui Khan

Wajid Ali Shah is said to have been introduced to this colourful aesthete at the house of a well-known courtesan of Lucknow.

As soon as he ascended to the throne, he appointed Ali Naqui Khan as his prime minister. The famous palaces and gardens at Kaiserbagh, where Wajid Ali Shah lived in a bungalow known as Khas Makam, surrounded by his wives, concubines, musicians and artists, were created under his supervision. Naqui Ali Khan had his offices established within the same area, near the grand gate with mermaids carved on it. His plea was that he must be on call for his boss at all hours. His daughter Akhtar Mahal was married to Wajid Ali Shah and was for long, his favourite wife and mother to the second-in-line, Prince Mirza Khush Bakht Bahadur.

Naqui Ali Khan moved with Wajid Ali Shah to Matia Burz, where out of the four bungalows made available to Wajid Ali Shah, one overlooking the river was given to him for his personal use. After his death, this bungalow continued to be occupied by his daughter Akhtar Mahal.

The Tilangas

These dreaded ruffians derived their name from the Telangana region, from where the British had originally recruited many of their native sepoys in the late eighteenth century. These troopers' sole concern, after gaining a victory for their masters, was to loot and pillage the vanquished region. Pillage was so much a part of the attacks by British-trained native troops that during the ghadar, the name of Madras regiment officer James McNeill and his men had become synonymous with terror. After the fall of Lucknow, the sepoys were joined by the mercenaries, the riff-raff and the cut-throats of the bazaar, and collectively, they were identified as tilangas. They joined in the native attack against the Residency when the native rebels had the upper hand.

Prince Birjis Qadr had to appeal to them to tone down their destruction and vandalism while the British side was on the run.

Matia Burz

After being exiled, Nawab Wajid Ali Shah and his entourage arrived in Calcutta on 13 May 1856. Arrangements had been made for his stay at a house in Matia Burz, also known as Garden Reach, then a suburb of Calcutta. The property belonged to the Maharaja of Burdwan who had leased it at a rental of 500 rupees per month. The nawab spent thirty-two years here. During his stay, Matia Burz became synonymous with hedonistic living and court intrigues.

Raja Razzak Baksh and Raja Naushad Ali of Jehangirabad

They were the rulers of Jehangirabad before and after the ghadar. Razzak Baksh had visited Sir Hope Grant and shown him great courtesy, bowing to him again and again and swearing everlasting loyalty to the British. He said he had come to offer them three cannons to help them crush the rebellion.

But when Sir Grant and two of his battalions reached the gate of his fort, they found it surrounded with a thicket of bamboos and thorny shrubs. Later, the British army hanged the raja and eighty of his men, and threw their dead bodies into the burning forest. By then, the Gurkhas and the Brits had gone on a rampage, looting and raping women from the palace.

It is hard to question the patriotic credentials of Raja Razzak Baksh from whose palaces seditious material was unearthed by Sir Hope's men, material that had almost managed to kill his army. But it is puzzling why the British later chose to anoint Raja Naushad Ali, a member of the same feudal family, as the next ruler of Jehangirabad. This makes Naushad Ali a curious character. According to descendants of Raja Razzak Baksh, when Naushad Ali went to Calcutta with the Nawab, he was actually spying for the British, and once Raja Razzak Baksh was killed, he received the throne of Jehangirabad as a reward for his services.

The new incumbent's original name was Farzand Ali, son-in-law to Nawab Naushad Ali who was pressurized by the palace into marrying his only child, Zaibunnisa, to him. This is also corroborated by *The Golden Book of India* by Sir Roper Lethbridge.

The Residency

The Residency was built initially on the banks of the river Gomti by the then British Resident of Lucknow. Before the ghadar, it had grown into a large imposing building to which successive residents added many wings and gardens. It finally had a guard house (called 'Beli Garad' locally, after its builder), a church, a banquet hall, an office, a large storehouse, stables and several private bungalows for high officials of the East India Company. It was badly ruined during the ghadar and preserved carefully thereafter by the British as a reminder of those terrible days.

Sir Henry Lawrence

Chief Commissioner of Awadh, promoted to the rank of a brigadier general with full military powers, when he arrived in Lucknow on 3 March 1857, just before the ghadar. He succeeded James Outram who returned to Britain on grounds of ill health. He was killed in the shelling of the Machhi Bhawan on 4 July 1857.

Amnesty

The proposal for amnesty was published as part of the general proclamation made in the name of Queen Victoria, at Allahabad on 1 November 1858, after the ghadar had been quelled. As announced by Viceroy Lord Canning, it extended an olive branch to the native aristocracy and promised to respect the rights of all individual princes as 'our own', and also that their lands would henceforth not be confiscated. This was, of course, subject to the fact that there were no charges against the princes and landlords of having murdered British officials during the ghadar.

Translator's Note

A Son Remembers

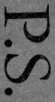

TRANSLATOR'S NOTE

The ghadar of 1857, the first public uprising against British rule, is a microchip embedded in India's collective memory of its struggle for freedom. The principality of Awadh, one of the biggest states in the north, was the mother lode of this revolt. There are good reasons for this. Ever since Lord Wellesley's 1801 treaty with Awadh (Oudh), this large, fertile and rich northern state seemed vastly important to the British, not because of what it was, but for what it offered them in the long run. Within the next fifty years Awadh was to become one of the largest sources of revenue for the East India Company's coffers. From the days of Robert Clive, it had already been a major recruiting centre for native soldiers for the Company's army. These soldiers were mostly from the rural Brahmin and Rajput families of Awadh and their long association with the British had bred a certain sense of resentment among them as they saw the men they had helped elevate from adventurers, begin behaving like demigods and potentates among the natives. When a young brahmin from a large contingent of sepoys serving in the Bengal Army and stationed at Meerut shot dead his British officer, the act triggered off the Mutiny in their camp at Meerut. After he was hanged, the fellow sepoys fanned out all over Awadh, soliciting finances and public support necessary for a major revolt against the British. Soon they found a willing leader in Begum Hazrat Mahal, the ambitious, young and spunky wife of the exiled Nawab of Awadh who was keen to have her infant son declared the regent of Awadh. And once the Begum joined the cause with Bahadur Shah Zafar, the last Mughal emperor in Delhi, the rebels were buoyant. By November 1857, 32,000 men, reportedly contributed by some thirty talukedars of Awadh, had joined the rebel forces in Lucknow.

Public pressure now began mounting on other rural talukedars and major landlords of Awadh to support the rebels, drive out the British and restore native rule. Like the soldiers, the rural public of Awadh too was prepared to sink all their former religious and caste squabbles at this crucial hour. The mutiny that raged in and around the capital of Awadh began to pull at all those that were sitting on the fence, enjoying the ease of a pensioned retirement or protected dependence, and compelled them to conform to noble ancestral traditions that had long been just a memory. The princes and landlords had little choice now but to throw in their lot with the rebels led by Begum Hazrat Mahal. A few secret conclaves of princes were held quickly in remote mud forts where some shrewd plans were finalized to protect the rebel leaders' families by allowing a few chosen rajas and major landlords to remain neutral and offer help and shelter to the beleaguered British officials in rural areas. This would ensure that if and when reprisals came and the properties of the rebel leaders were sought to be confiscated, these deemed loyalists would escape punishment and be suitably rewarded by the grateful British. They in turn, would then go on to care for all the families of the fellow nobles, who had survived the trauma of the mutiny.

A hundred years after the 1857 uprising, when not quibbling over an appropriate label for the ghadar—was it a sepoy mutiny, or India's first war of independence, or a mere upsurge of ire among a few disinherited nobles—the academic discussions centred largely around the role played in it by the nawabs, rajas and the urban nobility. Many of our school books in 1957 talked of a few martyrs, of national pride and dramatic and famous last words. Much more space was devoted to discussing the new British bandobast that followed and modernized India. There was absolutely no mention of how the ordinary people in the countryside may have experienced the uprising and its aftermath, and how it had been described to the generations that followed.

In the late sixties, when this writer was in college, there was little available by way of detailed studies of rural Awadh, its native rebel leaders, and the contribution of hundreds of small cultivators, artisans, priests and even landless labourers towards keeping the fires of the ghadar alive even after the British had recaptured Lucknow and forced the native leaders and their supporters to go on the run. Most available explorations into the whys and wherefores of the ghadar came from the victorious side and were available only in English. Writers like G.B. Mallesan and Col MacKenzie, C. B. (Hon. ADC to the Viceroy) had us chuckling and shaking our heads in disbelief at the sheer ineptitude of the rebel leaders, the decadence of the Awadh Nawab's court and the internecine squabbling among various religious and caste groups among the natives. Since almost nothing was available by way of Indian testimonies in Hindi or its dialects (except for Sepoy Sita Ram's autobiography which largely praised the bravery and generosity of the British army officials and of which only the English translation was available), the heart-rending grief of vernacular Awadh remained outside the pages of accepted history. The parting couplet of the deposed Nawab of Awadh, Wajid Ali Shah:

'Be happy my fellow countrymen,
alas we must leave on a long journey.'

(*Khush raho ahl-e-watan /Hum to safar kartey hain*) or the daring behind the widowed queen of Jhansi's declaration, '*Main apni Jhansi nahin doongi!* (I shall not give up my Jhansi!), sounded mostly melodramatic and colourful in English, almost like popular songs from a Parsi theatre play.

The history of the Awadh countryside hit me like a punch in the face when I chanced upon a copy of *Ghadar Ke Phool.* This slim volume by the eminent Hindi writer Amritlal Nagar was published by the government of Uttar Pradesh, way back in 1957 (and reprinted later by several other private publishers). The year 1957 being the centenary year of the ghadar, the state government of Uttar Pradesh in independent India, began planning several steps for commemorating the mutiny that had first erupted in the state. As his son describes (see *A Son Remembers*), the government's Department of Publicity in Lucknow offered to arrange for free travel and boarding and lodging facilities for Amritlal Nagar to enable him to go around rural Awadh and compile the hitherto unrecorded fund of stories of the uprising from farming families, folk singers and traditional storytellers into a volume. The remuneration offered was very small, but Nagar, an astute storyteller, could see that here was an excellent opportunity to access rare material he had longed to gather for creating a trilogy of novels about Awadh in the nineteenth century.

In May 1957, with a home-made shoulder bag containing a change of clothes, his pouch of tobacco and areca nuts, a couple of notebooks and a sturdy old pen, Nagar set out on an ambitious tour of the area that made up the erstwhile principality of Awadh before it merged into the United Provinces and is now Uttar Pradesh. Through some of the hottest months in the continent, Nagar travelled from village to village, town to town in ramshackle vehicles and with local guides of varying intellectual capacity that the government provided him. He painstakingly gathered reminiscences and popular ballads about the revolt, its celebrated and little known native leaders, its survivors and martyrs, and where and how various battles were fought after the fall of the capital city of Lucknow. He also managed to locate and dredge up a horde of facts that revealed the missing links between events as they unfurled over the vast region for nearly two years. Together, his stories manage to convey even to the lay reader that when the time comes, a major popular revolt long brewing in the air may suddenly make landfall in some remote army cantonment, gather force as it moves from one village to another, ultimately turning into a whirling tornado. Under his persistent questioning, several stories about how this dark column may have taken shape and then swept through Awadh, came pouring out from the mouths of humble farmers, Hindu and Muslim priests, erstwhile princes and major landlords, most of them now living in penury. After the ghadar, considerable properties of most of the major rebels were attacked and many of them were hanged, or captured and died en route, or within the infamous Andaman jail. Many precious old documents, deemed incriminating, were hastily hidden or thrown away, or burnt by families to avoid arrest. But enough was still available to enable a sensitive writer to recreate the dark period as experienced by the ordinary men and women of Awadh. Even ageing courtesans, bedridden octogenarians and nameless singers could recount stories about what remained to them one of the most glorious moments in the history of Awadh, even though for decades they were not allowed to say so.

Since he had to meet a deadline, Nagar-ji kept recording the ghadar stories without spending time organizing them in an orderly manner, or by writing footnotes. He just concentrated on recording the stories and fragments of old ballads as meticulously as possible. He wrote sitting upon string cots placed hastily under trees, in waiting rooms at railway stations, little shops in lanes of old bazaars, visiting feeble centenarians, and engaging caretakers of ruins and old, abandoned villages in animated conversation. He already had a rich fund of stories about Lucknow during the ghadar, gathered from many loquacious neighbours from old families of both Hindus and Muslims who were his neighbours in the historic Chowk area of the old city. By August 1957, Nagar-ji had managed to cover the districts of Barabanki, Bahraich, Balrampur, Faizabad, Gonda, Hardoi, Lakhimpur Kheri, Pratapgarh, Rai Bareilly, Amethi, Sitapur, Faizabad, Sultanpur, and Unnao. Since the monsoon downpour had blocked roads to a couple of villages by this time, he had to be content with people who belonged to the region and were willing to fill a few gaps. He however managed to sneak into Tulsipur Dang area in Nepal, a part of the Awadh principality up to the ghadar and later presented to the King of Nepal as reward for help rendered by his forces in quashing the ghadar.

As his son testifies, each day after he returned to his

lodgings in the evening, Nagar sat down to work from his notes and meticulously record the stories he had heard during the day. These handwritten papers, often written in the light of hurricane lanterns in makeshift guest houses, had to be rushed swiftly to the publishers at the government printing press in Lucknow. The publishers, working on a tight schedule, processed the material as soon as the chapters were received. Nagar-ji appended his own treasured posse of ghadar tales handed to him by his grandmother, old family retainers and numerous Hindu and Muslim friends from Lucknow's old families in the last chapters and the little document was ready, as promised, by September 1957, to be released as desired, during the centenary year. Sadly, the trilogy of novels did not get written.

Like many others in my generation, I had long puzzled over the swiftness with which the anti-British fires of the ghadar spread across Awadh even though the state was riddled with a long history of poor governance and many caste and communal tensions. What passion could have caused the warring factions to unite in both the urban and the rural areas so unhesitatingly? After all, Awadh had been one of the earliest subordinate allies of the British East India Company. And army recruits from Awadh had enjoyed the rare right of accessing their Nawab directly by filing their petitions in the special court of the British Resident in Lucknow. Stories that emerge in *Ghadar Ke Phool*, answer these queries by bringing to light the rebel sepoys' emotive devotion to their native villages, their clans and the local rulers. The book also reveals how the fabled annexation of Awadh, first planned by Lord Dalhousie, and later operationalized by his successor Lord Canning's government, was a sudden, crudely handled affair that showed little regard for the sentiments of natives. Unlike the states of Malabar and Sindh, the annexation process in Awadh was not even handled personally by the governor general.

The Resident, Colonel William Sleeman was asked to operationalize and oversee the entire process initially. This, Lord Dalhousie warned him in a letter, might be somewhat 'anxious work'. But, 'You will laugh,' the governor general's letter to Sleeman goes on with cool effrontery, 'to think of ... bowling about kings and kingdoms as if they were curling stones!' Sleeman was followed by Sir James Outram from Calcutta whose summary dismissal of the Nawab of Awadh was followed by the Summary Settlement (1856-57) of land. Together, both these steps threatened the age-old Mughal patterns of governance, land ownership and assessment of taxes and went on to cause great distress to the farming community that occupied about sixty per cent of the total land mass.

The native sepoys in the British army (who outnumbered the white soldiers nine to one) belonged to the rural peasant stock and were bound by strong ties of namak halali (loyalty for one whose salt one has eaten) to the badshah in Delhi, the Nawab at Lucknow and the local talukedar or raja. Their royals' public humiliation when coupled with the sudden hike in taxes and a loss of their ancestral land seemed to them a direct assault to their own honour. The Resident publicly accused the Nawab's administration of being corrupt and clueless, and asked Wajid Ali Shah to accept the blame even for petty incidents (such as an accidental firing of the musket by a drunk sentry posted at the outer peripheries of the Residency). He ordered the

Nawab to erase the word ghazee (a hereditary title) from his seal, actively encouraged defiant landlords like Hanuwant Singh of Kalakankar in his refusal to pay annual taxes to the native Aumil (revenue collector) from the Nawab's court, and instituted several enquiries against the court nobles and officials, dismissing them merely on the basis of some stray charge from one of his British officials.

The nazim or the collector of revenues had always been a much feared and hated representative of the rulers in Lucknow. But soon after the Nawab's exile to Calcutta (February 1856), the old nazims yielded place to Company's representatives who were even more arrogant, and driven by orders from their British masters to enforce compliance across landlords and princes to the new taxation regime. Even under Muslim rule, old ties between land owners and peasants were respected and a certain leniency was shown during bad years. The Mughals had respected these ties that guaranteed a remarkably harmonious and secular environment in ethnically and culturally diverse village societies throughout Awadh. With the new regime, the talukedars and powerful clans (mostly Rajputs who had long maintained personal empires within the empire in rural Awadh) faced a new system that destroyed their age-old proprietary rights, created new laws and appropriated all agricultural surpluses from their lands.

'We must admit,' says the secret letter from East India House, London to the Governor General (18 April 1958), 'that under these circumstances, the hostilities which have been carried on in Oude, have rather the character of a legitimate war than that of rebellion.'

The bare bones of the story of the great ghadar of 1857 in India are as follows:

+ On 30 January 1856, Major General Outram, the resident chief commissioner for the East India Company stationed at Lucknow, sent for Syed Ali Naqui Khan, prime minister to Nawab Wajid Ali Shah, fifth king and tenth Nawab of Awadh. Upon his arrival at the British government headquarters at the Residency, Khan was given the bad news. He was informed in grim tones by General Outram, that due to the 'prolonged and profound misgovernance' of the province by the Nawab, a non-negotiable decision had been taken by the governor general that he must forthwith proceed to take possession of the kingdom of Awadh. A strong brigade of British troops had been sent for and was crossing the Ganges to march to the capital to prevent any trouble during the takeover.

+ Three days later, on 4 February, General Outram, accompanied by two officials, arrived at the palace of the king at eight in the morning. He now announced formally to His Majesty King Wajid Ali Shah that as per orders from the Governor General Lord Dalhousie, the king must prepare to delegate power. The king, already greatly distressed by what his prime minister had reported to him after his earlier meeting with the resident chief commissioner told General Outram that he planned to challenge the decision which he felt was grossly unfair. He would leave immediately for London and seek justice for his case at the throne and parliament of England.

✦ On February 7, Major General Outram issued a proclamation that put the king and his trusted nobles and ministers under constant surveillance and barred any of them from leaving the city. It was simultaneously announced that Awadh was henceforth to be ruled not by Nawab Wajid Ali Shah, but by the governor general and officials of the East India Company. With this bloodless coup, the British East India Company ended the century-old nawabi rule in Awadh that had begun with the ascension of Sadat Ali Khan and had taken ownership of more than sixty per cent of the total landmass of India that was home to three quarters of India's total population.

The aggrieved king, reduced to being virtually a prisoner in his own palace, decided that a high powered royal delegation led by the queen mother must leave immediately for London to petition the British queen and request restoration of her son's kingdom. This was duly done. Dowager queen Janab-e-Aliya-Taj Ara Begum accompanied by the Prince Regent Mirza Hamid Ali Khan, her younger son General Mirza Sikandar Hashmat, nine daughters, twenty-one female servants, seven eunuchs (including a seven-feet-tall nubian), her personal interpreter, Englishman Capt. John Rose Brandon, Wajid Ali Shah's negotiator Maulvi Masih-ud-Din Khan Bahadur and numerous other aides, set sail for London immediately. She and her entourage may have been saved the humiliation of being banished to Calcutta with the deposed Nawab, but soon after their arrival in London, on 30 May 1857, the mutiny broke out in Awadh (while matters were being debated and after the exiled Nawab meekly signed the agreement for living as a mere pensioner, a few honourable steps to salvage his honour were being considered by the courts).

As news of British casualties began arriving in London, the case was summarily dismissed and a dejected dowager queen and her men decided to return. Unfortunately, she and her brother died on the way and both were interred in Paris.

- ✤ The humiliated Nawab now began life anew in Calcutta with several of his wives, many of his numerous children (twenty-five sons and forty-five daughters), concubines and loyal courtiers.
- ✤ Back in Awadh, the Company sarkar moved swiftly and replaced the old civil administration and army structures with its own. It introduced a bewildering array of foreign laws and several new taxes. Under the new dispensation many landed properties were summarily confiscated or divided, and many high and distinguished nobles who were suspected of having sympathized with the native militants in 1857, were put under surveillance and deprived of their properties. Lawyers of the British government played a major role in these confiscations and the divisions and sub-divisions of old principalities, citing the new laws that none of the affected parties understood fully. The revolt in Awadh as Rudrangshu Mukherji astutely points out in his seminal *Awadh in Revolt 1857-1858*, 'pertained to the people as a whole and was carried out by people...'
- ✤ On the face of it, the ghadar in Awadh followed no predictable pattern as it spread. But events reveal that Lucknow, after the collapse of British authority,

became and remained the fulcrum and the symbol of native authority and honour. As the British forces led by Havelock and Outram managed to beat back the native rebels at Chinhat and reasserted authority in Lucknow, the rebels headed by the deposed ruler's wife Begum Hazrat Mahal and the Prince Regent Birjis Qadr, dispersed into the countryside where the already disgruntled talukedars and peasantry joined the native soldiers. Pitched battles were fought in village after village by rebels who had surprised the British forces by emerging as excellent garrison troops in the hinterland, in mud forts, jungles, ravines and hillocks they knew like the back of their hand. Finally, by 1858, Lord Clyde had managed to quell the revolt in rural Awadh, and the Begum and several of her supporters from the districts and villages departed for Nepal. The British now circulated the famous Awadh Promulgation announcing lavish rewards for loyalty and severe punishments for rebellion. With the fall of the final bastion of the rebels at Baiswada, the revolt had more or less run its course. A period of ruthless reprisals followed. There were mass public hangings and confiscation of rebel properties and several rebel leaders were sent to the infamous Kalapani jail in Port Blair. The loyalists, meanwhile, were richly rewarded.

✦ Finally an 'English peace' was restored. But not before Awadh had established how deep and widespread the popular rejection of an alien order was, to all native Indians.

Nagar-ji has not tried to record the historic sequence of the popular revolt as it unfurled in Awadh. He tries, instead, to jog public memory through stories that have multiple narrators and speak polyphonically. In the process, he brings to the surface acts of collective defiance and individual bravery, tales of loyalty and betrayals, sung and unsung folk heroes and villains and their roles in the complex matrix of the ghadar. It was a time when all native structures were being deliberately discredited and pulled down by an alien power and oral narratives had become the preferred mode for preserving and transmitting the history of the vanquished. Nagar-ji's work highlights the historic processes of dispossession and its backlash, while exploring the popular character of this unique public uprising. It helps us see, much more than any formal academic treatise, how the defeated side perceives victory and loss, and how some, like the nameless fakir at Ramnagar village, simply refused to accept the inevitable and sheath their swords. Loyalty and betrayal are here described against the age-old standards of namak halali (being true to your salt provider) and namak harami (betraying one whose salt you have eaten). Public memory guarantees that namak harams of the ghadar, such as Vizier Naki Miyan, Raja Roshan Ali and Raja Man Singh would always be remembered in rural Awadh as gaddaars. And even after a century, their homes shall be pointed out to the visitors as *gaddaaran ke ghar* (homes of those who betrayed their masters).

In telling these tales, Amritlal Nagar chose to lean on the ancient Indian *vacik parampara* (oral tradition). As the *katha vacak* (teller of tales), he can assume a dual role: one, as teller of the narrative, and two, of a creative writer who can afford to step in occasionally, to insert his own reflections upon the times, and while at it, also insert a few tales of his own. We constantly see the teller and the listeners swapping roles, casually digressing from pure Hindi prose into Awadhi songs. Often they pause together and savour a particularly good joke or shake their heads in awe over some grim curse that had destroyed a whole family or royal line. On occasion, even the certifiably dead may simply refuse to fall down after being decapitated, and return to the battlefield at night, riding their ghostly steed, demanding that a shopkeeper hand them a roll of paan.

Seasoned Indian audiences will not find this format too strange or unsettling. Given their famous argumentative capabilities, they are content with, and even admire stories that recreate a complex world through point and counterpoint. There is trust that all complexities can be handled skilfully by a good storyteller and that as listeners they are free to interrupt and cap an incident with a similar one, or join the narrator in song, clap to keep time, and spontaneously invoke god's name at all particularly moving junctures in the tale. Everyday poetry flows from the mouths of ordinary people: farmers, artisans, barbers, sellers of perfumes, gardeners, erstwhile princes, landlords and priests. Mendu Khan, a local wit, when warned by the police official about his imminent hanging, replies, 'You will see sir, I shall come out of the case as a honey bee from a pot of honey. You will see!'

'Stay for lunch,' a lonely old dowager in her tumbledown rural fortress says coquettishly to the great hero Rana Veni Madhav Baksh Singh, who is about to leave for the battlefield. 'If you do not eat our royal repast, we shall chop off your horses' tails before you leave here.'

'But of course Aji (grandmother),' says the affable Rana and sits down for what is perhaps his last royal meal in a kitchen about to be demolished with shelling from British cannons.

Still smiling, the dowager queen is carried off to safety a little later by two burly soldiers from the Rana's army as the British rush into her fortress, while a little nameless girl gravely predicts to the Rana, 'Do not worry, this battle is not going to be lost.'

Like most regional writers, Amritlal Nagar is a listener of local history as also a witness and storyteller. He can maintain the objectivity of writing in English but lets on that he is too deeply moved by the stories not to take sides. Images of love and longing, death and bereavement, loyalty and betrayal are unfurled in tale after tale without moralizing. Even delightful trivia: an invaluable pearl necklace given to a Kashmiri family in Faizabad gets left behind during the ghadar riots and the young son resorts to fake lunacy to re-enter the town torn apart by riots and manages to retrieve and depart to the forest with the priceless family jewels tucked in his muddied loin cloth, begins to glow and emit a strange light when set against the backdrop of a true public rebellion. The Jekyll and Hyde characters too are viewed sympathetically: Lone Singh, the opportunistic Raja of Mitauli, the sadist Rao Ram Baksh Singh of village Dondiya Kheda and Farzand Ali, son-in-law to Raja Razzak Ali, who ensures his rise like a male model today, using sex, guile and treachery. Then there is the touching tale of conjugal misery from the village of Kathwara, where the ruler's alienated wife ceased to speak to her husband long before her death and willed that she be buried with the family pets but not her husband! A wall was erected between the two graves within the mausoleum and the wife was buried near the graves of Khan Bahadur's favourite dogs, parrots and nightingales.

What stories these graves hide!

The sequence of events and battles varies from village to village. After a hundred years, half a dozen versions of the battles fought at villages Ruia and Semri and Manva Ka Kot are doing the rounds. The exact route taken by Begum Hazrat Mahal's entourage as she came to attend the princes' conclave at Bondi, or later when she and some of her loyal talukedars escaped into Nepal, are also hotly debated. Even the officially announced deaths of venerable heroes such as Nana Saheb of Bithur or Rana Veni Madhav Baksh Singh are laid open to doubt because there are stories from multiple quarters about some mysterious sadhu or fakir suddenly surfacing in a far off place, and villagers swearing upon holy books that they were none other than Nana Saheb or the Rana in disguise.

A frequently asked question was *why* did the Indians massacre so many white men, women and children so ruthlessly during the ghadar? Why indeed. As Inayat Hussein of Sultanpur tells the author: because the whites had killed the natives just as ruthlessly. It's a closed circle of revenge that these stories from rural Awadh unfurl before us. Poor farmers and their families, mercenary soldiers, artisans, courtesans and prostitutes, sick of their exploited lives, wordlessly suffering under both the nawabs and the British chose to go with the native offensive when the opportunity presented itself. As the native side lost, the urge to pillage, loot and burn, to knock down the whole goddamned chess board, no matter how ill-tempered and vulgar, was immense. You cannot win the game, so why not overturn the board, pawns and king and queen and all!

The reorganization of Awadh that followed the suppression of the ghadar is usually seen as another necessary step in the direction of unification and modernization of a backward land divided by its ancient traditions and ethnic strife. But another question several of the stories raise in *Ghadar Ke Phool* has seldom been answered: how did the traditional Indian police and courts locate and implement the British laws in their cultural world? Wars that our ancestors lost or where they survived by lying or betraying their own, do not make for an appropriate subject for discussion in the presence of the younger generation. The terror, the guilt, the shame and vulnerability those memories may trigger off, must not, wisdom goes, be allowed to be passed down generation after generation. Hence the excuses given repeatedly to the writer about how written family records, the letters the rebels wrote to each other and the formal firmans sent by the queen of Awadh while on run, have not survived. Many talk frankly about how the fear of British reprisals loomed long after the ghadar had been quelled and fathers or grandfathers were sent out when eye witnesses in the family talked of the ghadar.

Ghadar Ke Phool also gives graphic details about the post-1857 reprisals visited upon the rebels. Many were hideously tortured and killed by the victorious British forces. Lands of rebel rajas were confiscated and many were executed or exiled to the Andamans. Villagers who were suspected of having helped or harboured the rebel leaders as they fled, were forced to vacate their ancestral villages and their meagre crops were destroyed.

As a writer, Nagar realized just as no political power on earth can stop history mutating into family lore, folk literature too cannot be prevented from choosing and immortalizing certain heroes and villains. Even a hundred years after the ghadar had been brutally suppressed and most records expunged from public arena, stories and ballads about local martyrs, their acts of bravery and betrayal continue to be transmitted through illiterate wandering poets, clerics, priests and of course, mothers and grandmothers. So we come across amazing cameos of little known or unknown men and women that challenge our fixed notions of survival and sacrifice in an age when everything seems to sway and crumble. We meet, many of us for the first time, almost unknown rural rebel leaders: Raja Devi Baksh Singh, Raja Veni Madho, Raja Haridutt, Thakur Balbhadra Singh , the Rani of Tulsipur, ordinary farmers and barbers and potters, courtesans and mercenary sepoys from hundreds of villages like Akauna, Charkhari, Maruadeeh, Rehua, Tifada and Bhinaga and Chinhat.

One of the most interesting features of this remarkable compilation is the key roles repeatedly played by a few spunky women who discarded the veil and led armies of rebels during the ghadar. In the nineteenth century, women's wrath, even that of queens', seemed to have had few acceptable uses. But in *Ghadar Ke Phool*, we repeatedly hear stories that link Lakshmibai, the Rani of Jhansi and her Muslim counterparts, Begum Hazrat Mahal of Awadh and the dowager queen of Awadh, Janab-e-liya Taj Ara Begum, mother of the deposed Nawab Wajid Ali Shah. She chose to sail all the way to London to meet the Queen and ask for a restoration of her son's unjustly confiscated kingdom. In these three mothers we meet women that may have spent their lives within the four walls of some royal harem. But as their ageing or ailing men begin to look for easy compromises or die long and lingering deaths, these women quietly step forward and assume charge. True, most rightful shedding of blood on battlefields is still reserved for men, but as persons in charge of the fate of millions, these mothers have full moral and cultural authority from the natives to lead men into intricate political negotiations and, if need be, into bloody battles.

As an imprisoned Nawab pours his heart out to his estranged wives in verse, fierce tilangas roam the streets, rebels are crushed under road rollers, tied to cannons and blown apart, as landlords lose or gain ancestral lands, fleeing queens bury their jewels in abandoned wells, shelled forts, temples and mosques and mothers send sons to war saying, 'I waive the price of my breast milk,' we realize how, despite the forced pace of his travels and paucity of necessary equipment such as a digital camera or a voice recorder, a good writer can gather hitherto buried stories and gently lend history a minimalist and graceful design that focuses not so much on the flow of events but on how they impacted people and changed lives. War and its companions, heroism and cowardice have haunted India ever since the hordes from the West rode across its borders. What happened to the people of Awadh has also been happening to other people in other countries in our times, and we may be sure will continue to happen.

One begs to answer the question therefore: how and when do the long-vanquished and meek people suddenly stand up to their tormentors, reassert their dignity, never mind the price they must pay? And what is the collective wisdom that makes them accept defeat temporarily only to resurface defiantly almost a century later?

Just as a needle's eye may usher one into heaven, these stories from a hundred terror-mirrored eyes will let the reader directly into the heart of 1857, a year that was great and sick at the same time. A year that, warts and all, was to be the crucible for India's struggle for independence in the twentieth century. That, rather than the ruthless march of an alien super power, is the true take-away from this gentle, loving and sorrowful gathering of the ashes of Awadh's ghadar.

A SON REMEMBERS

Stories about ghadar, the great Indian uprising of 1857, had obsessed my father ever since he was a child. He used to tell us, how, when he was staying with his grandfather at Allahabad, each night they would hear the howling of jackals coming from the park opposite their house. Matadin, their old family retainer, told him that this area used to be a thriving bazaar, but the British butchered many after the ghadar. After the massacre, the whole area was razed and bull dozed and it is believed that the howls they heard, came not from jackals, but the unhappy souls of those that had lived there once upon a time. My father's grandmother also told him many stories about those disturbed times. In my father, grandmother had discovered an avid listener of her stories. Stories such as how her own grandfather had left home after a tiff with his wife during the ghadar, and then her grandmother's father had rushed out to search for his missing son-in-law. Another source of ghadar tales, father said, was an old watchman known as thakur. Apparently, his whose body trembled as he recounted hair-raising stories from the mutiny, and his face would turn red in anger.

In 1944, when father was in Bombay, his friend and admirer, the Marathi writer Sham Rao Nilkanth Oak presented him a copy of *Maaja Pravas* (My Journey) by Vishnu Bhatt Godshe Varsaikar, a travelogue by a Marathi brahmin who had witnessed the ghadar during a visit up north in 1857. Father was so enchanted by that book that he wrote to his closest friend, the Hindi writer, Dr Ramvilas Sharma that he had to translate it into Hindi so that friends like Dr Sharma could also read the rare memoirs of an ordinary traveller. He shared the completed manuscript of the Hindi translation with Dr Sharma who was equally enchanted with the first ever record of the great historic rebellion, even though it was written by a simple Marathi beggar. Five years later, it was published by the great art historian Rai Krishna Das's publishing house as *Mera Pravas*, and then reprinted in 1963 from Lucknow under the title *Aankhon Dekha Ghadar*, and a third edition was later published by New Delhi-based Rajpal and Sons.

In April 1956, my father resigned from his job with All India Radio. He had been somewhat uneasy with the ever-increasing pressures of being a salaried servant of the government. But with the source of a regular income gone, the going got tough for him and his family once again. His most recent novel was very well-received, and boosted by this surge of confidence, by January 1957, father had begun planning a trilogy on the ghadar.

As the idea grew, he realized that one had to do some fieldwork and gather fresh and original material directly from the source: the villages of Awadh where most of the battles had been fought in 1857. He was, he wrote to Dr Ramvilas Sharma, getting more and more obsessed with the idea of travelling to as many villages of Awadh as he could, to tap public memory and gather whatever stories, ballads and memories about the ghadar that had survived. To him, it would be like gathering the ashes after a loved one's cremation, he said.

When he discussed this with his friend, Bhagwati Sharan Singh, the director for information and publicity for the government of Uttar Pradesh, he was enchanted. He urged my father to leave without losing time and promised to provide him with the basic minimum: a jeep for travelling, a district level official to take him around. In return, he made father promise that he would hand over a complete manuscript based on his field notes by September, which could be eventually published as a handbook during the centenary year of the ghadar. For his efforts, father was told, he would receive a total amount of a thousand rupees as advance royalty. Father immediately came home and told Ba, my mother, of this proposal. Ba was happy at the thought of my father's story-gathering efforts being facilitated by a government grant that would go on to produce an additional handbook. What also pleased her was the thought that the thousand rupees father would get as advance royalty would considerably ease the financial pressures our joint family had been undergoing ever since father resigned from government service. Father told Ba that his travels would be rushed and involve at least three major forays to various places. She should pack his bags accordingly. Ba had knitted a beautiful jute bag for carrying father's clothes when he had travelled to Chennai in 1946. The bag was taken out and found space large enough for three to four changes of father's clothes, his books and last but not the least, his precious box of paan. On 4 June 1957, father left for the first lap of his travels, to Barabanki.

Father carried no tape-recorder or camera that could have facilitated his gathering of the material. We simply could not afford them and the department of information and publicity did not consider providing him with any of these either. My father's childhood friend Gyan Chandra Jain, who was then working for a Hindi daily *Dainik Navjivan*, presented him with a precious sheaf of foolscap paper and a few small notebooks for taking notes during his travels. To this cache, father added a few pencils, a pencil sharpener, a pen and a couple more school notebooks. His arsenal thus completed, father left home to tour and survey the villages of Awadh. He was dressed as usual, in a simple pair of cotton kurta pyjama and a pair of slippers.

Father's three-day trip to Barabanki ended on 7 June. During this period he visited the villages of Dariyabad, Bhayara, Jehangirabad, Kursi and Mahadeva. Thereafter, between 8 and 9 June, he toured the districts of Sultanpur and Faizabad.

The second lap began on 15 June and lasted for three days. During this period he toured the districts of Bahraich and Gonda. Then from 26-28 June, he toured the district of Sitapur.

After visiting six districts, my father returned home and began working on the chapters using his handwritten notes for reference. He was very excited about the material he had collected, in particular, the role played by the weakest part of Indian society, its women. He was fascinated by the great organizational capabilities that a purdah-bound Begum Hazrat Mahal had shown as a leader of the rebel forces. In a letter to his dearest friend, the great scholar Dr Ramvilas Sharma, father wrote:

'... I wish to understand the society which was the crucible for the ghadar, in particular the biggest social problem that stared it in face: the caste system and casteism. Even at a time when the ghadar is challenging the system, I find the castes becoming more powerful, more rigid, in particular where the marriage system is concerned. The caste system's intricacies make it almost impossible to trace its simple and basic contours. It feels as though we are looking at the country through a moving body of water.

Brother! Queens like Lakshmibai of Jhansi and Begum Hazrat Mahal of Lucknow, along with the courtesans of Kanpur, ordinary housewives in Awadh, Bundelkhand and Jagdishpur, could not have taken to streets under ordinary circumstances. Who knows what prolonged oppressions they were out to avenge. The ghadar gave them an opportunity and almost overnight, turned them into aggressive Durgas lusting for battle...'

Many years later, once while straightening my father's papers at home, I came across some field notes for *Ghadar Ke Phool*, scribbled on a sheaf of foolscap paper and a school notebook. Where is the completed manuscript? I wanted to know. Father said that he did not have either the time or the money to have his manuscript typewritten. And producing another handwritten copy for his personal records would have been both tedious and time consuming. Since the state department of information and publicity was keen to publish the book during the centenary year of the ghadar, he decided to keep forwarding the handwritten chapters one by one to the publishers to facilitate printing within the given time span. What corrections he had to make, could be made on the proofs rushed to him by the publishers. There was thus no complete manuscript available.

The notes taken down hastily in pencil by father while he heard the tellers recount the stories are all nearly illegible by now. I once asked him why he had scribbled them in pencil.

He said that he liked to watch and record the faces and gestures of the storytellers as they spoke. He had therefore perfected the art of writing without looking down at the notepads as he jotted his notes. In his experience, a pencil ran on its own, unlike a fountain pen that could suddenly run out of ink and was therefore preferable. Each time he returned, he would sit down immediately to make out a 'fair copy' in ink using those hastily pencilled notes, which was then rushed to the publishers. I must mention here that father wrote a beautiful discursive hand and even if he wrote on a plain piece of paper, his lines ran without dipping down or coursing upwards. This fact must have made his proofreaders happy.

On 11 July, father left Lucknow again and headed for the district of Rae Bareilly. He was thereafter planning to tour the districts of Unnao and Hardoi. But unusually heavy monsoon rains put his plans to rest. This made him quite upset and he always regretted his inability to have toured these two areas.

Meanwhile, the department of information and publicity that had facilitated his travels was getting restless and wanted him to complete and hand them the manuscript for publication as soon as possible. Father sat down to write the remaining chapters on 21 July 1957 and managed to complete the job within a month, on 16 September. He dedicated this book to the young martyr, the Raja of Chahlari, Balbhadra Singh and 600 Hindus and Muslims who had laid down their lives to liberate their motherland from foreign occupation.

Dr Sharad Nagar
29 September 2012

ACKNOWLEDGEMENTS

I must begin by expressing my thanks to the late Sharad Nagar who warmly welcomed my offer to translate *Ghadar Ke Phool*, which is among his father's lesser known works, into English. Despite ill health, he also managed to send me a beautifully evocative piece (*A Son Remembers*) in Hindi, about how this little gem took shape. Both of us shared a deep love for Awadh and a profound admiration for Amritlal Nagar's writings that gave voice to this fascinating part of north India, a scene of many epic battles and churnings that have shaped this nation's destiny.

When I first began checking for an exact rendering of various names, titles, revenue systems and linkages, and connections between various rural estates and principalities mentioned in the original, I was greatly helped by Rudrangshu Mukherji's seminal study of rural Awadh (*Awadh in Revolt 1857-1858*, Oxford University Press), *Purana Lucknow*, an excellent Hindi translation of Abdul Halim Sharar's nineteenth Urdu classic, *Guzishta Lucknow* by Noor Nabi Abbasi (National Book Trust of India, 1971) and Hindi writer Yogesh Praveen's *Dastan-e-Lucknow* (Lucknow Mahotsav Patrika Samiti, 1986). I am most grateful to all of them.

I am also grateful to the ever-patient V.K. Karthika and her team of editors at HarperCollins especially Arcopol Chaudhuri whose unflagging enthusiasm and encouragement saw to it that after translating the Marathi eyewitness account of the ghadar (*Maaja Pravas*), I should go on to translate this rare collection of reminiscences about the ghadar from rural Awadh, gathered by a writer, a hundred years later.

And last but not the least, thanks are also due to Arvind, my husband and constant companion, who as always, held my hand, laughed off my tantrums and moments of jitteriness, and kept gently pushing me into finishing what I had begun.

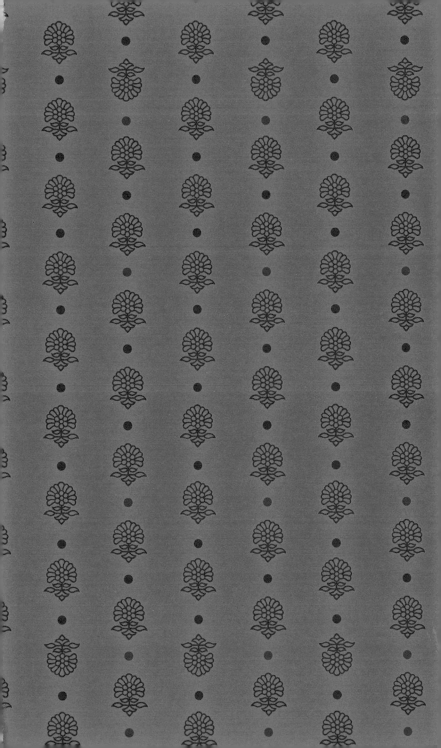

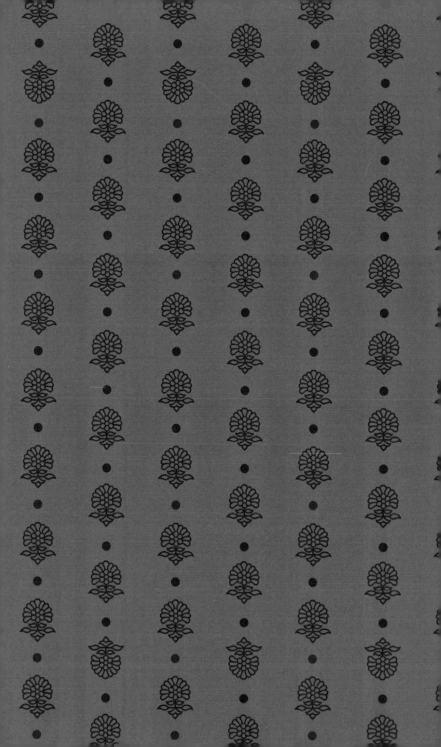